Brian Selvia

W9-BJG-940

# All the Moves

# All the Moves

*A History of College Basketball*

## Neil D. Isaacs

J. B. LIPPINCOTT COMPANY
Philadelphia & New York

U.S. Library of Congress Cataloging in Publication Data

Isaacs, Neil David, birth date
  All the moves: a history of college basketball.

  Includes bibliographical references.
  1. Basketball—History. 2. Basketball—United
States—History. I. Title. II. Title: College
basketball.
GV883.I82         796.32′363′0973        75–6574
ISBN–0–397–01045–1

For Jonny
in a love we share
and
To the Joys of One-on-One
everyone, everywhere

# *Acknowledgments*

For great generosity with their time and assistance I am grateful to Red Auerbach, Dick Comer, Lefty Driesell, Ned Irish, K. C. Jones, Sam Jones, Mack Posnak, Mark Splaver, Lee Williams, and Jack Zane and many of his (COSIDA) colleagues.

For various kinds of help, advice, and information I am also grateful to Lucius Allen, Bernie Bickerstaff, Tom Boerwinkle, Jack Bryer, Phil Chenier, Bob Ferry, Gus Ganakas, Ronnie Hogue, Rod Hundley, Dee Jackson, Sharon Landolt, Ray Mears, Bob Pettit, Mike Riordan, Linda Robinson, Tom Rollefson, Don Ruck, Honey Russell, Jack Russell, Charlie Rutherford, and Jerry Sloan.

Thanks for their confidence and efforts in support of this project to Ed Burlingame, John Kinney, and Ellen Levine.

Special thanks to the world's loveliest detective-researcher, Esther Isaacs.

# *Photo Credits*

*Numbers are page numbers. When more than one credit is given for the same page, they are listed in the same order as the photo subjects in the list of illustrations, page 11.*

16, Courtesy of University of Houston. 20, From Andrew J. Kozar, R. *Tait McKenzie, Sculptor of Athletes* (Knoxville: The University of Tennessee Press, 1975). 25, Courtesy of University of Southern California; courtesy of University of California. 27, Courtesy of University of Kansas. 31, Courtesy of Hiram College. 33, Courtesy of Georgetown University; courtesy of the College of the Holy Cross Archives; courtesy of the College of the Holy Cross Archives. 42, 47, 48, Courtesy of University of Wisconsin. 50, Courtesy of Davis and Elkins College. 51, Photo by Warren William Cross, Jr., courtesy of Butler University. 54, Courtesy of University of Pittsburgh. 58, Courtesy of Purdue University; courtesy of Purdue University; photo by J. C. Allen and Son, courtesy of Purdue University. 60, Courtesy of University of Rhode Island. 62, Photo by Duke D'Ambra, courtesy of University of Kansas. 64, Photo by Matt Grimaldi, courtesy of University of Kansas; courtesy of University of Kansas; courtesy of University of Kansas; courtesy of University of Kansas; photo by Duke D'Ambra, courtesy of University of Kansas. 65, Courtesy of City College of City University of New York. 72, Courtesy of St. John's University. 78, Courtesy of UPI. 83,

Courtesy of Clair Bee. 85, Courtesy of Seton Hall University; photo by Van Photo Service, courtesy of Seton Hall University. 89, Courtesy of University of Wyoming. 90, 91, Courtesy of UPI. 94, Courtesy of Lew Andreas; courtesy of Lew Andreas and the *Syracuse Herald-Journal*.

96, Courtesy of Western Kentucky University. 98, Courtesy of Bradley University. 99, 101, Photos by Charles Varon, courtesy of City College of City University of New York. 107, Courtesy of UPI. 110, Courtesy of Bradley University. 113, Courtesy of Stanford University. 122, Courtesy of Indiana University; courtesy of Stanford University; courtesy of Stanford University. 124, Courtesy of University of Illinois. 125, Courtesy of University of Utah. 131, Courtesy of Oklahoma State University. 134, Courtesy of Oklahoma State University; courtesy of UPI; courtesy of UPI. 137, Courtesy of University of Kentucky. 140, Courtesy of Special Collections, University of Arizona Library. 143, Courtesy of University of Kentucky. 146, Associated Press Wirephoto, Courtesy of Bradley University. 148, Courtesy of University of Kentucky. 150, Courtesy of George Washington University. 152, Courtesy of Western Kentucky University. 153, Courtesy of Indiana University. 161, 163, Courtesy of College of Holy Cross Archives. 166, Courtesy of Kentucky State University. 169, Courtesy of Pan American University; photo by Tim Schermerhorn, courtesy of University of Evansville. 170, Courtesy of University of Evansville. 171, Courtesy of Southern Illinois University. 173, Courtesy of Columbia University. 176, Courtesy of Seton Hall University. 177, Photo by Van Photo Service, courtesy of Seton Hall University.

181, Courtesy of West Virginia University. 186, Courtesy of University of Massachusetts; photo by Reisner-Simms, courtesy of Davison College; courtesy of St. Bonaventure University; courtesy of La Salle College News Bureau. 187, Courtesy of University of Massachusetts; courtesy of Western Kentucky University; photo by Rorabaugh and Millsap, courtesy of Wichita State University; courtesy of Niagara University and *Niagara Gazette*; courtesy of University of Kansas. 191, Courtesy of Loyola University of Los Angeles. 194, 195, 196, 197, Courtesy of University of San Francisco. 201, 203, Courtesy of University of Cincinnati. 204, Courtesy of University of Cincinnati; photo by Ed Kirwan, courtesy of University of California. 206, Courtesy of Photo Archives, Ohio State University. 216, Courtesy of University of California; courtesy of University of Detroit. 223, Courtesy of La Salle College News Bureau. 224, Photo by Mike Maicher, courtesy of La Salle College News Bureau. 225, Courtesy of University of Pennsylvania. 226, Courtesy of La Salle College News Bureau. 227, Photo by Bernard M. Nunez, courtesy of Villanova University. 228, Courtesy of Villanova University. 230, Courtesy of Clemson University. 231, Courtesy of North Carolina State University. 232, Photo by Danegger, courtesy of University of Maryland. 233, Courtesy of University of North Carolina. 235, Photo by Jim Keith, courtesy of Wake Forest University. 236, Courtesy of University of North Carolina.

237, Courtesy of North Carolina State University. 238, Courtesy of Davison College; courtesy of University of Maryland; courtesy of University of Maryland. 241, Courtesy of Auburn University. 243, Courtesy of LSU Sports Information. 244, Courtesy of Georgia Tech University; courtesy of Vanderbilt University; courtesy of University of Georgia; courtesy of University of Tennessee. 246, 247, Courtesy of University of Tennessee. 250, Courtesy of University of Kentucky. 253, Courtesy of Michigan State University. 254, Courtesy of Purdue University; photo by Jesse McGreevy, courtesy of Purdue University. 255, Courtesy of Purdue University. 256, Courtesy of Indiana University; courtesy of Michigan State University. 258, Courtesy of University of Michigan Athletic Department. 264, Courtesy of Dartmouth College; courtesy of LSU Sports Information; courtesy of Marquette University; courtesy of University of Miami. 265, Courtesy of Dartmouth College; courtesy of Columbia University. 266, Courtesy of Dartmouth College. 267, Courtesy of Princeton University. 272, Courtesy of Providence College. 276, 278, 280, 287, 289, Courtesy of University of California. 291, Photo by Malcolm W. Emmons, courtesy of University of Houston. 295, Courtesy of University of California. 299, Courtesy of University of Notre Dame. 302, Courtesy of North Carolina State University.

# Contents

# *Illustrations*

# Part 1

# The Name and Nature of the Game

BY ALL reasonable measures, with a single electronic exception, basketball is the most popular sport in the United States. Basketball has the highest level of participation of any sport: there are more players playing more games on more teams in more leagues at all levels of play than in any other sport; and the organized games themselves are outnumbered by the informal play in driveways, schoolyards, playgrounds, and gyms. As for attendance, more people go to watch live basketball than go to see any other sport, and no sport turns away as many would-be spectators as basketball because of limited seating facilities. Early in the fifth decade of its existence, that is, by the mid-Thirties, basketball had become the number one participant/spectator sport in the country, and it has widened its lead ever since. Basketball has at least as good a claim to the title of American Pastime as any other.

Television ratings, however, do not support this claim. Basketball does not command the TV audience of football or baseball. Not only does it lack the more elaborate spectacle and ritual elements of the other major sports, but it has a structure less conducive to commercial TV format. Where football and baseball employ the brief-action-and-pause arrangement of play to consider, reconsider,

Houston Astrodome, filled to capacity of 52,693 for basketball, saw Houston beat UCLA 71–69 in January 1968.

anticipate, rerun, and comment (not to mention advertising breaks that seem not to interrupt the rhythm of the game), basketball is basically a continuous-action sport like hockey, lacrosse, and soccer. The dramatic potential of football and baseball, then, is developed by the artificial means of the medium, augmenting the pauses between action to stimulate whatever suspense the game may suggest and to develop the context of spectacle and ritual by drawing attention to the "color" surrounding the actual play. In basketball, the dramatic potential is fulfilled in the continuous action of the game itself. Its rhythms are subtler because they are inherent in the play rather than imposed by an abstract structure. The time and space divisions are there, but they *serve* the action rather than divide it.

Basketball could be much more successfully televised than it is, but the production would have to take the nature of the game into account—and this has not yet been done. First-rate telecasts of football and baseball use six to eight cameras. Basketball generally scrapes by with two or three, and they are in the wrong places. Most of the action is shot from a camera high above floor level and at midcourt. The high angle is a mistake because it loses the needed perspective on relative size, which is obviously one of the most important dimensions in the sport. A projection that levels out the height differential, for example, among 6-foot 5-inch Bill Bradley, 6-foot 7½-inch Dave DeBusschere, and 6-foot 10-inch Jerry Lucas—to the point where they may be confused on the screen—cannot do justice to basketball. And the midcourt position is a mistake of equally basic import, based I suppose on the faulty analogy of 50-yard-line seats. But the center jump occurs no more than four times a game, so that for more than thirty-five years basketball has been much more of a half-court game than a full-court game. The main cameras should be set at the free-throw lines, as high as the tenth or twelfth row up from the floor. The other commonly used setup is an endline camera at floor level. Forget it. Even the most experienced basketball fan is disoriented by the cut from high-angle midcourt to floor-level baseline. At this position one cannot view *any* significant aspect of the play. Instead, the endline cameras should be elevated to backboard level, slightly off-center to maintain some depth perception of the basket, and with a wide enough angle to take in both corner men. This way the cuts from side view (at the free-throw line) to front view can provide natural continuity, plays can be seen developing and followed through to completion, and the action under the boards can be fully appreciated. In addition, by employing many isolated shots, focusing properly on the important one-on-one aspect of the game, basketball could rival the TV triumph of football—the home viewer could follow the game better than the fan in the stands.

But set aside the dramatic packaging of the sport and consider the reasons for its popularity. It is, first of all, simply fun. I can think of no other game that allows a player to practice the simple skills—his moves, his shots—by himself and at great length and enjoy doing it. The stories of young Bradley and Mount and Maravich spending hours in all weather, alone, throwing the ball in the hoop are not at all exceptional. Even in solitary practice, there is the challenge of hitting a target. Add a friend and there is a game, one on one, or at least companionship and competition in the practice of skills. But any number can play, up to the full complement of ten, and basketball is just as satisfying—half court as full, pavement as Tartan, schoolyard and driveway as the Garden.

The individual aspects of basketball, the fact that it is so fundamentally a sport played one against one, are heightened by the physical skills required for success. Basketball demands the basic athletic skills—running, jumping, throwing to a target—in such a way as to balance size, strength, and speed with coordination, cleverness, quickness, and timing. And all of this simplicity, this elemental single-ness, is rendered intricately complex when the individuals are placed in the context of a five-man team and a five-against-five system. However familiar the basic patterns are, the possibilities for variation are infinite. Whatever mystical powers are inherent in the pentangle, the quincunx, and the Pentagon, they have carried over to this five-man game, where arrangements signified by such labels as one-three-one, pinwheel, four-corner, and box-and-one suggest designs for movement, intrigue, and pleasure.

The cerebral dimension of basketball, where mental processes of recognition and response, invention and analysis, acknowledgment and analogy must be as strong and quick and complete as the physical, contributes greatly to the enjoyment of both player and spectator. Where the strategies of baseball are themselves part of the ritual function of the game and are more like slow-motion checkers than championship chess, and those of football are like projecting tic-tac-toe to the level of war-game spectacles, the thinking parts of basketball, in actual play, are like combining the lightning attack and response of an épée duel with finding the optional solutions to a sequence of variable algebraic/geometric problems. Scouting reports and statistical studies in basketball do not determine precise courses of action as they do in baseball, but they do suggest probabilities for success in determining a style or tempo or general plan of play. Unlike football, a basketball play is a pattern with multiple variations, with each variation having a number of options measurable only by the number of moves each player can make times the moves of his teammates times the possible defensive adjustments.

But the intellectual element is inseparable from the physical in basketball, the smarts from the moves. Indeed, the beauty of the sport lies in its integration of all the elements of athletic appeal, including psychological, emotional, aesthetic, and philosophical. Above all, its attractiveness lies in its unique blend of individual and team aspects, an integrity with built-in tensiveness. It is this charged tensiveness, I believe, that makes basketball the most beautiful and the most exhilarating of our major sports.

# 1

# *From Springfield to the World*

THE INVENTION and spread of basketball is a story of a remarkably fortuitous set of circumstances. The Young Men's Christian Association school in Springfield, Massachusetts, was a training school for athletic directors and YMCA secretaries. Its graduates not only went to posts all over the country, taking their Springfield routines with them, but also often returned to the school like former seminarians seeking guidance from the seat of their order. Besides, they all kept abreast of what was going on at Springfield by means of *The Triangle*, a monthly newsletter.

James Naismith, who had come from Bennie's Corners in northern Ontario to study for the ministry at McGill University, decided that there was great potential for spiritual leadership in athletics and enrolled in 1890 at the Springfield school under Dr. Luther Gulick. He stayed on as an instructor the following year and was given two difficult assignments by Dean Gulick: (1) to devise an indoor activity to sustain athletic interest in the long New England months between football and baseball seasons; and (2) to restore order in an unruly gym class of hyper-competitive types who were bored with gymnastics. Naismith solved both problems with the invention of basketball.

A decade later Naismith's job would have been much easier. In 1900 the

Mayan city of Chichen Itzá in Yucatan was discovered to have had a walled-in "ball court" of about 100 by 500 feet some fourteen centuries earlier. Beneath the stone grandstands, wall-carvings depict a sport in which seven-man teams shot a ball, probably of crude rubber, at vertical rings about 12 feet high. Naismith, however, lacking this native American inspiration, looked to football, rugby, soccer, water polo, field hockey, and his favorite lacrosse for suggestions, but he substantially created the game by a rational process of itemizing his requirements and finding answers to those needs.

Naismith's basic perception was that athletic interest could not be sustained in a gym class without a ball in a game, and he had tinkered with the idea of throwing a ball into a receptacle target even before leaving Montreal. It followed, then, since the idea was to play indoors, that the ball should be large and light. With no bat, stick, or racket, the ball would be handled with the hands, but to eliminate a primary potential for roughness there would be no running with the ball. Both teams would occupy the same area and no man would be restricted from getting the ball, but there was to be no contact. The ball would be put into play with a center jump as in water polo or rugby, but with only one man from each side. Finally came the crucial and distinctive feature that improved on all ball-goal games, even that of the Mayas: the goal would be elevated and horizontal.

With these principles in mind, Naismith drew up the original thirteen rules and posted them for the class. Mr. Stebbins, the custodian, was asked to supply boxes for the goals, but he had none of suitable size and suggested two peach baskets. These were fastened, at about 10 feet, from the track balcony that encircled the gym, and the first game was played December 21, 1891, with the eighteen-man class divided into teams of nine.

*The Tarbell Medallion, designed for Springfield College by Naismith's friend, R. Tait McKenzie, was first awarded to Naismith himself in 1935.*

Success was instantaneous. Frank Mahan, one of the leaders in the class, suggested "Naismith Ball" as the name of the new sport, but when the inventor demurred, Mahan offered the alternative "basket ball." Within a couple of weeks, starting during the Christmas vacation, the game was introduced in several hometowns by members of Naismith's class. In 1892 basketball caught on in several places across the country, largely under the auspices of the YMCA. Naismith took a team on tour to play exhibitions in Albany, Troy, Schenectady, Providence, and Newport. C. O. Beamis saw a game in Springfield and introduced basketball at Geneva College, where he was physical director. H. F. Kallenberg, a former instructor at Springfield, received the rules in the newsletter and introduced the sport at the University of Iowa. By April the Brooklyn YMCA was playing games with several other New York branches, and they had a championship tournament in the city the following year.

Basketball proved immediately attractive to spectators as well as to players. From the beginning, when the excited shouts of Naismith's class drew passersby into the gym balcony, people enjoyed watching. Maude Sherman, an early fan, became not only a player on one of the first women's teams, but she also became Mrs. Naismith. Indeed it is from this early spectator interest that participation multiplied so rapidly and led to the early organization of college teams. Smith and Vassar were among the first, and Amos Alonzo Stagg, a colleague of Naismith at Springfield, organized play at the University of Chicago in 1893. In the same year, W. O. Black graduated from the Springfield school and brought basketball to Stanford; his classmate, W. H. Anderson, introduced it at Yale the following year. By that time Vanderbilt had already beaten the Nashville YMCA, and Hamline had lost to the Minneapolis YMCA.

Basketball was being played at colleges in these early years, but without organized competition. The YMCAs were far ahead in this regard, having progressed from regional leagues and sectional championships as far as an American championship tournament in 1896, while even the Denver high schools had a formal league that year, playing their games at the local YMCA under Naismith's direction. There is very little record of intercollegiate play at all. On February 9, 1895, Hamline lost to Minnesota State School of Agriculture. On March 23, 1895, Haverford beat Temple. The earliest known game to use five-man squads was Chicago vs. Iowa, January 16, 1896, but the Iowa team, though all university students, was actually a YMCA team. The March 20, 1897 game, in which Yale beat Penn 32–10, has long been regarded as the first five-man intercollegiate game. If it was not the first, however, it was nevertheless a fountainhead. Yale pioneered the five-man game, scheduled many games against club teams (as did Minnesota and others on a less ambitious scale), and initiated intersectional play with a western tour in 1900.

Basketball was less than a decade old, but it had come a long way from the Springfield peach baskets from which the ball had to be lifted after every score.

Lew Allen of Hartford made cylindrical baskets of heavy woven wire in 1892, and the next year Narragansett Machine Company of Providence pioneered the modern basket with an iron rim with cord basket. Naismith's gym class had used a soccer ball, but in 1894 the Overman Wheel Company of Chicopee Falls put out a slightly larger ball, the ancestor of the modern basketball, although the weight was not increased to the present level until 1909. Backboards were introduced in 1895 to prevent interference from the gallery, indicating that the home-court advantage is as old as the sport.

Basketball became so popular that it monopolized gyms to the detriment of all other activities, and this led the Philadelphia YMCA, for one, to ban the game. As usual in such cases, the banning was a boon to interest. Independent teams moved into warehouses or hired dance halls. Spectators came in ever larger numbers and crowded the floors, so that the playing area was eventually enclosed with chicken wire. Fred Padderatz, a carpenter who managed the Trenton team, built the first cage, though it is not clear whether he was inspired by the Trenton *Daily True American*'s trenchant remark that "the fellows play like monkeys and should be put in a cage." An actual steel cage was first used, naturally, in Bristol, Pennsylvania.

There were actually four types of play before the turn of the century. One was the cage game with continuous play; the second had no restrictions on dribbling so that it was almost like football; the third was a passing game with restrictions on dribbling; and the fourth was the so-called "recreative" game in which the court was divided into sections and each player required to stay within a section to prevent massing. This last was a reaction to the idea that any number could play simply by dividing into two teams. A Cornell gym class probably holds the record with fifty-man teams—there happened to be one hundred students in the class. But out of this chaotic situation gradually came reasonable accommodation if not a perfect order. The sideline game assimilated the cage game, though cages were still employed occasionally as late as the Twenties. The recreation game was relegated to women's basketball, where it died a lingering death only very recently. The dribbling disputes bounced back and forth for years until a suitable compromise was reached. And a basketball team became a five.

# 2

# *Of the Rules and By the Rules*

NAISMITH invented basketball with a mere thirteen rules. There have been thousands since, proposed, refined, rejected, revived, and revised. Some have altered the course of the game, and some have been emergency measures to forestall revolutionary developments. A brief review of these changes encapsulates the sport's history, but many of Naismith's original dicta remain. The ball may still be thrown or tipped in any direction but never punched (Naismith's rules, numbers 1 and 2). The officials still determine possession, violations, and fouls—including responsibility for physical contact that is other than incidental—and players may foul out of games (5, 10, and 11). Traveling is still a violation (3), the defense still cannot interfere with the goal or a ball in contact with the goal (the original goaltending rule, number 8), a team still has but 5 seconds to put a ball in play from out of bounds (9), and the winner is still the team with the most goals or points (13).

Among the earliest refinements were measures to relax the prohibitions against running with the ball. A pivot was ruled not to be a traveling violation in 1893, but more important was the discovery of dribbling. Apparently it was used first as a defensive maneuver, but by 1896 Yale was employing the dribble as a standard means of attack. The loophole was never completely plugged, but it was considerably stopped up by a variety of prohibitions. The overhead dribble was outlawed, in 1898 the double dribble became illegal for most games, and the two-handed dribble was often banned. For seven seasons, 1901–1908, the dribbler was not allowed to shoot, and it was only in 1915 that this restriction was permanently removed. But attempts to steal the action of dribbling continued until 1927 when the National Association of Basketball Coaches was organized specifically to pro-tect the game from a limitation of dribbling to one bounce. The last skirmish in this battle took place at the 1928–1929 meeting of the Joint Committee. Doc Meanwell of Wisconsin led the way to a nine to eight vote to eliminate the dribble. The group adjourned to see the Celtics win the professional title from the Cleveland Rosenblums, and Meanwell exulted in the champions' ability to move the ball by passing, not dribbling. But Nat Holman, still playing with the Celtics while coaching CCNY, asked the Joint Committee to reconsider, arguing that college kids should not be expected to play like the Celtics. The vote was reversed, and the bounce has never been taken out of basketball.

The matter of team numbers, left to chance in Naismith's plan, was settled finally at five in 1897 after some experimentation with sevens and nines according to the size of the court. But the matter of how to put the ball in play was in dis-pute for much longer. With cages there was no out-of-bounds problem, but in the sideline game the first man to the ball would put it in play. The scramble over the lines became the roughest part of the game, and awarding the ball to the first man over was an unsatisfactory solution, so that in 1913 a new rule awarded the ball to the team opposite the one that last touched it. After a goal, however, the ball was still put in play by a center jump. By the Twenties, the center jump was already under fire, but it wasn't until the Thirties that the campaign gained sub-stantial support. The rule seemed to put too great a premium on height, and with the great improvement in scoring it seemed too dull and repetitious a way of slowing the action. Naismith himself argued that timing was more important than height and that inequities could be eliminated simply by higher tosses; but the opponents, led by Coaches Sam Barry of Southern California and Nibs Price of California, prevailed: the center jump was eliminated after free throws in 1936 and after all goals the following year.

The beheading of the center jump celebrated the tenth anniversary of the National Association of Basketball Coaches, but until 1927 responsibility for rules had been passed around a great deal. The YMCA unloaded it early to the AAU, but the pros kept their own rulebook going from 1901 to 1927, the *Reach Official Basketball Guide*. In 1905, when there were already many leagues and conferences operating at several levels of play, Spalding initiated its *Official Collegiate Basket-ball Guide* with six Ivies (Yale, Harvard, Princeton, Columbia, Cornell, Pennsyl-vania) and one Western Athletic Conference member (Minnesota) providing the aura of authority. The same year there were other defections from the AAU and

*The campaign against the center jump was led by Coaches Sam Barry (left) and Nibs Price.*

the formation of the Protective Basket Ball Association of the Eastern States, which published its own rules designed to combat fights and mobs, not to mention "trickster managers, dishonest officials, unprincipled players."

The buck was passed to the NCAA in 1908, but in 1915 as the world chose up sides and the nation began to build a facade of unity, a Joint Basketball Committee was formed with representatives of the NCAA, AAU, and YMCA. Strength in union led to an expansive spirit; in 1927 the Chartered Board of Officials and in 1929 the National Federation of State High School Athletic Associations and the Canadian Amateur Basketball Association were also seated. But union and inclusiveness have never meant unanimity, nor have joint collectives been profoundly prescient. Problems with rules have persisted.

The accidental addition of backboards back in 1895 brought a new dimension to the game that to a certain extent undercut Naismith's intention for horizontal goals: to reward skill rather than strength. The first "boards" were screens, but their obviously unfair inconsistency led to the use of wood. Glass was first used in 1909, with the spectators in mind, but had to be dropped in 1916 when the news rules committee, seeking uniformity, legislated white paint for all. The Protective Association had tried to limit the use of the backboard on field goals by requiring a 12-inch extension of rim from board and by outlawing any carom on free throws. But they did not prevail in this any more than they did in trying to eliminate the 6-foot foul lane. The latter remained until 1955 when Coach Howard Hobson of Yale led the successful drive to make it a 12-foot lane.

The lane had become the focal point of action—of offense and defense and rebounding and therefore of fouls and unacknowledged dirty play—by the mid-Twenties when much of the country had been treated to the sight of the Celtics running their pivot-post plays. To combat the roughness, especially after movies of lane violence were screened at a rules meeting, and also in part to limit the big man on offense, the 3-second rule was introduced in 1932 and permanently adopted in 1936. Then, as now, stalling was feared as a possible killer of basketball. Supposed cures were a 5-second backcourt held-ball rule adopted in 1930 and the present 10-second rule adopted in 1932. A bewildering variety of devices to prevent stalling has been tried in recent years in college basketball, but every attempt has been foiled by clever coaches and ballhandlers and by officials' failure to enforce rules vigorously, in part because they are asked to keep too many sets of time clocks running in their heads. The pro leagues and international competitions have solved the problem with a mandatory shot clock, but so far the colleges have been unwilling to accept the side effects that go with this specific cure.

The stall arose in the first place to counteract the zone defense, developed around 1914 and dominant throughout the Twenties. The 10-second rule fought the stall but not effectively because the burden of tempo remains on the defense, as Naismith continued to point out as long as he lived. By the same token, the 3-second rule and the elimination of the center jump failed to dampen the influence of the big men. Rather, by doing away with their specialized functions, the rules forced them to develop all-around basketball skills. Thus the big men dominate the game now much more than they did before; every restriction has made them better. But in the Thirties, when the restrictions were against height on offense, the big men became defensive specialists. Warner Keaney of Rhode Island, Mike Novak of Loyola of Chicago, George Mikan of DePaul, Don Otten of Bowling Green, and Bob Kurland of Oklahoma A & M were goaltenders who batted away or simply caught attempted shots before they could reach the basket. These maneuvers forced defensive goaltending legislation in 1944 (the "Mikan rule") and subsequent refinements dealing with the use of the backboard in goaltending and extending an imaginary cone over the rim. One of the most difficult judgment calls for a basketball official is to determine just when a shot begins its downward path.

Probably no single player has had such a great influence on rules-makers as Wilt Chamberlain. He played only two varsity years at Kansas and was legislated against no fewer than three times: his foul-shooting technique was banned by a new foul-line rule; some of his scoring moves were outlawed by an offensive goaltending rule; and a play designed for him was scrapped by a rule preventing an inbounds toss over the backboard. Even the "Alcindor rule" banning the dunk shot in 1967 was doubtless passed with the specter of Chamberlain's slams and dippers hovering over the board meeting. The antidunk rule has its advantages and admirers, but like other antitall legislation, it doesn't hurt the 7-footers, who

*The player with the greatest influence on the rules—Wilt Chamberlain.*

get their inside points anyway. It really hurts the moves of the 6-foot playground stylists and can thus be condemned as a racist rule. Most of all it hurt Coach Ray Mears who had choreographed a crowd-pleasing warm-up drill at Tennessee around the dunk and was informed he would be assessed a technical foul for every dunk tried in practice. But spectacle counts for too much in Big Orange Country for a mere rule to beat the showman in Mears, who had a portable basket wheeled out on the floor before each game so that the act could be performed for the Vol fans.

Personal fouls have always been at the heart of most basketball disputes. As Naismith envisioned his new sport, and as the early handbooks describe and illustrate it, the physical offenses were likely to be egregious. But free throws were assessed for technical violations as well, so that relatively minor or incidental contact—particularly on defense—was more likely to be whistled than blinked. This situation tended to encourage offensive blocking and screening designed to draw fouls, especially since players could be fouled out of games—a cumulative structure more like a penal system than any major sport. And the action was continually interrupted with tedious parades from foul line to foul line.

Much legislation has limited these defects, but much remains to be done. A giant step was taken in 1923 when free throws were no longer awarded for violations, like traveling, that were not personal fouls. But games were still won by excessive foul-shooting. Phog Allen remembers when little Louis Rabbit Weller of the Haskell Indian Institute beat Washburn College with a 5-point play in 1929: he made a basket, was fouled, was awarded two free throws, made the first, and deliberately missed the second which was tapped in by a teammate. It wasn't until 1949 that deliberate misses were discouraged by a Pacific Coast Conference experiment of giving defensive men both inside rebounding positions on free throws. Several rules permitting the waiving of free throws were tried, but they never seemed to discourage frantic fouling late in the game and they even abetted stalls or freezes. All such options were eventually abandoned.

Coaches' laments about officiating share an often-repeated refrain about consistency. It comes through especially loud and clear with regard to intersectional competition. In 1937, Phog Allen observed that in the Midwest too much contact was allowed and traveling too lightly limited, while in the Far West guarding was called more closely than elsewhere. Two years earlier, Adolph Rupp had brought Kentucky into Madison Square Garden for the first time and described the game as "one of the roughest and most rugged exhibitions of pivot play that has ever been shown." At the same time he discovered that the screening used in Kentucky's plays, while "perfectly legal in the Middle West and the South," was called for fouls in New York, including the game-winning whistle with 8 seconds left. And Doc Carlson in 1938 noted that on judgment calls involving contact, the defense was given the break in the East, the offense in the West.

28

Such regional characteristics die hard, especially in reputations. Big Ten basketball still seems to many more physical than other conferences. In the South, on the other hand, offensive rebounding is permitted to be more aggressive, according to invaders from elsewhere. In large metropolitan areas accustomed to NBA and big-time playground ball, traveling does not seem to be watched very carefully. But by and large these provincial distinctions fade a little more each year.

At present, despite certain anomalies among levels of play in high school, college, AAU, international, and professional basketball, there seems to be a logical progression of rules. As time periods get longer from high school through college to pro ball, it takes more fouls to disqualify a player. As the caliber of play improves, it becomes easier for officials to apply a no-harm no-foul standard. The pros have instituted a shot-time clock and outlawed the zone defense, but high schools cannot cope with the first and need the other. The colleges have not yet found an appropriate middle ground on these two matters. But there was a time when this kind of hierarchical structure would have made no sense at all—1901, when the high school team from Holyoke, Massachusetts, beat both Dartmouth and Holy Cross.

# 3

# *Toward Structure (If Not Order)*

THE MANIFEST destiny of basketball extended its sphere of influence from coast to coast within two years of its invention. But its lightning spread produced parochial pockets instead of a uniform arena. Enthusiastic acceptance of the game itself seemed to divert attention from the desirability of an orderly framework within which it could be played. When leagues were formed they tended to be closed, provincial groups of neighbors who played only among themselves. Even where football conferences had already paved the way on campuses, there was not likely to be an impetus toward truly national competition. The Western Conference as a whole adopted basketball, but in the East football rivalries did not carry over. Thus the Intercollegiate League, formed in 1901, consisted of Yale, Harvard, Princeton, Columbia, and Cornell, and the New England League, beginning play in the same year, included Amherst, Holy Cross, Williams, Dartmouth, and Trinity.

In July of 1904, while *The New York Times* was blithely reporting the successes of the Haverford cricket team, several basketball teams were meeting in St. Louis at the Fair. The Louisiana Purchase Exposition and World's Fair was host to Olympic Games that were primarily exhibitions of American athletes, and the basketball was no exception. On July 11 and 12, on a 50-foot by 70-foot outdoor court in the stadium, five teams played an abbreviated round-robin tournament, with the Buffalo German YMCA team winning four games and the gold medals. Then, on the same court on July 13 and 14, three colleges competed for what the winner's banner called the Olympic World's College Basket Ball Championship. Hiram College, Wheaton College, and Latter Day Saints University (now Brigham Young) took home the gold, silver, and bronze medals respectively. They comprised what could hardly be called a representative field, yet Spalding's *Guide* predicted that the tournament was the beginning of "what may in the years to come be an annual fixture, namely—A National College Basket Ball Championship held annually between the colleges of the U.S. played in alternate years in the East and West."

Such optimism was accurate but quite premature. At the time, college teams played YMCA teams, club teams, and pro teams much more often than they played each other, and this was true even among those colleges in the three organized leagues. Intercollegiate conference play began to stabilize around 1905, and it is with that season that a history proper of college basketball may begin (as

*Hiram College, Olympic champions, 1904.*

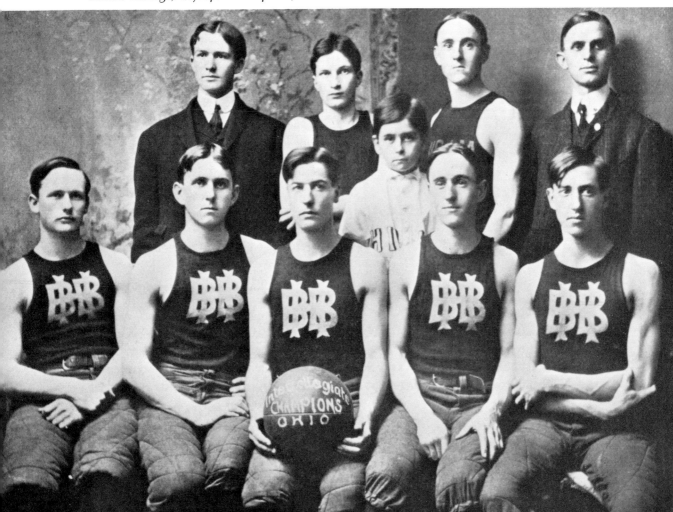

manager-coach Lew Wachter. Into the 1914–1915 season, they won thirty-eight straight games and demonstrated to the country such original and borrowed skills as tight man-to-man defense, fast passing upcourt (the ancestor of the quick-breaking offense), the bounce pass, and the screen. Lew Wachter later coached at Dartmouth, making them a championship team, and his brother Ed, Troy's star player, spent twenty-five years in college coaching at RPI, Williams, Harvard, and Lafayette. In addition, Bill Hardiman coached Union College for twenty years, and Chief Muller coached Manhattan College.

By the time the Troy team disbanded there had already been spawned at a settlement house on Manhattan's West Side the team that would epitomize basketball throughout the Golden Age of Sport. The influence of the Celtics cannot be overemphasized as for nearly two decades they sustained interest in the sport they dominated. But there was a negative factor in their dynasty; as absolute rulers they repressed dissent, and it was only after they were deposed that free rein in the development of other styles and new techniques allowed the rapid emergence of modern basketball.

Whenever sectional distinctions are made, the eastern style that is described is based on the Celtics. Adolph Rupp describes it as five-man offense built around the give and go. Ben Carnevale says it consisted of "the give-and-go cutting style; the one-on-one, man-to-man matchups; fast, accurate passing; quick, expert footwork and the 'picks' and screens so closely associated with basketball when played in close quarters." Nat Holman, personally responsible for bringing the Celtics' style to his City College teams, sees the only valid distinction as that between the "precision drive set style offense of the west and the free style spontaneous play-making of the east." Joe Lapchick, Holman's Celtic teammate and long-time rival coach at St. John's, capsulized the whole idea as "making the ball sing."

Doc Carlson, however, says that the major eastern contribution to basketball was the development of the three-man offense, that is, two little men cutting off the big pivot. The origin of the pivot-post play is obscured in a morass of conflicting legends. In Kentucky they believe Rupp invented it, but in Kentucky they think Rupp invented basketball. In Missouri they say a gym in Lathrop had a concrete pillar that was used as a post to pick off defenders, but anyone not from Missouri would have to be shown. Most credit it to the Celtics, but under a variety of circumstances. Whether it was in Rochester, Chattanooga, or Jacksonville, in 1924 or 1925, and whether the team was worn out from all-night travel or just big Dutch Dehnert was out of shape, there are certain constants in the story. A big standing guard was making trouble for the Celtics' attack. Dehnert backed inside, took a pass from Holman or Johnny Beckman, and passed off to one or the other as they cut past, picking off the defender, or, if the standing guard committed to one side, Dehnert would turn to the basket the other way. The play was so successful that it became the backbone of most offenses, enriched by a basic double-post variation, and it remains a staple of modern basketball.

Around 1930 two momentous developments took place: zone defenses began to move and the fast break began to fly. For fifteen years, zones had been stationary, aided by small floors, low ceilings, the general style of offense, and rules against offensive stalling and screening and occupying the lane. But as the facets of and facilities for basketball moved into the modern era in the Thirties, the zone had to learn to shift with the times and the offensive moves. And from a moving, shifting, collapsing zone defensive set, the fast break became a logical reality. Lapchick claimed he was introduced to both the shifting zone and the fast break on the same night in 1930 in Sandusky, Ohio. The pro champion Cleveland Rosenblums (led by three stars of the broken-up Celtics) were beaten by a team of college all-stars playing a 2–1–2 zone. Whenever the ball was passed inside, they converged on the ball and outraced the pros downcourt.

An offensive weapon that was successful against a team of touring pros became part of their own arsenal, while at the same time they would contrive a way to defense it. And this was the primary means of transmission of techniques, as the gospel of the game was preached by the practice of pros like the Celtics, the Rosenblums, and the fabulous Renaissance Big Five. But before the decade was over all this had changed—the product, the packaging, and the merchandising—and college basketball was big time.

Foresighted folks at universities in Iowa, Minnesota, Washington, Pennsylvania, and Oregon built fieldhouses designed to seat over ten thousand spectators for basketball. Ned Irish introduced intersectional double-headers to Madison Square Garden, featuring metropolitan area teams and opposition from all other parts of the country. These houses were often sold out: the attractions were a far cry from such famous CCNY games in 1926 as the 13–12 loss to Carnegie Tech and the 15–14 win over Temple. Now there were fast breaks, a point a minute, even 2 points a minute, the good big man on offense and defense, and the greatest phenomenon of all—Hank Luisetti.

Luisetti was the first basketball superstar to become a glamorous national hero. With his one-hand shooting, his speed, his all-around floorplay, and especially his charisma, he was a publicity man's dream. Imagine a college roundball player from California exciting the New York press as well as the public. In the wake of Stanford's eastern swing in 1936 there was a newly awakened sense of basketball's potential. To complete the equation, attraction plus arena plus publicity, there needed to be only a showcase—and so the idea of a national tournament was reborn.

The first truly national tournament, and in some ways still the best, was the NAIA. It originated in Kansas City in 1937 as a replacement for the national AAU tournament which had moved to Denver. Thirty-two of the finest small college teams, most determined by preliminary conference or regional tournaments, come to Kansas City every year for a week of total basketball immersion. In 1938, the Metropolitan Basketball Writers Association promoted the first NIT at Madison

Square Garden. It was so successful that the embarrassed writers turned the event over to the local colleges for the renewal. The success and prestige of the NIT continued until NCAA regulations relegated it to second place. The NCAA's own championship tourney began a year later, and through a roughly geographical elimination presumes to crown a national champion. To complete the national championship picture at every level, a national junior college tournament began in 1948 and an NCAA College Division tournament in 1957.

Academic institutions and schedules being what they are, the commercial success of these tournament ventures insured a proliferation of such events over Christmas and New Year's weeks. Some of these have provided outstanding competition, notably the Dixie Classic, the Sugar Bowl, the Kentucky Invitational, and the Holiday Festival tournaments in New York and Philadelphia. But it has gotten so now that every team with a hope of half-filling a fieldhouse will get three other teams together and proclaim its own classic. Then the following week it will be off to Hawaii or Long Beach or Knoxville for another two games (classic). These trips, scheduled years in advance whenever possible to sign prospectively attractive opponents, are often used as recruitment bonuses. Too often they are simply ways of padding a preconference record for a home team with homer referees or a canny visiting coach who has picked his spots, or a subsidized junket for a hard-playing squad (plus top administrators), rather than an opportunity for top-level intersectional tests. And the word *classic* has been cheapened by sport more than any but the word *great*.

Even on the international level an equivalent proliferation has taken place. After U.S. teams played exhibition games at the Olympics of 1904, 1924, and 1928, and led by Phog Allen's vigorous campaign, basketball became an official event in the 1936 games in Berlin, with twenty-two countries entered (only twenty-one competed because the Spanish team was summoned home when the Civil War began), and James Naismith a proud and honored guest. A little over four years earlier, at the First International Basketball Conference in Geneva, the FIBA (Fédération internationale de basketball amateur) had been established. And ever since, the sport has increasingly been included in such international events as the Pan-American Games, the Maccabean Games, and the World University Games, and there have been more and more frequent goodwill tours by national and representative teams abroad. In four decades, membership in the FIBA has grown to 132 national associations. Unfortunately, international basketball has gone its own separate way in terms of rules-making and officiating, compounding the difficult struggle toward sensible uniformity.

Ironically, World War II, which crippled other major sports, was a booming period for basketball despite some problems of travel, schedule, and facilities. High-pressure recruitment evolved quickly at a time when a boy over 6 feet 6 inches was exempted from the draft. The wartime context of these developments was at least partly responsible for two potentially destructive by-products. First, the sharp increase in gambling and the bad companions of loose money and loosened standards of behavior brought dangers to college basketball that were hinted at in 1945 and partially realized in 1951 and again in 1961. The game may have learned and recovered from these frightening experiences, but the second danger, in recruiting practices, is a destructive force even now. Recruiting abuses, despite attempts at legislation and punishment that often seem hypocritical in their application, are so thoroughly institutionalized that a cynical public accepts the unethical, covert payment to student athletes as a matter of course. But in a society where sport is big business, where business dictates to government, where government manipulates the worst in the people, and where the people look to sport to epitomize their ethic and their mythos, nothing could be more natural.

This process of organizational refinement, this building toward a monolithic superstructure, has built up tremendous pressures in the game, on coaches and on players. As Nat Holman pointed out in 1950, major stadiums made for longer schedules; transportation costs meant more games per trip; increased spectator interest added greater emotional stress to the greater physical stress; and emphasis on international play and national recognition put a higher premium on winning. Recognition of these factors in the media serves only to reinforce the process, so that scheduling and recruitment are even fiercer in the quest for rankings and tournament invitations. The AP rankings began in 1949, the UP (now UPI) in 1951. Public television of basketball began as early as 1940, but even before that there had been closed-circuit telecasts from Madison Square Garden.

A positive and cumulative effect of many of these developments has been progressive standardization, the breaking down of provincialism in a national game. The media and the structuring systems of intercollegiate basketball have virtually eliminated geographical distinctions. It has not, fortunately, been a matter of leveling, but one of learning. Within the range of styles and techniques available to a regularized sport, no team—no coach or player—does not have access to every option. Two other recent phenomena have contributed considerably to this educational process, the clinics and the camps. In the one, there is a cultural exchange for coaches embracing all the lore from sage advice on fundamentals to the most sophisticated techniques of pattern variations. In the other, there is the distillation of that exchange, that cumulative store of lore passed on to the younger levels of play and out into schoolyards and driveways where it is applied and redeveloped. Eventually, with new vigor, it will rise to the collegiate gym, where in 99 percent of all institutions of higher education in the United States organized basketball is played.

# Part 2

# Patterns and Pioneers

THE COMPLEXITIES of basketball, involving the integration of individual moves into team movement, make it a sport uniquely dependent on the direction of coaching. In its first decade, basketball coaching was negligible, most teams having at best a manager and a captain. Even in the second decade, following the establishment of regular intercollegiate play after the turn of the century, basketball coaching was a haphazard matter. Most schools had no official coach at all, and when they did he was likely to be a recently graduated star or captain of last year's team.

The play of the game was erratic, spasmodic, rough, and so totally unpatterned as to be called chaotic. Football, itself not yet having attained a modicum of discipline, was often the principal model for players and their actions. Regional characteristics were already clearly established, but they were attributable to varying interpretations of the rules rather than to the influence of individual styles and techniques taught by coaches. In the East, there were dribbling, free-lancing, two-handed shooting, and individual effort, with some teamwork in short passing; in the Midwest there were less holding on defense, less dribbling, more long passing, and one-handed and pivot shooting; and in the West there was the prototype of the fast break, with all five men running whenever the ball changed hands.

But from about 1905 on, the significance of coaching has been recognized and has steadily grown to the point where, instead of style and system labeled by region or team or school, style and system are labeled by the coach who developed them, taught them, or applied them with success. This evolution, more than any other, has made basketball what it is, but it was no sudden awakening of mind over material or strategy over force. In the fifth year of the (Eastern) Intercollegiate League (1905–1906—hereafter, the season is dated by the year in which it ends), four of the six teams were coached by graduate players and Princeton by a pro, but Cornell played without a coach. Penn led the league for the first time, coached by Russell Smith, one of the pioneers in college basketball. Columbia, second after two straight championships, was coached by former star forward Harry Fisher. Harvard, back in the league after a year's absence, was coached to third place by C. W. Randall, the best all-around Crimson player they had ever had. Yale, champions the first two years of the league, was fourth, coached by another pioneer, Roswell B. Hyatt. Princeton, with their pro coach, was fifth, and Cornell, coachless, was last, characterized in the Spalding *Guide* as utterly lacking in team play. This result, said the *Guide*, "should prove conclusively to the Ithaca institution that a coach for the players should be secured."

The lesson was not quickly learned either in Ithaca or elsewhere. In the Spalding *Collegiate Basket Ball Guide* for 1908–1909, for example, a table lists sixty-six schools: all but five list captains, all but eight list managers, but only thirty-one list coaches. Even where a coach was an established feature of the sport, there was no stability in the position. A school might have a coach for a season, then another for the next, and then not have one at all, like Iowa in 1912. Indiana had nineteen different coaches over a twenty-five-year period, and Northwestern had one a year for seven straight years. For a long time the position was voluntary, anyway, and coaches maintained amateur status for their own athletic careers. And as late as post-World War II it was still possible to find many schools whose basketball coaches were part time, often primarily doing other jobs in other fields with the basketball duties thrown in. Indeed one can find a direct correlation of basketball success with the acknowledgment that the basketball coaching job is worthy of full time (and high salary).

This section will examine some of the important stabilizing figures in the coaching ranks, the successful innovators who influenced generations of followers and led basketball into a new era of achievement. The establishment of coaching is one significant phase; another, to come much later, is the coaching establishment, in which a basketball program must have four coaches if it is not to be regarded as bush league.

# 4

## *Ever the Twain*

THE ESSENCE of championship play, however keen the conference rivalry, is intersectional competition; and the pinnacle of interest in any sport is attained when the best meets the best, each side representing one side of a tensive, polar system of opposing forces. The system may be a natural or geographic one, like east–west or north–south, or it may be wholly artificial, like the color war in a summer camp or the phratries of a totemic society. The point is that the system works because its structure is a universally appealing construct of our awareness or perception of life, not merely of sport.

Among other reasons, the year 1905 is significant because for the first time a team had a good claim to a national collegiate championship. In the Eastern Intercollegiate League, grown to six teams the season before when Pennsylvania was admitted but shrunk again to five by Harvard's withdrawal, Columbia had completed its second straight unbeaten season. In the West, not yet organized into conferences, Wisconsin had come to prominence under coach Emmett Angell to challenge Chicago and Minnesota for supremacy with star players Chris Steinmetz, who scored 44 against Beloit in an 80–10 win, and Bob Zuppke of football fame. During the 1905 season, both Wisconsin and Minnesota came east to chal-

*Chris Steinmetz, sent by Coach Angell to high-scoring fame.*

lenge Columbia and both were beaten, 21–15 and 27–15. Since both had beaten Chicago, Columbia could claim to be the best, East or West.

On Thanksgiving Day, 1905, the Universities of Chicago, Illinois, Purdue, Minnesota, and Wisconsin met to form the Western Intercollegiate Basket Ball League. Other leagues had preceded it, but none would survive continuously. Even the Eastern—ultimately the Ivy—League dropped formal competition in 1908–1910 and again in 1918–1919. The New England League, as ancient and ivied as the

Ivy, was short-lived. Only two of its members, Dartmouth and Williams, survived the first season to join with Wesleyan in a Triangular League that lasted only two years, and Dartmouth eventually joined the Eastern in 1911. Most of the New England schools continued to play each other, with upstate New York teams—Syracuse, Colgate, Hamilton—also regularly on their schedules.

Minnesota was the Western League champion in 1906, led by R. T. McRae and Garfield Brown, despite a strong challenge from Wisconsin. It was Chicago that had the two best players, however, in James McKeag and John Schommer. There was no postseason playoff between Minnesota and Penn, however, so that no national championship could be claimed. At any rate, there would have been at least one other contender for the title in Dartmouth, led by all-star George Grebenstein, with a 16–2 record. The home-court advantage was already very well established. The Spalding *Guide* noted that the "Hanover court is notoriously difficult for an opposing team" as was that in Williamstown, and said that a team's own floor was "easily worth fifteen points to the home team," a striking figure in 1908, when 15 points could still be a winner's total. Yet Dartmouth in 1906 went on the road to beat Manhattan, Princeton, Columbia, and Yale, and then beat Williams home-and-home to be acknowledged best in the region. An earlier New England traveler, the 1904 Holy Cross team, had gone on the road to beat Dartmouth, Yale, Harvard, and Hiram twice, and even split with the Buffalo Germans.

Meanwhile Yale had gone much further down the road, inspiring a great deal of increased play in the South. The Southern Intercollegiate Athletic Association was formed, with Auburn taking the first championship over Howard College, Georgia Tech, Georgia, Tulane, Vanderbilt, and Mercer College. The two Auburn forwards, Ware and Woodruff, also played for the Birmingham AC which beat Yale that season on its second southern tour. Most of the colleges in the country were not yet organized in leagues and played most of their games against non-collegiate opposition. Canisius, for example, played an eighteen-game schedule, opening with the Buffalo Germans and including high schools, clubs, and YMCA classes, but only one college, their neighbors at Niagara.

The following season brought little change, except for the first formation of a freshman league. CCNY played eight games, losing only to Fordham. Harvard rejoined the Eastern League but had a losing season, as Yale beat Columbia for the title, despite Penn's all-star Charles Keinath. In a newly reformed New England League, Williams beat out Dartmouth as both had midseason wins over Yale. In the Western, a three-way tie among Wisconsin, Minnesota, and Chicago was not resolved. The best chance at intersectional play was a challenge from the Southwest, where a paid coach named Phog Allen had led Baker University of Baldwin, Kansas, to an undefeated season and had scheduled a trip to Chicago. Unfortunately, an epidemic of the mumps kept Baker from the Midway.

A year later the second city came first. From coast to coast, colleges were playing basketball and organizing leagues. In the Northwest, Oregon Agricultural College was the first champion in a league that included Idaho, Whitman, Oregon, Washington, and Washington State. Down the West Coast, California won the first Pacific Athletic Association championship by beating the Columbia Park Boys' Club team in the tournament finals, after the undefeated Stockton YMCA All-Stars had to withdraw because of injuries. In the South, Georgetown had the best record until displaced by the 1910 Navy team with guards named Wills and Jacobs (playing a different net game from that of the Helens who launched a thousand lobs). In New England, Williams remained on top, though the quality of play failed to keep pace with Ivy and Western improvement. Notre Dame, beginning in 1907 the kind of ambitious scheduling that would make them the most traveled of all college teams, met teams from Pennsylvania to Oregon and Kalamazoo to Birmingham, winning thirty-three games in the 1909 season while losing only seven including two to the Buffalo Germans. Yet with all this, the national championship would come from the meeting of East and West.

Penn, led by Keinath, was clearly best in the East. After losing two of their first three games, they won twenty-two straight games, including all eight conference games. But in the West there was more difficulty selecting a representative. Minnesota had slipped considerably, but Wisconsin and Chicago tied in the league at 7–1, having split their series. Wisconsin may have had a slight edge in previous years, particularly under Angell's coaching, although Chicago upset them at Madison to break an eight-game streak in 1906. But with Schommer, Chicago was at least a match for Wisconsin in 1907. They tied in the conference, splitting their series, but Chicago's overall record was 21–2 compared to Wisconsin's 11–3. Then, when H. O. Page joined Schommer in 1908, with a promised playoff against the Eastern champion at stake, they split again and again tied. But now Chicago had a perceptible edge in the most outstanding coach of the whole prewar era, Joseph E. Raycroft.

The playoff was held in Madison before 1,500 fans, and against Jumbo Stiehm, Biddy Rogers, and company, only the inspired play of Schommer and a last-minute shot by Pat Page won for Chicago, 18–16, the right to play Penn. Raycroft's strategy had nullified the prevalent setup of basket-hanger and standing guard which had reduced most offenses to three moving men. The mobility of 6-foot 3-inch Schommer and the quickness of Page had made five-man play feasible for Chicago, and it was five-man play that won them the title. At home in the first game they beat Penn 21–18 in a game featured by four Schommer field goals and Page's basket shot from under his legs when he was about to be tied up. In Philadelphia it was even closer, tied eight times before Chicago wrapped it up by a point, 16–15; and the championship, their record of 22–2, and their ability to win the big games and the close games mark them as the great team of the period. Along with Schommer and Page, Raycroft's team had Bill Georgen, Doc Falls, and Art Hoffman as starters.

The next year was Schommer's last, his fourth as an All-American, and Chicago went 12–0 in the conference, which had added Indiana, Northwestern, and Iowa. Columbia was the best in the East, with Williams perhaps close, but there was no formal league and no playoff. Despite the continued presence of Penn's Keinath, the All-East team picked in the Spalding *Guide* consisted of the whole Columbia team, not just the stars, Melitzer and Cerussi, but Kiendl, Ryan, and Kimbel as well. It should be noted that the selections were made by Columbia's Harry Fisher. Kansas had risen to prominence in the Midwest but not so as to challenge the Western Conference. Chicago, until proven otherwise, was number one. Even after Schommer's departure (he later invented the modern backboard), they won another conference title in 1910, with Bob Harris and Ed Hubble assisting Page in Raycroft's last year. Through 1921, Chicago had only winning seasons: their coaches were Schommer for a year, Page for nine years, and—in that last winning season of the streak—the man who had brought the game to Chicago in the first place, Amos Alonzo Stagg. And it was Stagg who, overwhelmed by increasing crowd disturbances at basketball games, called out to the house, "Ladies and Gentlemen, *be* ladies and gentlemen."

The 1911 season may be regarded as an interregnum. Chicago's power was dissipated, but Wisconsin was not yet ready to assume the crown. Undistinguished teams from Purdue and Minnesota tied. The Eastern League was reorganized and Columbia, led by Ted Kiendl, won again but declined to wait for the Western Conference to select a representative. Dartmouth was admitted to the league for the following season and almost upset Columbia right away, but there was no question of challenging the new power in the West, undefeated Wisconsin.

The nature of this power will be discussed in the following chapter as, more and more, the important coaches came to dominate the scene; but a couple of observations remain to be made about the preceding period. Harvard's withdrawal from competition drew attention to the roughness of play. President Eliot had called the game "even more brutal than football," and this occasioned some tightening of the rules and taking charge of their own game on the part of the colleges. Increasingly, there was need for intersectional play to determine rankings, as more and more colleges made reputations as independents, including Swarthmore, Carlisle, Westminster, and Wabash. It was an alumnus of the latter, Homer Stonebreaker, playing for the Fort Wayne Knights of Columbus team in 1921, who beat the touring Celtics 24–17 on five two-handed underhand set shots from past midcourt. But it was hard to do anything twice to the Celtics. The next night, Chris Leonard played defense all over the court, held Stoney scoreless, and the Celtics won 48–19.

# 5

# *What's Up, Docs?*

IN DEVELOPING the idea of a basketball coach as choreographer, probably no two men have been as influential over several generations of coaches as Walter E. Meanwell and Henry C. Carlson. Their contributions to establishing set patterns of movement on the court, however, were primarily concerned with the offense. To complete the roster of pioneer contributors to deliberate styles, defense must also be taken into account, so this chapter will include, in addition to the review of Doc Meanwell and Doc Carlson, a brief discussion of George Keogan, Cam Henderson, and John Lawther.

Meanwell became coach at the University of Wisconsin for the 1912 season. He preached close teamwork and his instructions concentrated on the short pass. The combination produced a precision drive-set offense that surpassed in efficiency any college team up to that time. In his first season, his team won all fifteen games, averaging 34 points, while their tight defense augmented by the ball-control offense held opponents to an average of 15. Purdue was also undefeated, but without the rigor of Wisconsin's schedule, while undefeated Wesleyan in the East scored more but allowed weaker opposition many more points. With teamwork as the watchword, Wisconsin's team nevertheless worked their star forward, Otto Stangel, free for a conference record 177 points.

*Doc Meanwell of Wisconsin.*

*Bud Foster as player for Meanwell.*

With the Doc's prescriptions doing their job, Wisconsin was even better the following year, making the conference title official, beating seven league opponents (Ohio State had joined up, but Northwestern was not scheduled). They didn't score quite as much, but their defense was even better. Allen Johnson, John Van Riper, and Eugene Van Gent were all outstanding players. Only in their last game of the season, with the conference title clinched, did they lose to Chicago and overconfidence. Navy also had an excellent team that year; undefeated and with a 52-point average, led by a small forward named Smith and big center McReavy, they whipped good teams from NYU and St. John's among nine opponents. In the Eastern League, with Yale temporarily gone, Cornell learned the lesson of a coach's value: they won the title, led by the Halstead brothers as guards, but most felt that the improvement was due to their new coach, Al Sharpe, the first one they had ever had, even if he was a Yale man.

By the end of Meanwell's third season at Wisconsin, there was no longer any doubt that he had not only the best team in the country but the best system yet for playing the game. Van Gent, Harper, Lange, Sands, and Hass all ranked among the top eight scorers in the conference while the team maintained their tight defense. Their crisscross patterns and short passes would free one of them for a good shot, and they had the patience to wait until it happened. Again they were undefeated, making Meanwell's record 44–1 for three years, but their pattern of play was even more notable than their pattern of success. The teaching of the "little Doc," who had never played the game himself, came to dominate an era and, in essence, remains one of the dominant philosophies of basketball now. Several branches of its descendants will be discussed in subsequent chapters.

Meanwell could not maintain his overwhelming initial success, yet his record continued to be remarkable. Wisconsin lost four games in 1915, including two to champion Illinois, but regained their regional and national prominence the next year with twenty wins and a single loss, later avenged, to Illinois. In two seasons at Missouri, Meanwell had identical 17–1 records and conference championships, and when he returned to Wisconsin in 1920 he resumed his winning ways, having only five losing seasons before he retired in 1934. He tied for the Big Ten lead with Michigan in 1929, losing only two, both to Michigan, the second time before 9,500 fans in Ann Arbor. Perhaps his biggest loss was in his struggle the year before to have the Joint Committee legislate against the dribble, which he saw as a threat to the kind of game he had taught to so many players and coaches. As late as 1947, Wisconsin was still doing very well playing Meanwell-style basketball under his disciple and former star, Bud Foster, but lost in the second game of the NCAA Eastern Regionals to CCNY in what Nat Holman called a "classic clash of basketball styles."

One way to stop Meanwell's patterned style was for defenders to maintain a set position counter to the setups of the offense and not to move when an offensive man made his cut or moved without the ball. From about 1916 on, for a solid decade or more, the standing zone was the prevalent defense, equally effective against long passes and short. Cam Henderson, first at little Davis and Elkins College in West Virginia and then at Marshall, made the zone work so well that other coaches adopted his arrangements after having tried to play against them. Henderson played his varsity basketball at Westminster College in western Pennsylvania, not to be confused with its tiny namesake in Denver where Bob Pettit's father played briefly before World War I nor with Westminster of Missouri where Forrest DeBernardi, later a perennial AAU all-star, in 1920 scored 50 points in one college game, a presage of things to come.

The big game of 1920, however, was a nostalgic throwback rather than a forward-looking spectacle. Just as in 1908, Chicago and Pennsylvania agreed to a postseason series. Penn was undefeated in nineteen games, coached by Lon Jourdet, an alumnus from the 1910–1912 teams. Winning the Eastern Intercollegiate championship for the third time since the league's reorganization in 1910, they retired the Heppe Trophy. The All-East team consisted of Penn's starters, George Sweeney and Emil Rosenast at forward, Bill Grave at center, and Dutch Peck and Danny

McNichol at guard (the latter a younger brother of Harry, Penn's 1908 star). Chicago's record was not so formidable: they were 10–2, having played no one outside the Western Conference and splitting home-and-home series with Iowa and Wisconsin. But they had a solid team with two veteran forwards, Birkhoff and Vollmer, and a high-scoring running guard, Tony Hinkle (whose subsequent success as coach at Butler for over three decades earned him his Hall of Fame niche). Chicago, too, was coached by a former star, Pat Page, All-American in 1908 and 1909, who later brought Hinkle to Butler as his assistant.

The first game was played in Chicago's Bartlett Gym, with Grave out of the Penn lineup because of measles (reminiscent of 1908 when McNichol had the

*In civvies with the Davis and Elkins 1937 squad are Coach Cam Henderson (right)* and Athletic Director Jennings Randolph, now senior senator from West Virginia.

*Tony Hinkle, protégé of Pat Page.*

flu) and Hinkle of Chicago weakened by illness. Vollmer and Birkhoff got Chicago off to an early lead, 17–6 at the half, and though Penn rallied in the last 13 minutes, led by third-string center Huntzinger, Chicago held on to win 28–24, Vollmer and Birkhoff scoring 12 points each. The second game was at Penn's Weightman Hall three days later. Huntzinger played the whole game for Penn; Hinkle started for Chicago but needed relief in the second half. They tied 10–10 at halftime, but Penn pulled away in the second half, mainly on the strength of Sweeney's fifteen free throws, to win 29–18.

The rubber game was on a neutral court, two nights later, at Princeton. Though the capacity crowd was largely from Philadelphia, both Penn and Chicago provided one official and they alternated halves as referee and umpire. Bill Grave returned for the Red and Blue and was the difference, restoring their cohesive teamwork and tight defense. Penn led 11–7 at the half, but Chicago came back to within a point, 14–13. Penn spurted out to 9 straight points and a ten-point lead with 9 minutes to play. Then they made the tactical error that has cost many a team many a game since: they tried to sit on the lead and the ball. Chicago came back again, but fell short 23–21 at the whistle.

The series may not have provided a national champion for 1920, but it provided a thrilling renewal of intersectional postseason play. The problem was that it looked no different from the basketball played in the earlier series and was perhaps not even as good an exhibition of that style as that shown by Doc Meanwell's first Wisconsin teams. One guard rarely advanced past midcourt, and the cutting and slashing and short passing were still reminiscent of primitive football and rugby. Meanwhile other leagues and independents in every region were playing at a level just as high as the Ivies and the Big Ten, and in many cases more exciting and advanced.

Outstanding in the early Twenties were Westminster of Missouri, South-western of Kansas (led by Edmund Cairns, an 85 percent free-throw shooter in 1920), Washington College of Maryland, Dana Bible's Texas A & M team, Stanford, California, and Nevada in the Far West, and little Franklin College in northern Indiana. The 1920 NYU team, led to a 16–1 record by Howard Cann, perhaps the best player in the country, won the national AAU title in Atlanta. NYU and CCNY played before a crowd estimated at 10,000 at the 22nd Regiment Armory, solidifying a basketball eminence that persisted for three decades. And in the Missouri Valley, once Meanwell brought his methods to Missouri and Phog Allen returned to Kansas, there was another conference worthy of consideration among the best. Into this grouping several others would have to be admitted, including teams coached by Dutch Hermann at Penn State, E. J. Stewart at Texas, Piggy Lambert at Purdue, Pete Vaughn at Wabash College, Bo Shepherd at North Carolina, and finally, once he arrived in South Bend in 1924, George Keogan at Notre Dame.

Keogan gave up dentistry to coach basketball full time, moving with varying degrees of success among six colleges before coming to the Golden Dome. There he stayed, dying at fifty-three during the season in 1943. His twenty-year record was 325–96 for a 77 percent average; he never had a losing season, and several of his teams in the mid-Twenties and mid-Thirties were regarded as the country's best. In forty games in the two years 1926 and 1927 they lost only to Franklin College twice, avenging both losses later in the seasons. In 1937, when they won twenty games against top-flight competition (Notre Dame's schedules have always been ambitious), many thought they could have given the best challenge to Luisetti and Stanford.

Keogan's reputation for strategy is based on his defenses, but he began coaching with primarily an offensive theory. It came not from his days as a student at Minnesota where he saw Western Conference basketball, but his nights as a fan when he watched the Celtics play, especially Dutch Dehnert. He worked patterns based on cuts off the post, but the prevalent midwestern zones effectively changed his thinking. Later, he turned his attention to the defense and was instrumental in making the zone move. He saw that the major advantage of the zone, which basically set up as a three-two, was in having two big men always underneath for defensive rebounding, but he also saw that its major weakness was a vulnerability to penetration by a third or even fourth man on offense. At the same time, most man-to-man defenses were vulnerable to screens and picks. His solution was a neat combination. The three up men set up in what looked like man-to-man coverage, but they switched men with every screen so that they maintained a relatively constant defensive position however much they shifted or dropped back on the court. The back line, however, was virtually stationary in order to control the boards and to initiate the quick-breaking offense whenever they got possession.

Keogan's success was matched by his influence. Ray Meyer adopted his methods in making DePaul a national power, and Ed Hickey used precisely the same three-two screen-switch setup in winning two NIT tournaments for St. Louis. By the end of the Twenties no effective zone defense was ever stationary any more, and the number of variations and combinations began to multiply. Keogan's thinking has been reflected or refracted wherever the zone is played, particularly in terms of quick conversion from defense to offense, and has had great success under such student-innovators as John Lawther at Penn State, Clair Bee at LIU, and John Wooden at UCLA, in shifting, trapping, and pressing zones everywhere.

Zone defenses all have one inherent weakness, which zoning coaches are reluctant to acknowledge, an inability to come from behind. Against superior teams, a zone can keep a team close or keep the score down, but it cannot play successful catch-up. Therefore, a good, confident team has always been able to get a lead and then hold the ball until the defense is forced to come out of their zone. In 1926 CCNY lost to Dickinson College's zone 29–24. When they played again in 1927, Captain Sam Liss of Nat Holman's team suggested that they get a quick 6-point lead and then just wait. The lead came at halftime, thanks to some vintage-City long set shots, and when they got the ball in the second half, they put it in a deep freeze for 12 minutes, winning 15–8.

Conversely, a team with a lead can afford to relax in a tightly zoned shell if the other team is stalling on offense. The fallacies of both these approaches to the game, tactics that tend to terrible tedium, have been pointed out by many an expert and coach, but never with such theatricality as that employed by Pitt's legendary Doc Carlson. Playing on the road once against a zone, he intructed his team to hold the ball throughout the first half with a 3–2 lead, and while the hometown fans showered abuse on the bench, Doc yawned and tossed peanuts to the crowd. Near the end of his career, after losing twice in the season to the Lawther zone as carried on by Elmer Gross at Penn State, Carlson tried the stall in their third meeting. Down 9–6 after three quarters, Pitt tried to pull it out in the fourth, only to have Penn State calmly pull away 24–9.

Carlson's color often provoked interaction with the crowd. After Pitt beat Washington and Jefferson one night, Doc was beaten on the head with an umbrella wielded by a matronly Pennsylvania lady. And in Morgantown, when he kept shouting "this burns me up" at what he thought was partisan officiating, a fan poured a bucket of water on him. Doc's book, *Basketball: The American Game*, has some wry observations about the game. He talks about the peculiarity of clocks in South Bend and the phenomenon known as Notre Dame time (echoed, in Ned Irish's memory, by the situation at City College with their faculty timekeeper):

The timer, his gun poised in the air, ready to end the game, was interrupted in the performance of his duty by a gentle tap on his arm. He turned toward the interrupter to find a little old lady who said only "Wait!" which he did. There was a fraction of a second's play, a shot was made, the gun discharged, the ball bounced against the bank board and into the basket—two points and a tie game.

*Doc Carlson: the Panther as Showboat.*

This otherworldly intrusion only delayed Pitt's win, a rare overtime triumph at South Bend.

It was not Doc Carlson's showmanship, nor even his 370 wins in thirty-one years at Pitt, that won him a place in the Hall of Fame. It was his development of that offensive style known as "continuity." In his sixth year at Pitt, he coached his alma mater to a perfect record. Their twenty-one wins against good teams from the East and the West gave them a good claim to a national championship in 1928. The team started Wallace Reed, Stanley Wrobleskie, Paul Zehfuss, Charles Wunderlich, and everybody's all-time All-American Charles Hyatt in his first varsity year. It was with this team, midway through the season in a game against Army, that Carlson said he saw the birth of system play in basketball.

Carlson's idea of continuity of attack consisted of a three-man figure-eight pattern while the other two men held position. Later, of course, coaches developed continuity patterns for all five men: Ken Loeffler a five-man figure eight, Garland Pinholster a wheel off a disguised 1–3–1 set, Adolph Rupp a guard-through rotation, Bruce Drake and Joel Eaves their similar "shuffles," and Bill Menefee a wheel-post variation. Often, Carlson's influence was direct, since he also pioneered the institution of basketball clinics at Pitt. Buzz Ridl, coach of Westminster's top-ranked college division team in 1962 and in 1974 himself coach of the highly ranked Panthers, remembers being a guinea pig as a high school freshman at one of those clinics, and his own deliberate offense is another descendant of the Doc's continuity, as is Vernon Drenckpohl's "Illinois Continuity" and Bill Healey's "Rotation" offense. Indeed Joe Lapchick says that Carlson's offense, "in some manner or form," is a part of every modern attack in the game.

After a brief falling off in 1929 (16–5), Pitt came back to 23–2 in Hyatt's last year (60–7 was his varsity record) and national prominence, ranking perhaps second only to St. John's. They beat Montana State, the previous season's "Wonder Five," among others on an ambitious schedule. Even after Hyatt's graduation, the system continued to win, twenty of twenty-four games in 1931. The following season was Carlson's first losing one at Pitt, and it would be five more years before there was another one, but in many ways it was a season of great accomplishment for the Panthers.

It was during this year that they blazed a trail for eastern basketball to the West, beginning with a three-game series against Allen's Kansas team and going on to Colorado, Stanford, and Southern California (two games). They won four in a row on this tough road, starting with the third game at Kansas, and thus contributed a standard of excellence against which others could be measured. But if continuity and national competition were firmly established by Doc Carlson and his Pitt teams by the early Thirties, another trend would begin to overshadow those accomplishments as the game entered its hurry-up phase of development.

# 6

# *Piggy and the Horses*

THE SPORTS cliché about coaches not being able to win without the horses originates in the debate about the relative value of jockeys in racing. In basketball, as in football, the phrase has taken on greater meaning by drawing on the symbolic associations of equine size and speed. Thus fast-break basketball is often called the racehorse game, and in looking back to the origins of this style, one discovers that size has often been an essential component of the running game. Probably the most influential coaches in this development were Ward Lambert and Frank Keaney, and their Purdue and Rhode Island teams provide perfect models for this notion of horses. Other early proponents of the big-man, fast-break configuration, such as Ed Diddle and Leonard Sachs, will be mentioned later.

When Piggy Lambert took over at Purdue, the Boilermakers had been suffering through bad times. Only once, in 1912, had they been close to the top of the Western Conference, when they won all twelve games, including ten in the league, but finished second to Wisconsin, which played a fuller schedule. Purdue sank slowly through the ranks until 1916 when, coachless, they finished last. Lambert brought them back to respectability with an 11–3 record, third in the conference. For two more lean years in Lambert's wartime absence they languished and lapsed, but again he led them back—to second in 1920 (they didn't play champion Chicago), to a three-way tie for first in 1921 (losing twice to Michigan but not playing Wisconsin), and finally to the title in 1922, when they lost only their conference opener by a point to Illinois and nonconference games to Wabash and DePauw. Not until the Forties did a Lambert-coached Purdue team have a losing season. They won 372 games, over 70 percent of all they played.

Piggy bucked the prevailing style of Big Ten basketball. While most teams were playing modifications of Meanwell's system and, later, Carlson's continuity, Purdue specialized in quick breaking whenever the ball changed hands. To make this system work they needed all-around quickness and balance and a dependable big man. The 1922 team had all-league Blair Gullion at center, but the defensive rebounding burden fell to Captain Ray Miller, whose strong backcourt play allowed Gullion along with Eversman, Masters, and White to roam and run and gun. This team was notable also for its unusually large squad—fourteen men until White became ineligible—and because its coach suited up and worked out with his men, unlike the sedate professorial doctors elsewhere.

Lambert's ideas were not radically visible in the Big Ten. His teams didn't roll up unusual scores, and from casual observation it was hard to tell their theoretical distinctiveness from the more traditional patterns of their opponents from Madison or Champaign. Indeed it was Illinois's Chuck Carney who set a conference scoring record in 1920, 188 points in twelve games, that wasn't broken for over two decades. Lambert just didn't have the horses to make the theory visible yet. Purdue stayed close to the top of the league, tying for first with three others in 1926, but then in 1928 the components were all there. Again they tied for the title, splitting their series with Everett Dean's Indiana team, but this time they had 6-foot 6-inch Stretch Murphy clearing the ball and Lloyd Kemmer leading the charge. For the first time they consistently scored near 40 points a game, and they even beat Wabash, Piggy's alma mater, who had always given them trouble in the past. The following year, with Murphy still leading the way, Purdue outscored their closest rival in the conference by 100 points, though finishing third.

When Murphy was a senior, he was joined on the starting five by Harmeson and Kellar at forward and at guard by Boots and one John Wooden, who had already become a legend during his high school career in Indiana. Purdue was undefeated in the league, the first time in eleven years that that had been done, and lost only to Butler and Montana State. Wooden's presence on the team brought the final dimension to the championship pattern: to rebounding strength and quick-breaking offense, add tight, aggressive defense. Two years later, after an interregnum for Northwestern's Cinderella Wildcats, Wooden led Purdue back to the top, assisted by Harry Kellar, Ray Eddy, and the new big man, 6-foot 4-inch Ralph Parmenter. They lost only once in splitting with Illinois; their seventeen victories included Notre Dame, Pittsburgh, Montana State, and Marquette; and they scored 41 points a game while holding their opponents to under 25.

Piggy Lambert.

Stretch Murphy.   John Wooden.

Purdue's defensive strength was misleading, in the sense that it disguised the significant differences of their overall play from that of all their conference except, on occasion, Indiana. They went on to further success, winning or tying for league championships in 1934, 1935, 1936, 1938, and 1940, yet it can hardly be said that Lambert and Purdue taught the fast break to the Big Ten and the Midwest, let alone the country as a whole. But perhaps they helped teach their neighbors. Ironically, in 1940, Indiana won the second NCAA tournament, though they had finished second to Purdue in their conference.

It remained for a greater showman than Piggy to show the horses in a way that would excite the public to the possibilities of fast-break basketball, Frank Keaney of Rhode Island. After a decade at little Putnam College, Keaney came to Kingston town in 1920 where his Rhode Island team celebrated his arrival by running up over 80 points against Providence in their opener. This was surely an omen of things to come, though they were a long time coming for this ebullient coach. Six mediocre seasons passed until they started to roll toward point-a-minute production in 1927, but they moved from there to the 1,000-point-season mark in 1937, to 70 points a game in 1939, and to an incredible 2,000-point season in 1945. Keaney won over four hundred games in twenty-eight years at Rhode Island, with a 77 percent winning record.

Keaney at courtside was a show in himself. He might dump jackets and towels and anything else he could find on the bench out onto the court and tell the referee, "You've taken everything else from us—you might as well have all this, too!" Once, against Northeastern, one of his players fouled out, and instead of sending in a substitute, Keaney put a folding chair on the court, saying, "Call fouls on that player right there if you want; that's my fifth player." Of course he had a big lead at the time, near the end of the game, but he liked to say that he had beaten Northeastern with four men and a chair.

Keaney hated the zone defense, thought it was ruining the game. Certainly it ruined the scoring proclivities of his team. One night Maine, against whom Rhode Island had been running up scores for years, went into an extreme deep zone to keep the score down. Rhode Island scored two quick baskets, got the ball back, and called time out. Keaney instructed them to hold the ball until Maine came out of the zone. For the rest of the half a Rhode Island player stood just over the time line with the ball under his arm. Other players were sitting on the floor. The substitutes on the bench were reading newspapers. The halftime score was 4–0, and Keaney was saying, "If you really want to play a zone, we'll help you."

It is said that he would inspire his team by reading poetry to them before a game. Frank McGuire decided to try this on his Tarheels before an important North Carolina game. On their way onto the floor, one of his players said, "We've *got* to win this one for Frank. He's gone nuts!" Keaney was always coming up with psychological devices to prepare his team. He invented a ring that would be placed inside the hoop to reduce the diameter and improve accuracy. And once he burned

*Keaney's* (left) *fastest horse came on to fill his shoes at Rhode Island—Calverley was coach and athletic director.*

smudge pots in the gym during practice to prepare Rhode Island for a game in smoky, smoggy Madison Square Garden.

But when he had the horses, his teams could fill the lanes on the fast break as it had never been seen before. He began to develop this style in the late Twenties, but it really began to open up in the Thirties and into the early Forties, when he had a succession of outstanding players at Kingston. First there was his son Warner, a 240-pound, 6-foot 6-inch giant. He instructed him to guard the basket and do nothing else. The other men were to play a pressing, harassing, gambling defense, and as soon as a shot went up, they were to break the other way. Warner would get the ball—on a rebound or out of bounds—and throw a long pass downcourt. This brought many a turnover but many a basket, and that was the idea— scoring and excitement.

When the others were players with the speed, moves, and accuracy of Chet Jaworski, Bill Rutledge, and Stan Stutz Modzelewski, the Keaney style usually won. They could drive at full speed from any angle and put up the soft shots. Finally there was Ernie Calverley, called by Red Auerbach the finest passer coming down the middle of the fast break in all of college basketball, surpassed only by Bob Cousy when the Boston Celtics were running. Calverley led a Keaney team all the way to the NIT finals in 1946, only to have Kentucky beat them by a point with a very deliberate game plan. But by that time all of basketball had learned the values of the running game.

# 7

# *The Phog Rolls On*

ACCORDING to Adolph Rupp, Forrest C. Allen was "not only one of the greatest coaches that the game has ever developed, but also the finest leader of men that the game has known." Only Rupp's teams won more games than Allen's 771. In his forty-eight-year career Allen produced outstanding coaches from among his players, including Rupp, Dutch Lonborg, Johnny Bunn, Lou Menze, Dean Smith, and Frosty Cox; in his thirty-nine years as head coach at Kansas, he won seven Missouri Valley titles plus one shared, eight Big Six titles plus four shared, two Big Seven titles plus two shared, and the NCAA championships in 1952.

Allen played under Naismith at Kansas and on the Kansas City Athletic Club team that beat the Buffalo Germans in a 1905 series. In 1907, still an undergraduate, he coached Baker University in Baldwin to an undefeated season that included wins over Kansas and Missouri. The following year he took over for Naismith at Kansas, continued to handle Baker, and then took on Haskell Institute as well for 1909. In those two years his teams won 116 games, losing only sixteen including two to each other. His 1909 Kansas team was 26–3, was considered the best in the Midwest, decisively avenging all three losses, and successfully defended their title in the Missouri Valley Conference formed just the year before.

This was a giant start toward his career totals of 771–233, a .768 percentage. For four years he studied for his medical degree at the Kansas City School of Osteopathy and then coached the Warrensburg Teachers College to 107–7 in seven consecutive championship years in the Missouri College Conference before returning to Lawrence. Here is where the major phase of the Phog Allen story begins.

During Allen's absence Kansas had slipped from champions in 1915 to consistent also-rans, losing more than they won both in and out of the conference. He brought back with him some sound, practical ideas on basketball and on training, and he carried with him a unique personality and a host of idiosyncrasies as well. His offense was a standard three-two pattern with a clear middle through which most of the plays were directed. His defense was developing a complex combination of man-to-man and zone techniques that he eventually came to call "Stratified Transitional Man-for-Man Defense with the Zone Principle." Exactly what this meant has never been quite clear, but some special defenses later used by Hank Iba and Adolph Rupp seem to exemplify Allen's conception.

A stickler for conditioning and training, Allen drilled his men with analogies of simians on the defense and a mongoose defeating a cobra. His authoritarian leadership extended to matters of diet for his players, with water by the quart as a staple—except during a game. Sometimes he would get a bit mystical and swear he could see "the victory light" shining in the eyes of those he picked as starters.

Winning was very important to this self-styled "Father of Basketball Coaches," in marked contrast with his long-time colleague at Kansas, the "Father of Basketball." Naismith believed in throwing up the ball and letting the boys have fun playing with it; Allen believed that Naismith's game was well designed for the exercise of strategy in achieving victory. Naismith, the chaplain-sportsman, advocated pure amateurism; Allen, the promoter-pubicist-progressive, pioneered recruiting and professionalism. On the issues of rules, they usually argued—with some degree of influence on both parts—on opposite sides, Naismith in defense of the old rules, Allen in favor of the innovations. Yet for decades they coexisted peacefully on the same campus, the one rather wistfully indulgent, the other respectful but condescending, and both proud—in their different ways—of what they had wrought.

However unorthodox Allen's methods were, they were successful. Missouri, under Meanwell, was way ahead of the league, but Kansas had a winning record in 1920 for third place, extending Missouri to an overtime game in their first meeting. Phog took only seven men on the road to Drake, and when two, Bunn and the star Scrubby Laslett, broke training rules, the stern coach announced that the other five—Lonborg, Rody, Bennett, Harms, and Fearing—would start and play the whole game. With 3 minutes left and Kansas up by a point, Rody was charged with his fourth foul, the limit at that time. Allen, believing the foul should have been Fearing's, started around the floor to explain the situation to Coach Solem, confident he would allow Rody to continue. But the crowd's reaction was so vehement that he turned back to his bench and sent Laslett in. Drake thought they would win now against a weakened opponent, but Laslett played, in Allen's words, "like a fiendish animal unleashed," scored or contributed to 16 points in 3 minutes, and Kansas drew out to an easy 19-point win.

After another mediocre (or what is often called a rebuilding) year, Kansas was again ready to challenge for the crown in a newly arranged double round-robin schedule. Offensive-minded Missouri led in the early season and beat Kansas at Lawrence by 10 points. Going into the rematch at Columbia they remained undefeated, while Kansas had lost only a nonconference game with defending AAU champions of the Kansas City AC. Just before the game, Kansas star forward

Lonberg (left) and Rupp.

Paul Endacott.

Dick Harp.

Ray Evans.

Phog Allen's legacy includes
great coaches and players.

Dean Smith.

Armin Woestemeyer was declared ineligible. Allen confused Coach Ruby and Missouri's defensive plans by having Woestemeyer warm up and his name in the scorebook, though not in a starting position. Kansas, with tight defense and ball possession, controlled the tempo of the game and won, 26–15. The star was not one of the regulars—Rody, Endacott, Wulf, or Black—but substitute Tusten Ackerman, who believed he was avenging the accidental football death of his boyhood hero, Tommy Johnson, at the hands of Old Mizzou.

There was no sharing of the title the following year as Kansas, with the same lineup that had earned a conference tie by beating Missouri the previous year, went undefeated in the conference. They lost only to the same Kansas City AC team that seemed always to tighten them up for league play. The game at Missouri was the toughest. It was the fourth game in five nights during an arduous Kansas road trip, and all five starters played the entire game with slight injuries. Moreover, they had not eaten a sit-down meal in over 24 hours. Down 16–10, they rallied in the last 5 minutes to take the lead 21–19. And in the last 2 minutes, All-American Paul Endacott bulldogged the ball on sixteen straight tip-offs to keep the game safe. Ironically, one of Phog Allen's proposed rule changes was a rotation of the center jump that would have made such inspired play impossible. The second Missouri game was saved by Charley Black's one-man freeze to preserve another narrow win 23–20.

Kansas dominated the league for four more years, never losing more than two conference games, until 1928 when Oklahoma took over. That was the last year of the old system, and the larger schools regrouped into the Big Six. The first year under the new alignment was a disaster for Kansas. It was the year when they had planned to unleash 7-foot Harry Kersenbrock, whom Allen had drilled into shape by working him against two tough football guards. But the gentle giant was lost in a drowning accident during the summer, and the grieved coach and team never recovered that year. They won only three games. Ironically, again, Phog Allen became an early proponent of a 12-foot basket, presumably to cut down the effectiveness of the big man.

The resilient Jayhawkers came back in 1930 to second place and then four straight championship years, led by such stars as Cox, Bishop, O'Leary, Johnson, and Ebling. In 1932, the league race was decided on the last night of the season against Oklahoma as Bill Johnson arrived from his father's funeral 400 miles away just 6 minutes before game time. The tip-off had actually been delayed a half-hour, ostensibly to get the Missouri–Kansas State results in advance of their own game. But the real reason was to get Johnson there from the airport where an alumnus' plane had flown him straight from the funeral. The 31–27 win might easily have gone the other way without him.

The year 1936 was a big one for Allen. His team went undefeated in the conference and was led by his son Milt. Phog had to bench his irrepressible son for insubordination during a practice, but he sent him in as a substitute in the Nebraska game to spark the team to a tough road victory. When Milt fouled out, the Lincoln fans gave him a standing ovation. The team, however, did not get great national attention for a variety of reasons. LIU in the East, Notre Dame, Indiana, and Purdue in the Midwest, and Stanford in the Far West were all outstanding (as were their coaches: Bee, Keogan, Dean, Lambert, and Bunn). And then, in the Olympic trials, after beating Utah State once, Kansas lost to them twice and was eliminated. Nevertheless, the inclusion of basketball in the Olympic Games was itself a triumph for Allen, who had campaigned vigorously for several years for the rulings and the funds that would make it possible.

In 1938 Kansas was on top of the conference again, with Fred Pralle and Dick Harp leading the way. They tied for the lead in 1940 (with another son, Bob, in uniform), 1941, and 1942, and then went undefeated in 1943. The 1940 team went to the NCAA finals, beating Rice and Southern Cal before losing to Indiana. But the 1943 team, with Ray Evans and another Charley Black, did not participate in postseason play, nor did the championship 1946 team. Phog believed that the 1943 team came together on a road trip, playing St. Bonaventure, Fordham in Madison Square Garden, St. Joseph's in Convention Hall in Philadelphia, and St. Louis in Municipal Auditorium. Traveling second-class by day with signs of wartime stress and casualties visible everywhere, and staying in railroad hotels at night, the coach could feel the petty jealousies giving way to larger thoughts. This story, Allen said, "should perhaps be accompanied by muffled drums," but in his book it is what led to a surprising ever-victorious season.

In the fifth decade of his basketball career, Phog Allen continued to field representative teams, to keep track of developments, and especially to have his foghorn voice heard on all controversial matters. When pressing zone defenses were shown to work, Allen perfected one of the best. He had supported the campaign for a 10-second rule but played reactionary in calling for the reinstatement of the center jump. The fan-shaped backboard was his innovation, but he opposed all bonus-foul rules with the quip that "only alcoholics want two shots for one." He continually looked for ways to hold down the trend toward the big man, yet he entered his sixth basketball decade with big Clyde Lovellette as the star who brought him the national championship in 1952. Dunking is not basketball, he proclaimed to all who would listen or read; yet when he was forced to retire at the age of seventy in 1956, it was with great reluctance, because he had recruited Wilt Chamberlain. Chamberlain played his two varsity years under Allen's former player and assistant, Dick Harp, and it is a final irony that Allen and Kansas indirectly brought about some reforms against the domination of the big man.

66

# Part 3

# The City Game

WITH APOLOGIES to Pete Axthelm not really necessary, I use the title of his excellent basketball book to label an entirely different concept. By "city" Axthelm means "an urban society that breeds invisibility," a place where basketball with its harsh rhythms and intricate patterns is perfectly suited to "a turbulent, frustrating existence," in which basketball can be a major part of the fabric of life. By "the City" I mean simply New York, except when by "City" I mean CCNY, now the City College of the City University of New York. By "the city game" Axthelm means simply basketball, whether played one-on-one on strips of asphalt or by NBA teams in sold-out arenas; by "the city game" I mean a style of play, developed in the metropolitan area, that was a dominant factor in American basketball for over two decades.

Yet we are not that far apart after all. Axthelm's book intercuts two main sequences of action: the championship drive of the New York Knickerbockers at Madison Square Garden and the continuing drama, breeding legend, of contemporary playground basketball played in New York. He thus juxtaposes the epitome of team play of the 1970 Knicks with the spectacle of individual feats like the Hawk hook-dunking over Chamberlain in a Rucker's game or the matchless moves of the fabulous Earl Manigault. And it is New York City basketball he is talking about throughout.

Leonard Koppett, too, in another excellent basketball book, says that the sport was "indigenous to the city, the game kids could play with a passion in school yards and settlement houses." He goes on to point out how that passion grew by a kind of implosion as city-bred boys became students and then alumni of NYU, CCNY, Manhattan College, Fordham, St. John's, Brooklyn College, LIU, and others. The good teams, the natural rivalries, and the rooting interests fed upon each other, and later the widespread media coverage helped fan these insular flames. Another important element is the prideful mark of distinctive ethnic contributions.

In the early Fifties, Axthelm finds the game feeding "the dreams of the Irish athletes on famous playgrounds . . . in Rockaway," while a decade earlier "in the Bronx, tough, aggressive Jewish youths grew into defense-minded, set-shooting stars [who] led the colleges of the city to national prominence." From the middle Fifties on, however, the great black products of the city's playgrounds have gone far afield to establish regional hegemonies in diverse provinces; but perhaps this trend can be considered the ultimate triumph of what we have both called the city game.

I can remember my camp counselor in 1945 who was a local hero because this wiry Jewish boy and Dick McGuire had picked up each other's moves in their neighborhood games in Belle Harbor. And watching Marty Karp play, one could understand perfectly what Ben Carnevale means when he talks about Frank McGuire's background: "His knowledge of the game was gained the hard way. He first played and fought on the playgrounds where the playing areas were congested, where a basketball was a prize to be fought for and where the competition was intense and cruel."

The basketball lessons learned in this milieu by Nat Holman, Joe Lapchick, Howard Cann, and Honey Russell, among many others, and passed on to their teams at the New York colleges, are the basic texts for this section called "The City Game." Its chapters will sketch a period of twenty-odd years when a significant, substantial portion of the whole American college basketball scene could be viewed in the old Madison Square Garden or within a radius of 25 miles. And the refinements and applications of those lessons will be seen to have produced a distinctive style that marked its time and place with what I call the era of the city game.

*Mr. City Basketball, Nat Holman.*

# 8

# *Buck Freeman's Wonder Five*

BASKETBALL, born 100 miles up the Connecticut River, found one secure home at the mouth of the Hudson. Throughout the metropolitan area, in YMCAs and settlement houses and school gyms, in lofts and armories and dance halls, basketball evolved a style in which New Yorkers excelled with their aggressiveness, quick hands, and ability to dodge. From the City, out the Island and up the River, the game became the favorite indigenous sport, and in this area the club, semipro, and professional teams early on established their supremacy.

The colleges of the area were relatively slow to achieve a parallel success, although Columbia was four times the Eastern Intercollegiate League champion by 1913 and was not until 1921 surpassed by Pennsylvania as the league's winningest team. In 1907 Columbia scheduled both CCNY and Fordham, and by 1918 they had been beaten by NYU, CCNY, and Brooklyn Polytechnic. In 1910 NYU was 14–3, beating both Princeton and Yale, while St. John's was 15–5, including easy wins over NYU by 21–12 and Navy by 31–14 (supposedly the best in the South). The Redmen averaged close to 40 points a game, running up a 96–5 score against St. Stephen's College. The following year St. John's won all fourteen games, beating many of the strongest teams in the East—Penn, Yale, Wesleyan,

Georgetown, and Colgate—while NYU was the only team to beat Navy at Annapolis.

If the team play at the metropolitan schools was erratic during the first quarter of this century, there were at least two good reasons. For one, many of the players were often playing with other teams—clubs, semipros—at the same time. And for another, they were all trying to play pro-style ball, that is, the precision give-and-go, quick-cutting, short-passing game that came to be known as the Celtics style; and they couldn't master it without the confidence and integrated skill born of repetition in game and practice with a constant lineup. Stability of a kind was established with the beginning of long-term coaching tenures—Nat Holman at City from 1919, Ed Kelleher at Fordham from 1922, Howard Cann at NYU from 1923, and Lew Andreas at Syracuse from 1924—but these positions were just part-time jobs for a long time. The coaches had other duties, other jobs, and other teams.

Holman could first claim a championship in 1922 with a strong six-man team led by Frank Salz and Jack Nadel, two 5-foot 5-inch forwards. At home they beat Princeton 18–15 with a freeze in the final minutes. Their only losses were by a point in a split series with Syracuse and to Holy Cross by 2 points. The return match at Princeton was, unofficially, for the regional championship, since the Tigers had clinched the Ivy League. With a starting team averaging 6 feet, Princeton successfully kept Salz and Nadel away from the basket, but with the score tied at 24 and time running out, Salz hit from midcourt to win.

Syracuse, NYU, and Fordham all had powerful teams at times in the Twenties, but although recognized by the Ivies, they rarely played anyone from west of Trenton. Pitt was the major exception, losing four of seven to Syracuse and beating Fordham once during the decade. Syracuse also won three of five games with Big Ten schools from 1926–1930. But for the most part the eastern independents and the metropolitan area schools played each other. The Hudson Valley and the neighborhood of its delta constituted a major force in basketball, but these colleges were outside the mainstream. Still, in 1927, Fordham, led by J. Zakszewski, may have been the best team in America, while Vic Hanson of Syracuse may have been the best player.

Well into the 1928 season, Fordham was unbeaten. The Rams, with Frank Dougherty, Bo Adams, Nick Landers, Morgan Sweetman, and Dan Reardon, led CCNY 24–12 with 6 minutes left. At this point, Holman sent Jack Sandak in for Lou Spindell with instructions not to drive on Landers. Sandak obeyed, hitting two quick sets from 25 feet and then two more baskets off the pivot. With 2 minutes remaining, Sandak hit another long one to cut the lead to two, but Dougherty's free throw made it 25–22. Julie Raskin then drove in for a layup, and on the following tip-off, Teddy Meisel fed Irv Goldberg to put City ahead. With only seconds left Landers tied Goldberg up, but deafened by the crowd Goldberg refused to give the ball to the referee and was called for a technical foul. Adams went to the line, but Holman, using a ploy that has since become standard practice

*St. John's squad includes the Wonder Five: in the first row, from the right, are Begovich, Posnak, Kinsbrunner, and Schuckman; Gerson is just behind Posnak; Coach Freeman, in sweatshirt, is at top left.*

in the ploybook of every coach, called time-out to let Adams think about the clutch shot. It was missed, and City gave Fordham their only loss of the year. The following year, NYU did the trick, but over a three-year span Fordham went 48–4.

Fordham may have been the big team of 1928, but they were not really the big basketball news in New York. Nor was it the foundation of LIU, which was to attain athletic prominence in its academic infancy. It was the arrival at St.

John's of six men, Coach Buck Freeman and five players. Matty Begovich, 6-foot 5-inch center, could not only jump well but also control the tap. The others were all 6 feet and under. Mack Posnak at forward was a good rebounder and defender and the best passer outside the pros. Rip Gerson at guard was the premier defensive specialist with the quick hands that held down opponents' top scorers. Allie Schuckman at guard had the original "quick release" that has become a sports cliché. And, perhaps best of all, twice All-American along with Posnak, was Mac Kinsbrunner, at 5 feet 8 inches the smallest of the five, rated by both Nat Holman and Red Auerbach as one of the greatest dribblers of all time.

St. John's had always tried to emulate the Celtics, and it is said that their 1926 center, Rip Collins, even improved on the original pivot-post play by developing a quick pivot shot. But now they had the personnel to carry it off, and Freeman experimented with a double-post setup to vary their standard ball-control-around-single-post offense. Their defense was tight man-to-man coverage, with switching when necessary. But the best part of their defense was preparation. Freeman scouted future opponents and often had his players there as well, studying the moves of the men they would cover.

Posnak relates amusingly the story of how they all got together, the coach, the big center from Hoboken, and the four Jewish boys from Brooklyn, at the Vincentian school at Willoughby and Lewis in Stuyvesant Heights. Freeman was a St. John's alumnus, and he was hired as coach with the idea that he would recruit ball players. Begovich joined up in a normal course of events, unlike the others. Gerson was already two years out of Commercial High School, where he had been a truly great prep player, and had since completed the two-year course at the Brooklyn College of Pharmacy. He came to St. John's and Freeman for the sole purpose of continuing his basketball, not his education. Schuckman and Kinsbrunner graduated from high school one semester ahead of Posnak and started college elsewhere, one at LIU and the other at Syracuse. Posnak was ready to follow along to Syracuse, but Kinsbrunner talked him out of it, saying no scholarship was worth the amount of work required.

Posnak enrolled at St. John's, and Kinsbrunner transferred there from Syracuse. Then Schuckman, who had played at Thomas Jefferson High with Posnak, decided to transfer to be with the others. Thus Freeman had his Wonder Five assembled in the little gym at Willoughby and Lewis, yet the four Jewish players were not enrolled there at all but at the accounting school at Borough Hall. Not that it mattered; they played very few games in the campus gym anyway, using the Armory at Bedford and Atlantic for some games and Arcadia Hall for others but playing as visitors throughout most of their impressive career.

In their first game together they upset a good CCNY team and went on to an eight-game streak before Fordham whipped them 32–20. They finished the season at 18–4, splitting series with St. Joseph's and Scranton and losing to the Crescent AC, a semipro team that made a habit of teaching the college boys a lesson. As freshmen they had averaged 36 points a game while holding their opponents to 26. More important, they had meshed as a unit. Learning what each other could do, they learned what they all might be able to do together, and they had the confidence to fulfill their high aspirations.

As sophomores they lost their third game to Providence College by two points but then went on to eighteen straight wins, mostly comfortable ones although NYU came within a point. It was Fordham that broke the streak, also preventing the Redmen from avenging all of their previous season's losses. They finished the season with three more wins for a 23–2 record. Their scoring had fallen off to a 32-point average, but their defense had been even better, so that their margin of victory was still better than 10 points a game. They had been drilled into marvels of ball control, and they made very few mistakes or turnovers.

Perhaps their only mistake in their junior year was to be overconfident in a return game with Providence, whom they had beaten early in the season. The Friars ruined a perfect record. The first seven games, including Columbia and Providence, were all fairly easy wins, and then they faced little Rider College from Trenton, which Clair Bee had turned into a powerful, high-scoring team. Rider was 18–3 that year and scored over 1,000 points. At the half Rider led by 2 but had been frustrated by St. John's defense and ball control. Rider scored to start the second half, but St. John's controlled the tap and then the ball for 11 minutes before working it in for an easy score The success of their patience seemed to rattle Rider, and St. John's scored twice again after taps from Begovich to Posnak and never relinquished the lead, winning 36–32.

Wins over Holy Cross and St. Bonaventure stretched their streak to thirteen, including the last three of 1929, before they came a cropper at Providence. Fourteen games remained on the schedule, and they won them all, including Crescent AC, NYU, and a 22–21 rematch with Rider. Their scoring dipped to 31 points a game, but this time their opponents averaged under 21, an incredible defensive performance even for 1929–1930, when there was neither boom nor bust in Stuyvesant Heights. For the first time they were recognized in Spalding's *Official Basketball Guide,* in a new section called "The Game in the East," though that traditionalist publication ranked Pitt ahead of them. Pitt was good (23–2) but had lost to Syracuse. Syracuse was good (18–2) but had lost to Columbia. Columbia was good (17–5 and the Ivy League champs), but the Redmen had handled them easily 28–19.

The senior year was the best. They played fewer games but a tougher schedule. The first thirteen games, extending their unbeaten streak to twenty-seven, included Providence, Georgetown, Niagara, Syracuse, and City twice. Then came the only loss, as Howard Cann's inspired NYU team beat them at their own game, 27–23. The grim grey Palisades echoed to the cry of this upset, but along the rippling Hudson shore no one else came close to St. John's for the rest of the season, eight more wins. In the second CCNY game they had held the Beavers scoreless for 38 minutes, winning 17–9 over a team that averaged 32 and had scored 56 against Dartmouth and 68 against Ursinus. In their final game the Wonder Five held a better than average Manhattan College team scoreless from the floor. Again their defense against scoring for the year was just under 21 points per game, and they won twenty-one games while averaging just 29 points themselves.

Four years together and eighty-six wins in ninety-four games, including a record of 70–4 in the last three years, were not enough. Begovich, Kinsbrunner, Posnak, Gerson, and Schuckman graduated together into the pros, forming their own team. Only one other time, two decades later, would a college five try the pro game as a unit, and with altogether less satisfactory results. The Wonder Five toured independently for two years and then played five years as the Jewels in the American League. Joined by George Slott and Jake Poliskin, both younger St. John's graduates, and Honey Russell, an experienced pro who had grown up in Brooklyn but instead of going to college had been a professional athlete in three sports since he was sixteen, they were often near the top of the league; and they stayed together through eleven seasons all told.

For five more winning seasons Buck Freeman stayed on at St. John's. His cumulative record of 179–32 was probably the greatest success of any coach whose teams were taught to play exclusively in the style of the Celtics and the Rens. And he was succeeded in due course by one of the premier younger-generation Celtics, Joe Lapchick.

# 9

# *Gotham as Mecca*

IT WOULD almost be possible to believe that it happened in a single, bold, imaginative stroke, that overnight New York City became the focal point of national interest in basketball, and that it was the night of December 29, 1934. The night's importance cannot be denied, nor can the great contribution of Ned Irish, but the match was a long time in the making.

The excellence of the City Game had long since been established, but virtually the only ones who knew about it were the local followers of the teams. Babe Ruth got twice the press coverage of the President of the United States, but few newspapers covered basketball on any kind of regular basis. Basketball fans were necessarily in comparatively exclusive company in the city. Only Fordham had anything like adequate facilities for its own students in its gym—2,500 seats—while in the Midwest fieldhouses already could accommodate four times that number.

St. John's great Five performed their wonders in relative obscurity, though fans were often turned away at the door. Game after game CCNY, NYU, and a dozen other teams in the area worked their pivot play, their give and go, and their controlled passing before rabid capacity crowds, all under fifteen hundred. In 1930, the powerful Rams were beaten in the last minute by City with the perfect execution of a center jump play that Holman had been working on in drills. Frank De Phillips tapped the ball toward Lou Spindell who tapped it aside to the cutting Art Musicant for a layup and a 24–23 upset. The event thrilled all of 1,200 people, and perhaps not many more than that read about it the following morning.

There were occasional exceptions. Early in 1931, a record New York crowd of 12,000 jammed the 106th Infantry Armory to see the Wonder Five beat CCNY 26–21. A more important exception, and a new record crowd, came shortly after, brought on by the conditions of the times. Mayor Jimmy Walker enlisted the aid of sportswriters to promote benefit basketball games in Madison Square Garden for the Unemployment Relief Fund. On January 19, 1931, a charity triple-header drew an SRO crowd of 15,000 to the Garden, with thousands more turned away, to see six local teams with a combined season's record of 45–8 among them square off: Columbia beat Fordham 26–18; Manhattan beat NYU 16–14 to remain undefeated; and St. John's extended their unbeaten streak to twenty-two at the expense of CCNY, 17–9.

Yet just weeks later, only the usual 1,200 faithful saw another classic City upset. With Holman at his sick brother's bedside, Mac Hodesblatt, his assistant and former captain, led the Beavers against Doc Carlson's Panthers. Pitt led 14–5 at the half; but City began to come back, patiently waiting for the good shot, giving no room at all on defense. Captain De Phillips scored on a set shot, Milt Trupin fed Davidoff for a layup, and De Phillips hit from outside again. Smith's basket for Pitt gave them a 5-point lead again, when Holman made his dramatic appearance. The timing was impeccable, the inspiration sufficient. Trupin hit a free throw, De Phillips a shot from the side, and Davidoff fed Trupin for the tying layup. Kowalis missed a foul for Pitt, and with time running out and Holman shouting, "Shoot!" from the bench, Lou Wisner hit the long set that won the game 18–16. City had allowed Pitt only 2 points in the second half.

In the next season, Wisner, along with Davidoff, Moe Spahn, Moe Goldman, and Johnny White, got City off to a good start, though there was an early loss to Temple. The crucial game was with St. John's. The Wonder Five, having beaten City three straight times, were gone, but with Slott, Poliskin, Lazar, Neary, and Smith, St. John's was still strong, coming into the game with an 8–1 record. The teams were virtually mirror images, Buck Freeman and Nat Holman thinking along identical lines. City led 9–8 at the half, and with 3 minutes left in the game and leading 17–14, they elected to go into a freeze. This tactical error, as it has countless times since, backfired. Neary intercepted a pass and scored and then Slott scored, but Goldman's free throw sent them into overtime. City went back into their patented attack, starting with a Goldman-to-Davidoff-to-Wisner tap play. White and Goldman added a basket and a free throw each, and Davidoff also hit from the field: it was 10–0 in the extra period for a 28–18 win. CCNY went on to a 16–1 season and in 1933 were 13–1 and rated the best in the East.

*Ned Irish.*

Twenty years later Holman still ranked Wisner among the greatest little men he'd ever seen.

During that season the Mayor and the sportswriters staged a marathon seven-game orgy in the Garden, drawing 20,000 people, again for Depression relief. Ned Irish, who helped promote all these charity affairs in the *World-Telegram*, didn't really need this lesson to teach him that newspaper coverage could sell games and fill halls. He also had great confidence in the drawing power of basketball. Starting as a stringer for five newspapers, he had been covering sports since he was in high school, making up to 100 dollars a week. As a college student at Penn, he covered Pennsylvania sports for most of the New York papers, while also working full time on the *Philadelphia Record*. Returning to New York in 1929, he took a substantial cut in salary to cover local sports for the *World-Telegram* at 60 dollars a week. In fact, for about two years, Irish and the *World-Telegram* were alone in giving regular coverage to metropolitan college sports.

Legend has it that Irish, with the doors locked at the crowded little gym in Riverdale where Manhattan College played, climbed through a window to cover his beat; that he ripped his pants doing it; and that he experienced an epiphany, the vision of thousands lined up at the Garden to see a college basketball game. Well, he did go in through the window, and he says now that it is "possible that the suit tore"—but the visionary revelation is pure press-agentry. The idea of promoting basketball at the Garden was already firmly established in Irish's thinking, and so was his belief in the value of the printed word in selling sports events to the public. Indeed, he was already writing publicity for the football Giants and later initiated the National Football League Press Bureau.

By the 1934 season, following the lead of Irish, most of the local newspapers were covering metropolitan college basketball, and some of the rest of the world was taking notice. Among the matters worth noting were two teams, outstanding among several good ones, CCNY and NYU. Holman and Cann had the Lavender and the Violet executing their precision games, winning them all, and heading for a climactic clash in March. With interest building for this game and a mythical City championship at stake, Ned Irish decided to promote it at Madison Square Garden. The only date available as far as the two schools were concerned was already booked for what Irish calls "a so-so heavyweight fight," and Harold Steinman, manager of one of the fighters, rejected a week's delay because it was infra dig for the sweet science to be preempted by a roundball game.

As it happened, the game was played at the 168th Street Armory, and Nat Holman made the mistake of getting tickets for his old friend Lazarus Joseph, New York City's Comptroller. NYU's Willie Rubenstein had been detained at the police station; Joseph arranged to get him out in time for the game; Rubenstein led Cann's team to a 24–18 upset. It was City's only loss and NYU could claim the local championship, but the really important event of the spring was Irish's definitive decision. His frustration over failing to promote that game provided the final impetus; he got six dates from General Kilpatrick to stage double-headers at the Garden during the following season, and he set about booking the teams.

Irish's instincts were right, his thinking almost prescient. It had to be, because promoting took so much phone time at the sports desk of the *World-Telegram* that Joe Williams, the sports editor, asked him to choose his career. Irish left the paper a month before opening night at the Garden. His idea was to ballyhoo intersectional matches between the popular local teams and well-known schools with star players from the provinces. For the feature of the first date Irish matched NYU, sure to be one of the strong teams every year, against Notre Dame's Irish, chosen because of its big sports following. The preliminary was even better, matching St. John's against little Westminster of Pennsylvania who happened to have Wes Bennett, probably the best pivot man in the country. And Bennett put on a show to whip Buck Freeman's Redmen 37–34.

The crowd was over 16,000 and the pattern was established: instant and lasting success; the best of the area against the best available from all other areas. As often as not the city schools were the winners, and the best of the rest learned that they had to prove themselves in the Garden. There were complaints about officiating and about adjustments that had to be made for playing in the City, but invitations were coveted. New York basketball had more than come into the mainstream; it had become a kind of fountainhead in the Garden.

For the second season the dates were doubled, and by the Forties there were twenty or more double-headers. But before that, Ned Irish was promoting twinbills in Philadelphia and Buffalo that were not only successful themselves but also cut expenses for teams from the West Coast and elsewhere to make a swing through the circuit. Eventually Arthur Marsh applied the proven formula in the Chicago Stadium. Meanwhile Irish and the Garden were finding ways of promoting their game into something bigger. One promotion method was radio broadcasts; the voice of Marty Glickman became familiar to all fans with his staccato calls, "Rebound up—missed—rebound up—missed—rebound up—goo-ood, like Nedick's." Another method was television; closed-circuit telecasts were pioneered at a theater on 53rd Street (sell-outs were a matter of course), and on February 28, 1940, NBC brought the Pitt–Fordham, NYU–Georgetown doubleheader into a few thousand New York living rooms.

The basketball played in the City during this period was at the highest level. Holman's and Cann's teams were consistently competitive. Other powers were a-building in the suburbs, under Clair Bee at LIU and Honey Russell at Seton Hall. St. John's was consistently strong; Freeman, incidentally, avenged the loss to Westminster a year later by devising a defense against Bennett, having his team drop off their men to help out, holding him scoreless and winning 35–26. Nor was there any weakening in the program when Lapchick replaced Freeman in 1937. Outstanding games, and sometimes seasons, were also produced by St. Francis, St. Peter's, and Manhattan. It seemed as if anywhere you turned in the greater metropolitan area, you could find a school playing the game as the city game was supposed to be played. A tiny school like Seth Low Junior College, for example, coached by Gordon Ridings, split series with St. Francis and Brooklyn College in 1936 and almost upset Frank McGuire's St. John's team. And in 1935 little Geneva College, under Ken Loeffler's tutelage, broke LIU's home winning streak and then upset City College 50–27.

The culmination of all this build-up was the inevitable postseason tournament. Sponsored by the Metropolitan Basketball Writers Association, the NIT began in 1938 with six teams. The two local entries played each other, NYU edging LIU, and Alfred Robertson's Bradley Braves (18–2) were eliminated by James Usilton's Temple Owls (23–2). The teams with byes were Frosty Cox's Colorado and Iba's Oklahoma A & M. One seeding was justified when Colorado beat NYU by a point, but the other fell as Temple beat Oklahoma A & M by 10. In the finals, Temple, led by Don Shields, Ed Boyle, and Meyer Bloom, shot down the Buffaloes 60–36, despite a charismatic athlete called Whizzer White.

The tournament's success was great in every respect. The NCAA was inspired to initiate its own tournament the next year. The writers, with an embarrassment of riches, turned the NIT over to the local colleges. And the growing legions of basketball fans enjoyed an extra dividend of Ned Irish's original investment— more action.

# 10

# *Bee and Honey*

NED IRISH put it very simply in answer to my question about the influence of Clair Bee: "He came to Long Island University and created a national reputation." The point goes beyond basketball to the many positive contributions an athletic program can make to an academic institution. Even the most cynical observer can appreciate the value of a gentlemanly, scholarly, innovative winner like Coach Bee.

He came to LIU from little Rider College, where for several seasons he had impressed metropolitan area teams, giving St. John's Wonder Five a much closer game than most. His Rider teams had emphasized offense, and by his third year at LIU (1934) the Blackbirds were scoring over 1,000 points a season. While City and NYU were attracting all the attention that year, LIU was winning twenty-seven games, losing only to St. John's. Of course they were playing mostly second-rate teams, but as they continued to win, Bee was strengthening their schedule. They went 24–2 the following year, losing by 1 point to Geneva and 5 points to Duquesne in the Garden. In 1936 they avenged both these defeats and played through twenty-six games without a loss. The Duquesne game, in the Garden, was won in the last minute on a tip-off by Marius Russo (later a great

Yankee pitcher) after LIU had come from 5 points down with 4 minutes to play. Big Ben Kramer was the pivot man on this team that also featured Jules Bender, Arthur Hillhouse, Leo Merson, and Willie Schwartz.

The winning streak ended at forty-three with a loss to Stanford, but it was another big year for Bee's team. They lost three of thirty-one games during the season, and then—even though the graduating seniors had turned pro—the rest entered the AAU tournament in Denver. They won their way into the draw by beating CCNY 28–23 and went to the quarterfinals before losing to the Denver Safeways, the eventual winners. LIU had become big time, and for the 1938 season they were featured on six of the twelve Garden twinbills. The first two of these appearances were losses to Minnesota and Stanford, but they won the others—against SMU, DePaul, Washington and Lee, and Duquesne in overtime. There were only two other losses on a twenty-seven-game schedule, but they were beaten by NYU in the first round of the first NIT tournament.

There was a total attendance of more than a quarter of a million for the complete Garden schedule of double-headers plus the NIT, and Bee, never happy with losing, was mortified at losses before huge galleries. In 1939 there were no losses. Twenty-two straight wins in the regular season, including five in the Garden, against the toughest schedule in their history, were recorded by Irving Torgoff, Art Hillhouse (a February graduate), Danny Kaplowitz, John Bromberg, Dutch Newman, Dolly King, Myron Sewitch, Ossie Schectman, Sol Schwartz, Si Lobello, Joe Shelly, Max Sharf, and Irv Zeitlin. This was not only a great team but a squad with such marvelous depth that Bee could not follow his usual practice of going with only seven men. He carried a squad of fourteen; twelve played in the NIT finals, and ten scored.

Particularly sweet during the season were wins over Southern Cal, Kentucky, Geneva, and Duquesne, but the only other metropolitan area team they played was St. Francis. Perhaps this was why they weren't seeded in the NIT, but then neither was St. John's. Joe Lapchick's team, featuring two sweet-shooting guards, Bill Lloyd and Dutch Garfinkel, had gone 17–2 during the season. Both local teams won easily in the first round, against New Mexico A & M and Roanoke, but in the semis they were challenged by Bradley and Loyola of Illinois. LIU got by Bradley, but St. John's fell to the Chicagoans, setting up a final match of two undefeated teams. The winner was LIU, 44–32.

Clair Bee approached the game with great intensity and devotion. Scouting was never left to others when he could do it himself. Against Loyola's great center, Mike Novak, LIU won by banking their shots high off the backboard, because Bee had studied Novak's success in blocking St. Johns's shots in the semis. Basketball was changing quickly, and Bee tried to keep ahead of the game. With the center jump abandoned, new styles of offense and defense were required. One of his developments, also used against Novak and Loyola, was the 1–3–1 trap zone, which will be discussed later. He was also the architect of the 3-second rule (and

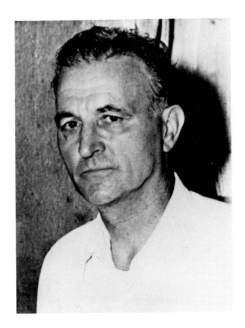

*Clair Bee.*

later of the 24-second rule that was to save and distinguish the game in the NBA).

In December of 1939, with the winning streak at thirty-one, LIU played Oregon in the Garden, opening the season's double-header schedule with a match between the defending NIT and NCAA champions. Down 15 points early in the second half, LIU came back to tie in the last minute. With 1 second to play a foul was called on Dolly King, the first black star to shine in the all-white college game, but the shot was missed. In overtime, LIU twice came from behind to tie, but with 12 seconds left Oregon went ahead on a free throw. Nine seconds later, King drove in for a scoop shot that bounced three times on the rim before dropping through for the winning basket.

Three games later it was bye-bye Blackbird streak at thirty-four, when Sam Barry's Southern Cal team, led by Ralph Vaughn, beat them 57–49 in the Garden before 18,245 fans. After seven more wins, LIU faced Duquesne whom Bee had thoroughly scouted. He planned a defense to stop Moe Becker's set shots, but the strategy backfired as Becker kept faking the shot to draw out the defense and then fed Paul Widowitz underneath. The only other loss during the season was to DePaul, starring Lou Possner, whom they had beaten earlier, but DePaul won the rubber match in the NIT first round. St. John's was also a first-round victim, but the best local team did not compete. NYU, one of Cann's best teams with Bobby Lewis, Ben Auerbach, and Ralph Kaplowitz, had gone undefeated to the last game of the season, beating Missouri, Temple, Notre Dame, and St. John's along the way. But in the last game an inspired City team (Babe Adler, Marty Scheinkman, Sam Deitchman, Julie Gerson, and Al Goldstein) upset them

36–24. Holman calls it one of his most satisfying wins, almost making up for 1924 and 1934, when NYU had upset CCNY to ruin perfect seasons for them.

Meanwhile, across the River in South Orange, another winning streak was being fashioned. Undefeated in 1940, Honey Russell had his Pirates off and running again. Like Bee at LIU, Russell had quickly moved Seton Hall into prominence by putting together an outstanding basketball team. After one losing season in 1937, he had been strengthening both the team and the schedule, so that his undefeated team, in just his fourth season, had beaten Tulane, St. Peter's, St. Francis, St. Bonaventure, and Canisius. But where LIU reflected Bee's intense concentration, Seton Hall was the free-wheeling reflection of the colorful Russell. He had been a professional athlete since he was sixteen, playing baseball with Shoeless Joe Jackson in the Coal League, football with George Halas in Chicago, and basketball with the Rosenblums, the Jewels, and others in half a dozen cities. As a player, though often a top scorer, he had the reputation of being one of the toughest defenders of all. In classic match-ups against Holman he had held the Celtics' star scoreless on occasion. As a coach he taught solid defense but concentrated on offense. Where Bee was scholarly, ingenious, and inventive, Russell was canny, jovial, and sound.

By the end of the 1941 season, the Pirates could no longer be denied their booty and were invited to the expanded eight-team NIT, which they entered with forty-two straight wins. But they were on a collision course with another fine Bee team, led by Schechtman, Lobello, and Hank Beenders, who had lost only to Michigan State in a split series and Duquesne by 2 points in a twenty-five-game schedule. City, with Red Holzman and Red Phillips, was also invited, having won thirteen of their last fourteen games. All three won first-round games, with Bobby Davies performing brilliantly in Seton Hall's 70–54 win over Rhode Island (with Stutz Modzelewski and Fred Conley), but only one survived the semis.

City was edged by Ohio University, 45–43, and in their long-awaited meeting the Blackbirds made the Pirates eat crow, dominating them completely, 49–26. Russell anticipated that Bee would double-team Davies when he had the ball, and Davies who was as clever a passer as he was a dribbler and shooter could take advantage of the situation by hitting the open man. To stop Ossie Schechtman, Russell assigned Bobby Holm. Schechtman had one basic move, the elementary one-on-one playground play: fake left and drive right; if the first fake wasn't taken, he'd hold up on the drive and shoot over the defender.

Russell told Holm to respond to the first fake with a step back to cut off the drive lane, and they joked about what would look like a dance step when Schechtman held up to start all over and Holm moved back into position. In the event, two things went wrong. Davies's ballhandling eluded Bee's defensive strategy, but his passes were too slick for his teammates. And Holm's effort was much less successful than that of his Aunt Eleanor's Channel swim: he went for Schechtman's first fake, and Ossie owned him the rest of the night. The wind gone from their

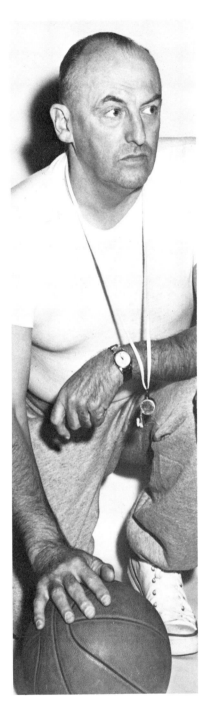

*Bob Davies, Seton Hall's Golden Boy, a pre-Cousy wizard.*

*Honey Russell.*

sails, Seton Hall also lost to City in the consolation game. It would be another twelve years before Russell would bring an NIT championship home to South Orange.

LIU won the finals easily, 56–42, though Ohio's Frankie Baumholtz won the most valuable player (MVP) award. Throughout the rest of the Forties, both LIU and Seton Hall continued to win. LIU won invitations to the NIT in 1942, 1947, and 1950 but failed to survive the first round. Seton Hall, canceling its schedule during three wartime years, nevertheless had outstanding records in 1942, 1943, 1947 (under Davies), and 1948 (under John Reitemeier), although they were not invited back to the Garden until Russell's second tour of coaching duty. Bee and Russell went on as would have been expected, the one taking everything to heart, the other rolling with the punches.

Bee never lost his commitment to every aspect of the game, including scouting. In 1948, having studied Duquesne carefully, as usual, he concluded that they had no outside shooting, so he prepared his defense to cut off all driving moves toward the basket and won an easy victory. A year or so later, Bee was in the hotel room of his old friend Sam Barry, the Southern Cal coach, the day before their game in the Garden. Barry had been promised a scouting report on LIU from Jack Gardner, whose Kansas State team had given the Blackbirds their only loss earlier in the season. But when Gardner's call came, Barry was being interviewed by *Time*. Bee took the call but didn't tell Barry about it until after the game. LIU won 70–45, breaking Southern Cal's twelve-game winning streak.

Probably no one was more shocked or hurt by the scandals than Clair Bee. He came to believe that the coaches had to accept responsibility for what had happened, not just for their ostrichlike ignorance but for their failure as teachers and leaders for their young men. An idealist, who had even written a series of boys' books about a Jack Armstrong type, he could not rationalize away the burdens of guilt. For Honey Russell, whose whole life had been devoted to sports, the fact that basketball was just another game was never completely lost. As an athlete and sportsman he maintained the equilibrium of his attitude and escaped the pitfalls of those who take their games so seriously that they become ritualistic devotees of a substitute religion.

# 11

# *Where the Action Is*

THE WAR had some effects on college basketball, but they were not all harmful to the game. The big men were too big to draft, and there were many ways to stay in school even while in service. Relaxed eligibility rules allowed freshmen and transfers to play, which provided some surprise bonanzas during the season. Three of the ten schools organized in the metropolitan association, the NIT sponsors, canceled their programs as did Seton Hall. In many other parts of the country, where travel was too difficult or expensive, schools curtailed intercollegiate competition. But not in the City. It was business as usual at Madison Square Garden. The NCAA tournament would not expand at all until the Korean War; the NIT was the one that kept the clout in the Forties.

City College remained a factor, even during three rare losing seasons, 1943–1945. The Beavers kept running a four-man weave around a post—the Holman wheel. And almost always they were outmanned and outsized. CCNY by necessity specialized in the long set shot and the clever little man, in a game of short pass, quick score, and dribble away to run out the clock. Sometimes more extreme methods were called for. Once a tall Dartmouth team was surprised when City consistently grabbed the unusually long rebounds. Congratulated by the losing coach, who commented on the lively ball, Holman explained that he was on the research committee of the Basketball Coaches Association and had decided to experiment with a few extra pounds of air in the ball.

Usually, Holman's success rested on the Holman-like player, comparatively small but a complete player, a Lou Wisner, a Red Holzman, a Sonny Hertzberg. Red Auerbach rates Holzman and Hertzberg with Bob Cousy among the masters of the freeze, but their shooting could also get the lead that the freeze would protect. Somehow, too, Holman would often come up with a substitute whose long set shots would save a game. In the 1942 game against St. John's, Dutch Garfinkel had the Redmen ahead of City's Reds—Holzman and Phillips—with a few minutes to play. But from off the bench and with his coach yelling "No! No!" Harold Judenfriend scored from 35 feet to send the game into overtime, and then again from 30 feet in a 2-point win that insured the NIT bid. In 1945, in a 42–41 upset of St. John's, it was Danny Markoff who came off the bench to hit the long shots. But there was no tournament bid for a team with a 12–14 record. A year later, with a record of 14–4, they were not invited because they hadn't played enough games.

That NIT bid in 1942 resulted in a first-round elimination by Western Kentucky, but a bigger upset had already taken place. Top-seeded LIU was beaten in overtime by West Virginia, the eventual winners. Seton Hall, despite Bob Davies's crowd appeal and a 16–2 record that included a 1-point loss to NCAA runner-up Dartmouth, had not been invited. A year later the metropolitan schools did much better. NYU, led by Jerry Fleishman, won seventeen games and became the first New York team to play in the NCAA, losing to Georgetown in the Eastern Regional semis. But they were not nearly the best team in the City. They had beaten Manhattan (18–3, a first-round loser in the NIT) but had lost to both Fordham and St. John's. This was Ed Kelleher's last Ram team, starring Robert Mullen, and they had gone 16–4 on a very difficult schedule. They edged Western Kentucky in the first round but in the semis were whipped for the second time that season by one of Lapchick's strongest teams at St. John's.

Niagara and Manhattan had beaten the Redmen earlier in the season, but they came on strong in the NIT with big Harry Boykoff winning the MVP. Hy Gotkin got them by Rice with a last-second basket in the first round, and Fuzzy Levane, the metropolitan player of the year, generaled the rout of the Rams in the semis. The championship game was easy too as Boykoff and Moschetti had 13 points each and Larry Baxter 8 in a 48–27 win over Toledo. A Red Cross benefit game was lost to NCAA champ Wyoming, but across the board it seemed that basketball in the City was stronger than ever or anywhere.

The level of play fell off considerably the following year. Manhattan, Fordham, Hofstra, and Seton Hall were missing from action, while neither City nor NYU could win more than half their games. LIU, under George Wolfe, went

*Tripping the light fantastic: Kenny Sailors (4) maneuvering for score in Wyoming's win over St. John's in the 1943 Red Cross game; teammate Milo Komenich (17) watches as Al Moschetti, Harry Boykoff, and Hy Gotkin defend.*

12–3 on an unimpressive schedule, but it remained for St. John's to uphold the metropolitan honor. With Boykoff gone, they had to rely on two freshmen, Dick McGuire and Bill Kotsores. They lost four games during the season, but only one decisively. That was to Army, where Ed Kelleher, having moved 50 miles up the Hudson, had fashioned a perfect season at West Point. In his two years there before he died, Kelleher lost only one game in thirty.

Despite wartime restrictions, the NIT field was unusually strong, and the teams were unusually big. The defending champions didn't seem to have much of a chance, especially since McGuire had entered service and been transferred to Dartmouth. But the Redmen became giant-killers. In the first round they stopped Bowling Green with 6-foot 11-inch Don Otten, while DePaul with 6-foot 9-inch George Mikan and Oklahoma A & M with 7-foot Bob Kurland were also winning. The other first-round game saw Vadal Peterson's top-rated Utah team, with Arnie Ferrin and Wat Misaka, get knocked out by Kentucky, with Bob Brannum. In the semis, while DePaul put down Oklahoma A & M, St. John's beat Kentucky 48–45.

*Joe Lapchick.*

The championship game was not really close, though it must have been exciting because Coach Lapchick passed out on the bench. He was out for 10 minutes of play, and during that time his team stretched their lead from 5 to 12 points, coasting home finally by 8. Kotsores was the MVP, despite the awesome presence of the big men. Gotkin also performed well, along with Wertis, Wehr, and Duym, but it fell to Ivy Summer—big but no giant—to take on the opposing centers, which he did remarkably well. Meanwhile Utah rebounded from their NIT elimination and won the NCAA, beating Dartmouth, with Audley Brindley (and Dick McGuire) by 2 points in the finals. Again St. John's lost the Red Cross benefit game to the NCAA champions, but their back-to-back NIT titles against overwhelming odds were outstanding achievements for Lapchick's teams and for the City game.

In the last wartime season, the giants had their day, Kurland leading the NCAA winners and Mikan outdueling Otten to win the NIT for DePaul. But again it was teams from the City that pushed them hardest. NYU came on strong at the season's end to win another NCAA berth. They beat Ohio State with Arnie Risen to advance to the finals and then took Iba's team down to the wire before losing 49–45. Al Grenert, Don Forman, Dolph Schayes, Sid Tanenbaum, and Frank Mangiapane made up this Cann team that narrowly missed beating Cecil Hankins, Kurland and company and then did beat Bowling Green in a preliminary Red Cross benefit game. Meanwhile, St. John's had beaten twenty teams, including NYU, before toppling to Bowling Green. But they too won their last game, the NIT consolation against Rhode Island. In that game, Rhode Island's speed came from behind to take a 3-point lead midway in the second half. Lapchick then ordered Summers to crash the offensive boards, even if St. John's scored, to cut off long outlet or inbounds passes and break down the fast break. The strategy turned the game around and gave the Redmen a 7-point victory.

The Garden was still where the action was. The double-header schedule went on, uncurtailed, the benefits were played there, and though the NIT had an eight-team draw like the NCAA, it often had a more difficult field. If there were danger signs, no one chose to read them or heed them. The gambling on college basketball in New York had gotten very big, and it was remarkably open. A brief scandal exposed Brooklyn College for point-shaving, but it was glossed over and virtually forgotten when attention was drawn to an attempted fix of a pro football championship during the next season. Memories seemed to get shorter as ostrich-necks got longer, and in the permissive atmosphere of the immediate postwar period the action grew bigger and louder and certainly no better.

There were thirty nights of college basketball at the Garden in 1946 as the NCAA followed the NIT on the Eighth Avenue boards. Bee was back from service to lead LIU, with Jackie Goldsmith, to a 14–9 record; Manhattan returned to action under Honey Russell, winning fifteen of twenty-three; Hofstra and Fordham also resumed schedules; and City's fourteen wins included one over NYU that broke a thirteen-game winning steak. NYU went to the NCAA anyway, but Tanenbaum, Mangiapane, and Forman couldn't get them past North Carolina in the first round. Harry Boykoff was back at St. John's, who won seventeen, but they lost to West Virginia in the NIT first round.

A disappointing 16–7 season, Boykoff's last, nevertheless won St. John's a sixth straight NIT bid, but they lost in the first round, as did LIU (19–4). Seton Hall, 24–3 under Davies, was not invited, nor was NYU, 12–9 in Tanenbaum's

*Howard Cann* (left) *and Dolph Schayes.*

All-American senior season. The City's best team was the City College team, though St. John's had beaten them earlier in a 15–4 campaign. Perhaps still miffed at not being invited the year before, they turned down the NIT bid and played in the NCAA. Again the championship would be played in the Garden.

Wisconsin, their first opponent, had a great height advantage, with 6-foot 6-inch Ed Mills, 6-foot 3-inch Glen Selbo, and 6-foot 2-inch Walt Lauterbach starting and reserves Bob Harlow and Don Rehfeldt, both 6 feet 6 inches. Wisconsin got off to leads of 22–6, 26–10, and 36–20, though CCNY closed to 37–27 at the half. Holman's assistant Bobby Sand diagramed Wisconsin's basic play that had Mills screening for his two corner men, Cook and Menzel, who had 10 points each. City loosened their center coverage so that defenders could slide through the screen. Paul Schmones held Cook to 3, Lionel Malamed held Menzel to 5, in the second half, and City took the lead 49–48 with 10 minutes left. They then scored 10 straight and drew out to win by 70–56, as Adolph Rupp, in the press box at halftime, had predicted they would. Holman called this a classic East-West confrontation, precision drive-set vs. free-style playmaking, that was twenty years in the making; but it was Bod Foster the disciple rather than Meanwell the mentor that bowed to Holman. That was the high point of the season. They next lost to eventual winner Holy Cross and then to Texas in the consolation game.

For a third straight year, the NCAA championship was settled in the Garden in 1948, but no City team was around. Lapchick had moved up to the Knickerbockers; St. John's was 12–11 under Frank McGuire. LIU (18–4), Seton Hall (18–4 under Reitemeier), and CCNY (18–3) were all distinguished by their absence from the NIT, perhaps because they had all been disappointing in intersectional matches at the Garden during the season. Manhattan, 23–6 in Ken Norton's second year as coach, went to the quarterfinals of the NAIA tournament in Kansas City. Only NYU, led by Don Forman, Dolph Schayes, and Ray Lumpp, upheld the honor of Gotham in the postseason big time. They beat Texas and DePaul before losing to St. Louis in the NIT finals, and the absence of Forman because of injury may account for the 13-point loss.

In part to accommodate the local fans, the NIT increased the field to twelve in the following season, the first in which the AP published its top ten rankings. Neglected by the poll, four metropolitan teams earned invitations with winning seasons, though none was outstanding. St. John's (16–9), NYU (12–8), CCNY (17–8), and Manhattan (18–8) all lost in the first round, to Bowling Green, Bradley, Loyola of Illinois, and San Francisco. It was no consolation that these four also upset the four seeds to gain the semifinal round; the entire preliminary round was called the Manhattan Massacre. But a year later the City game would be redeemed in the eyes of the sporting world, if not in the judgment of the pollsters.

92

# 12

# *The Brief Reign of Cinderella*

BY TOURNAMENT time in 1950, the seeding committee of the NIT found themselves with an embarrassment of riches. In the metropolitan area they really had little problem. NYU had had a rare losing season, so had Seton Hall though Honey Russell had returned from the pros, and Manhattan had a mediocre record. LIU, with Sherman White, earned an invitation with twenty wins but no seed because they had not played a challenging schedule. CCNY was 17–5, including a win over St. John's that broke a twelve-game streak for Frank McGuire, but the Beavers were not highly regarded. The Redmen themselves were ranked ninth in the AP poll and were given the fourth seed. From upstate came little Niagara, who had rolled up twenty victories under Taps Gallagher, and mighty Syracuse, with seventeen wins on a customarily stiff schedule. This was Lew Andreas's last year as the Orange coach, and he retired with a twenty-six-year record of 364–145 for a .715 winning percentage. Playing the best opposition he could schedule year after year, he consistently had sharp, well-prepared teams; Andreas is probably the most underrated coach of the whole period.

Top seeding was reserved for Forddy Anderson's Bradley team, top-ranked in the nation, led by All-American Paul Unruh. Second and third were Kentucky

*Syracuse Coach Lew Andreas and his greatest player, Vic Hanson.*

and Duquesne, ranked third and sixth in the poll. The rest of the draw included Western Kentucky, San Francisco, La Salle, and Arizona, of whom only Newell's Dons had won under twenty games but were back with nineteen as defending champions. This may have been the strongest draw in NIT history.

In the first round Ed Diddle's Hilltoppers eliminated Niagara, Syracuse beat LIU, and La Salle beat Arizona. The winners scored 79, 80, and 72 points, respectively. In the other game City dominated the defending champions with remarkable ease, 65–46. Earlier in the year City had played Oklahoma and lost 67–63 because they were unable to switch men and adjust their defense to Bruce Drake's shuffle offense. This was a continuity pattern designed to set up screens in all their play variations. But by tournament time, Holman had the Beavers ready, and San Francisco's screening plays gave them no trouble.

The City team was young, with only Irwin Dambrot an experienced hand, but it was taller than a typical Holman team and more versatile. During the season five different men played pivot—Dambrot, Ed Roman, Ed Warner, Al Roth, and Norm Mager—while one of the tallest on the team, Floyd Layne, could move to corner or backcourt. In the quarterfinals they faced a Kentucky team that liked to screen, too, and was smarting over an NCAA snub. Defending NCAA champs, with a 25–4 record, Kentucky was stunned when the district's invitation went to North Carolina State.

The Metropolitan Basketball Writers voted Rupp the college coach of the year, and he was proud of his team that included 7-foot center Bill Spivey, 6-foot 6-inch forwards Shelby Linville and Jim Line, 5-foot 10-inch guard Bobby Watson, and 6-foot 2-inch Dale Barnstable. In the game heavily favored Kentucky scored only 50 points (Spivey and Linville combined for 28), while CCNY rolled up 89. It was Rupp's worst defeat ever and an incredible performance by a Nat Holman team that had apparently mastered the full potential of the contemporary game. Ed Warner had 26 on a variety of shots; the Wildcats began by sagging in on him in the pivot, so he moved outside and hit two 30-footers. But most impressive was the variety of plays, playmaking, and shotmaking employed by the whole City team. Rupp, whose team had beaten top-ranked Bradley early in the year, predicted flatly that the unranked Beavers would win the tournament.

In the other quarterfinals the seedings held up. St. John's beat Western Kentucky 69–60 as Zeke Zawoluk bested Bob Lavoy in their match-up. Bradley ended Lew Andreas's career by beating Syracuse 78–66. And despite Ken Loeffler's ingenuity (this was the first of his six remarkable years at La Salle, 145–30 for 83 percent, one NIT and one NCAA championship), Dudey Moore's Duquesne team narrowly won 49–47. This no doubt made a lasting impression in Philadelphia because Dudey Moore was brought to La Salle from Duquesne in 1959.

In the semis Bradley's powerful, balanced attack put away St. John's 83–72, while City added yet another upset by beating defense-minded Duquesne 62–52, despite a fine performance by Chuck Cooper. This set up the storybook finals

between the number one seed and the Cinderella team. In addition to Unruh, Bradley had a strong center in 6-foot 7-inch Elmer Behnke and at guard Gene Melchiorre, whom Holman has placed in his own pantheon of great little men along with Wat Misaka, Rene Herrerias, Kenny Sailors, Ralph Beard, Red Holzman, Lou Wisner, Barney Sedran, and Vic Hanson. CCNY had trouble early when they missed seven of their first eight free throws, seventeen of twenty-eight altogether. This handicap had to be overcome by superior floorplay, but they were struggling to stay close, playing catch-up throughout the first period. Down 30–27 at the half, they came on strong after the break. Bradley kept the game close all the way, but Dambrot, Warner, and Roman combined for twenty-five field goals to match the whole Bradley team. And at the end, under the short-lived 38-plus-2 rule of jump balls after free throws in the last 2 minutes, 6-foot 3-inch Warner outjumped 6-foot 7-inch Behnke seven times to control the taps and preserve the 69–61 win. (The City's honor was reinforced by St. John's consolation victory over Duquesne.)

Then they started all over again, Bradley courting revenge and CCNY out to prove they were for real. Bradley went west and had to face seventh-ranked UCLA. Wooden, in his second year in Westwood, had won the Pacific Coast crown on a 50-foot shot by Ralph Joeckel against Washington State. The Bruin star was George Stanich, an Olympic high jumper in 1948, who could dunk the ball off a drive whenever he had an opening. Bradley beat them easily, 73–59, then had some trouble with Baylor before winning a trip back to the Garden, 68–66.

The Eastern Regionals had second-ranked Ohio State, fourth-ranked Holy Cross, and fifth-ranked North Carolina State to burst the Cinderella balloon. The opening game was the toughest of all the postseason matches. Tippy Dye's Buckeyes played ball control, running plays off a shifting double pivot with All-American Dick Schnittker and Bob Donham, who made up with savvy and drive what he lacked in native ability. On defense Ohio State dropped deep to defend tightly around the basket and across the lane. Schnittker set up right at the foul line, and the other four played a sagging man-to-man defense. What this accomplished was to force City into one of the more traditional facets of their game—the set shot from 25–30 feet out. Dambrot, Roman, and Warner were held to 8 points each, but Mager had 15 including five long sets and Layne 17 including four bombs. CCNY narrowly survived 56–55. North Carolina State, meanwhile, handed Holy Cross an 87–74 defeat to end Bob Cousy's college career disappointingly.

Rupp may have had just cause for his bitterness over the selections, but Everett Case had a fine team at Raleigh. They could run a fast break on occasion

*Sky-hook, vintage 1950: Bob Lavoy of Western Kentucky.*

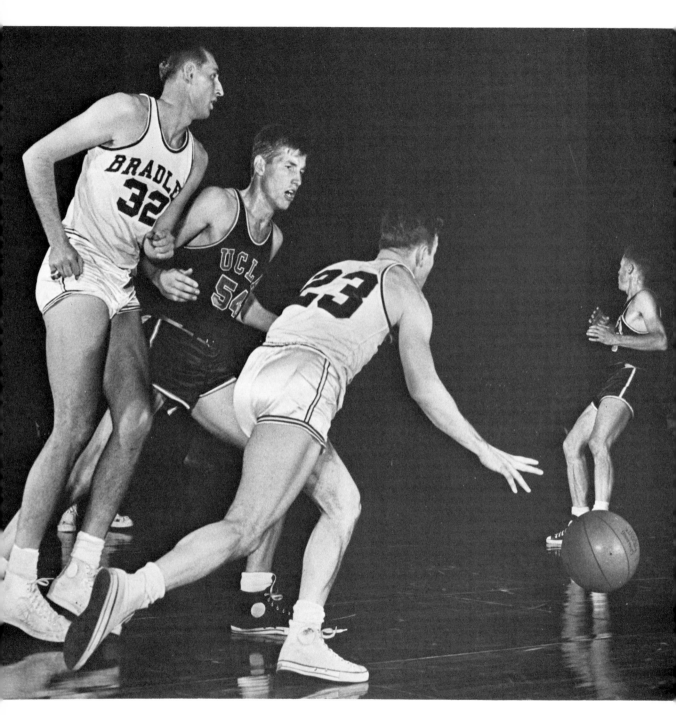

*Melchiorre (23) fast-breaking, helped by Behnke's (32) block.*

*Ed Warner (4) spins in to score, despite Dickey (70), Bubas (78), and Harand (80) of North Carolina State.*

but for the most part played an organized offense with set patterns to make use of screens. CCNY was now confident of handling switches on defense, and their scouting convinced them they had good match-ups. Floyd Layne was assigned to Sam Ranzino, who liked to shoot a one-hander from 25 feet and then drive in to follow the shot. Layne simply boxed out long enough to prevent Ranzino from rebounding and then released to lead a fast break downcourt. At the other end Ed Roman took Paul Horvath to the high post, faked him out, and drove by for crucial layups. It was City by 78–73.

One last time the NCAA championship game was played in Madison Square Garden, and once again it was Bradley against CCNY with both teams having much to prove. For the most part it was a rerun of the first game, though the scoring was redistributed. Unruh and Behnke were shut off effectively, but Bradley's scoring was picked up by Melchiorre, Preece, and Chianakas. For City there was great balance, with Dambrot, Roman, Warner, Mager, and Layne all scoring in double figures. With just a few minutes left the score was 69–61, just as it had ended in the NIT, but Anderson sent his Braves into a full-court press. Their pressing defense had already caused many fouls, but now it was causing turnovers and they closed to 69–68. One last time they got possession, but as Melchiorre drove for the basket, he lost the ball to Dambrot who hit Mager with a lead pass for the final score of 71–68.

It is difficult to assess just how good this team was, and I'm not questioning their excellence. Under the greatest of pressure they won through two tournaments in which all ten of the country's top-rated teams were playing. They beat the previous year's defending champions from both tournaments and twice beat the number one team. Their grand slam was a once-in-history feat and will never be challenged unless there is a very unlikely change in the rules for postseason play. And they did all this with only one experienced player when they started the Cinderella season. What must make one wonder just how good they were is the fact that they compounded their pressures and obstacles by shaving points and controlling spreads in several games during the season. In a sense, abstract if not cynical, this argues that they were even more skillful than their record indicates.

*Warner (8) driving, Floyd Lane (right) preparing to follow.*

# 13

# The Serpent in the Garden

EVEN IN the lucid vision of hindsight the basketball scandals appear distorted by a variety of prejudices. The sociohistorical view sees a situation caused by the loosened moral standards of the immediate postwar period and the deterioration of the quality of urban life. The amateur athletic apologists see naive players seduced by smooth city sharpies insinuating themselves into inexperienced lives with smiling assurances of the good life and easy consciences. There is a tendency still apparent in mainstream, waspish Middle America to blame the whole thing on the evil ambience of New York City. On the other side are those who blame the repressive poverty of ethnic ghettoes for making it natural, even inevitable, for poor boys to take easy money.

Interesting insights into the conditions are found in remarks of Nat Holman. Writing in 1950, at the time of the major point-fixing, but before the investigations had begun and certainly before he had any inkling of involvement by his own Cinderella champions, Holman talked about the pressures of contemporary basketball. He talked about physical pressures: players did more traveling to play more games and put in more playing time on larger playing surfaces. He talked about financial pressures: higher costs of travel added to higher costs of all education-related programs, with promotion needed to sell more tickets and fill larger houses. And he talked about emotional pressures: increased spectator interest (including TV) and increased emphasis on winning with the possible rewards of national recognition, rankings in the polls, and tournament bids.

The point of Holman's remarks is simply that college basketball had become big business, a very profitable industry. Teams "produced," coaches "turned out products," and schools became known as athletic "factories." But it was an industry peculiarly blind to two by-products: the disproportionate growth of gambling associated with it; and the incongruous diminution of the actual participants, the players, in terms of rewards and values—they were progressively dehumanized.

The excitement generated by the game itself has always been increased by the conditions for viewing it. From the time in January of 1892 when two hundred people crowded into the balcony of the gym on State Street in Springfield during the noon hour to the present sell-outs for all games at Pauley Pavilion, basketball crowds have pushed themselves toward hysteria. And, as Leonard Koppett has also pointed out, there has been a long history of ticket scandals with players taking advantage of opportunities to turn a little profit by scalping. But if betting on the games was hardly necessary to build up interest, it was nevertheless an ever-present factor and by no means a regional peculiarity.

Ever since medieval theologians legislated gambling into a major sin by elevating it to a prime type of Sloth, one of the Seven Deadlies, there has been a basis for a moralistic argument against betting in any form. Yet the ethics of gambling are themselves as high-principled as the pure and purely abstract rules of any game or system. Betting on basketball is a good example. An independent board of experts, taking all known factors into account, rates a team against its opponent. The experts then publish a line or spread which indicates how many points, according to their form, the favorite should win by. Using this differential as a handicap, a bettor should have an equal chance with either team. Since it is in the enlightened self-interest of the bookmaker to encourage betting on both teams, the point spread should be as nearly accurate as possible.

An honest line is the bookie's best asset. An ideal situation for a bookie is to have equal amounts bet on both teams: as a businessman he makes his profit on a percentage, the vigorish, taking every bet at 11–10; he prefers not to gamble himself but profits from the gambling of others. Clearly as a businessman he wants to encourage others to gamble. Therefore he works as hard as he can to make the best possible sporting proposition, and if his labor is fruitful, the result of every basketball bet will be in doubt until the final buzzer.

Simple and straightforward as it is, this system should operate successfully in this best of all possible worlds. That it does not work is less a property of this world's not being a just one than it is a result of pure idleness being itself corrupted by two other of the Seven Deadlies, Pride and Avarice. In the first place, since modern moralists have legislated the Sin of gambling into a Crime, the rules of play cannot be abstractly exposed to the objective correction of the public marketplace. Then, since large sums of money may be involved, the activities labeled sinful and criminal stand a good chance of becoming corrupted. And finally, if players are so good that they are rated 19 points better than their opponents, then they must be good enough to make sure they win by, say, 13 and make some money for themselves instead of for the promoters and the institutions, for individuals instead of the establishment. Where's the harm—never mind sin and crime? Clearly, harm lies in the corruption of the game—using it or selling it for something else; in the corruption of the players—again a matter of use or sale that hastens rather than arrests the dehumanizing process; and ironically in the corruption of the gambling itself—a self-destructive abuse of what is premised upon honest sport.

Today there are very few bookies in operation, in the sense that bookies have balanced, two-way action on every game. The gambling tax, 10 percent of gross, makes a balanced book a losing proposition. But the application of interstate-commerce doctrine to gambling makes two-way action a practical impossibility anyway. The Crime Control Acts of 1968 and 1970 made gamblers easy prey for government snoopers and permitted the federal government to enforce local gambling laws. The results have been to turn most bookies into gamblers, with one-way action predominating because of local interest, and to drive the big surviving bookmakers underground because the wagering taxes are crippling.

It is axiomatic that wherever games are played there will be action, and it is no semantic accident that action is a synonym for gambling. Basketball provides an ample arena for action, for all. Attempts to influence the gambling action inevitably interfere with the game's action, and unfortunately there are no geographical limits to such attempts. None of the seven deadly sins nor any crime known to man has a definitive provenience. But where there are the most people and the most games, there will probably be the most action and the most attempts to subvert both the sport and the sporting chance.

In 1945 reports of a fixed game between Brooklyn College and Akron leaked out, causing violent fluctuation in the point spread. The game was canceled, but five Brooklyn players admitted taking bribes to throw it. In the summer of 1946, Bob Cousy was playing for the Tamarack Lodge in the Borscht Belt in a league including George Mikan, Ed Macauley, Dolph Schayes, and Don Forman. Heavy betting among resort guests was common and common knowledge. When the story of a dumped game was exposed, the players involved were fired from their summer sinecures, and the fixer-guest was kicked out of the resort. In 1949 a George Washington player reported a bribe attempt. These isolated events aroused their respective flurries of indignation, but they were not seen as symptoms of a general, pandemic condition.

The next time an attempt was reported it was Junius Kellogg of Manhattan College talking to the Bronx District Attorney. Unfortunately, two of Kellogg's teammates had accepted the bribe. Frank Hogan, the D.A. in Manhattan, then took over the investigation, and before he was finished he had probed over one hundred suspicious games over a span of four seasons. More than thirty players from seven schools—CCNY, LIU, Manhattan, and NYU in the City; Kentucky, Bradley, and Toledo from the rest of the world—had conspired, according to his findings, to fix scores of games in over a score of cities in seventeen states.

The shocks and aftershocks were felt deeply this time, cutting through all sorts of pieties and hypocrisies. The whole Cinderella team of City College was involved; Holman couldn't believe it, many skeptics couldn't believe he hadn't known, and he went on wondering why he hadn't known. None of the City players would ever play pro ball; Floyd Layne, for one, looked to some like the prototype of the modern pro player. Layne continued to devote his time to basketball and also to community service, and he returned to City College as head basketball coach in 1974. LIU was perhaps hardest hit, because Clair Bee took it to heart. He spoke as a moralist, taking the responsibility for not teaching or communicating with his players; yet his very moralism acted as protective blinders against the intrusion of unpleasant realities in the total environment of his sporting world. His star, the great Sherman White, was accused but never convicted. Banned for life from the NBA, he played some professional ball in the Eastern League but never could fulfill all the promise. LIU, which had grown as a university on its basketball reputation, dropped intercollegiate play for six years. St. John's and Fordham were under the metropolitan cloud of suspicion, but no hard evidence was brought against them. Ken Norton at Manhattan and Howard Cann at NYU carried on with their programs through the troubles.

While the attention was focused on the City, basketball people in the rest of the country took a kind of grim pride in their own and a twisted satisfaction in blaming the evil environment of Madison Square Garden. Adolph Rupp sounded the watchword of arrogant parochialism: "They couldn't touch our boys with a ten-foot pole." It is the measure of the unrealistic attitudes that prevailed that this was the honest expression of a generally held view. But when it was over, the great Kentucky team was shown to be the busiest offender. Groza, Beard, and company apparently had set up shop as soon as they returned from the Olympics, and their splendid 1949 season is all the more amazing when it is remembered that they won thirty-two of thirty-four games while controlling their point spreads and that their NIT loss to Loyola was a game they fixed too well to win. Bradley, top-ranked in 1950 and losing finalist to CCNY in both tournaments, were dumpers too, so Cinderella may have been crowned by overly generous Braves passing for Prince Charming.

Groza and Beard, already NBA all-stars with the Indianapolis Olympians, had their careers terminated, and their team survived only a short time without them. Bill Spivey, whose testimony conflicted with that of teammates Line and Barnstable, pleaded innocent. His jury was hung (reported to have stood nine to three for acquittal) and he was never retried, but despite polygraph support he was also banned by the NBA and played some in the Eastern League. Kentucky sat out a year's suspension by the NCAA and SEC. Bradley and Toledo continued their programs.

It is widely believed that only a small percentage of the corrupt and their corrupters was exposed. People clung desperately to the belief that the exposures and prosecutions and punishments would put an end to the practice, that the risks would seem far greater than the rewards. But surely this rationalized prop was washed away in the wake of subsequent scandals; in 1961 and 1965, thirty-nine more players were implicated in twenty-three schools. Yet the reformers attacked only symptoms, and it may be that the whole syndrome has yet to be properly identified.

In the frenzy of anti–New York feeling, Madison Square Garden and its NIT were declared off limits for many schools. But if there seems to be a lot of gambling in New York and on Garden events, the fact is that comparatively few gamblers have ever looked to New York for the line on their action. The line used to come from such places as Cincinnati, St. Louis, Kansas City, and Minneapolis, with even the Coasts looking to the heartland for their numbers. Now, under restrictions of federal laws, every gambler must have a source in his own state. And if New York newspapers were the first to publish point spreads, it has become such common practice that syndicated columnists, usually with a Nevada dateline, now have their numbers printed across the country.

College players were forbidden to play in organized summer leagues, theoretically to insulate them from undesirable contacts. But play they do—without supervision, without regulation, without public exposure, and therefore without protection from anyone who wants to contact them. The proscription is analogous with seeking to remedy war crimes by rules against fraternization.

Kentucky and CCNY were primary targets of the investigation. Their tradition of success and their current championships, along with the aura of superiority exuded by Coaches Rupp and Holman, made them worthy of treatment as examples or even scapegoats. And so the point-shaving inquiry was diverted to an examination of unprincipled approaches to winning at all costs. Kentucky was nailed for illegal payoffs; players were subsidized beyond allowable limits. They were not talking about thousands of dollars, but about an extra 50 dollars for spending money in New Orleans after the Sugar Bowl tourney. Rupp knew about it and considered it small change and too trivial to be considered more than the most technical of violations, but it was this knowledge that cost suspension, not all the dumped games.

At CCNY, a school much prouder of its academic heritage than its athletic accomplishment, the offenses were much more grievous. Without Holman's knowledge, but with the deliberate involvement of an assistant to whom he delegated

*Jack Molinas*
*liked to play more*
*than one game*
*at the same time.*

authority, some of his players had been illegally recruited, their transcripts and records falsified. Of course it is completely unrealistic to suppose that these violations were isolated instances or limited to champions. But it was open season for the snipers, and Wildcat and Beaver were fair game.

The scandals threatened college basketball, but the game survived and thrived. It was too successful a business to fail because of some under-the-table transactions. But it is a system built on property values. High school players are courted as if the best deal will determine the decision, regardless of any individual values. And once signed, the players become the chattels or at best the Hessians of the institution. Besides the support promised in their deals, they are protected as valuable commodities—not only medical attention but the best food in town, not only costs of education but extra privileges of courses and registration and tutoring and even grades. Moreover, a whole set of procedures has evolved to protect the players from such temptations as precocious professional careers. The system protects its property, without regard to the sport.

The irony is so plain and the hypocrisy so blatant that it produces callousness at best, cynicism at worst. Gambling, though involved with money, depends for its sporting chance on the honesty of the sports. The corrupters of the gambling, on the other hand, operate on the same value system as the illegal recruiters and subsidizers and standard-benders. Association with the one is banned, with the others is blinked. But as long as the sport is susceptible of corruption, the players will be susceptible to corrupters. The lessons of the scandals have yet to be learned: the shaving of points is not a passing phenomenon, the betting remains widespread and underground—therefore unpoliced, the recruiting is more cutthroat than ever, and the property value on the player is still in an inflationary spiral.

# *Part 4*

# *Kentuckiana: Heartland Coast to Coast*

ALL THE WHILE that the City Game was dominating the development of the traditional style to its peak, a revolution was going on out there in the country. Madison Square Garden saw a fusion of the old polarity, the East of the Ivy and the West of the Big Ten, in a game of short pass and dribble and two-hand shot. But as every good dialectic would have it, this synthesis became part of a new set of polarities. Out there in heartland fieldhouses, a new game was being played, a game of long pass and running and one-hand shot. And this was the game that would assimilate or cannibalize the City Game.

A confrontation of great significance in the new polarity took place when Stanford met LIU in the Garden and introduced New York to Hank Luisetti and effective one-hand shooting. Stanford had to play 3,000 miles east of Palo Alto to win their number one ranking, proving their extraordinary skill to the metropolitan press and fans. But in that same season, 1936, three of the country's best four or five teams were playing their home games in the state of Indiana, in South Bend, in Bloomington, and in Lafayette.

Kentuckiana basketball was the quintessence of that increasingly dominant style of the late Thirties and Forties. Perhaps in no other part of the country was basketball taken so dearly to heart as in Kentucky and Indiana, and it was not just a matter of people adopting one or two teams as state heroes. In the Commonwealth of Kentucky, besides Coach Rupp's Wildcats, there have been outstanding teams and players at Eastern Kentucky, Western Kentucky, Centre, Georgetown, Kentucky Wesleyan, Morehead, Murray, Transylvania, Kentucky State, and of course Louisville.

In Indiana, the big three at Purdue, Indiana, and Notre Dame have sometimes been outshone by stars at Wabash, Evansville, Valparaiso, Butler, DePauw, Earlham, and Franklin. In Kentuckiana, state high school tournaments excite the interest and coverage of a Super Bowl or a World Series elsewhere. There may be some argument from Kansas, but Kentuckiana is the geographical center of heartland basketball, particularly when the region is extended to include bordering areas of Ohio and southern Illinois.

This section, appropriately the largest in the book because of its significance, chronicles the eminent domain of the new style as it is embraced by the whole continent. There is a distinct geographical orientation here, as various regions come into basketball prominence—Pacific Coast, Rocky Mountains, Missouri Valley, Philadelphia, New England—but there is also the presence of the two wide-reaching dynasties of Adolph Rupp and Hank Iba. Primarily, though, the focus will be on the prominent, evolving elements of modern basketball—one-hand shooting, the mobile big man, and the organized fast break.

*Will it play in Peoria? Basketball? BIG! Heroes' welcome for Bradley's Western Regional champs in 1950.*

# 14

# *Look, Ma, One Hand*

IN THE mid-Thirties, star quality could be instantly recognized if not defined. You didn't have to be an Irving Thalberg to look at Hank Luisetti and know that he was something special. Strikingly handsome with dark hair, brilliant dark eyes, and a flashing smile, he moved with the grace and strength of a thoroughbred champion. Add to the charismatic appearance the facts that he did what he did—play basketball—better than anyone else around and that he did it with a markedly individual flair—the one-hand shot—and you have all the ingredients of an instant folk hero. This is, indeed, what Luisetti became, and so it is necessary to separate the unreal legendary qualities from the real qualities that gave the legend substance.

When Luisetti came down the peninsula to Palo Alto from his home on Telegraph Hill in San Francisco, Stanford basketball was not prospering. Only once, in 1920, had they won a Pacific Coast title, and though they had brought in a Phog Allen product to coach them in 1930, they had not acquired the Kansan winning habit. His first four seasons were all losing ones for Johnny Bunn, but though his fifth was also dismal, at 9–16, he couldn't be unhappy because Luisetti's freshman team went undefeated, with Hank averaging 16 points a game, mostly with one-handed shots.

Luisetti did not invent the one-hand shot. Thirty years before he came to Madison Square Garden, the Spalding *Guide* identified a "Mississippi Valley style" with "long, swift passes [and] one-handed throws for shots at goal." The point is that he developed consistent accuracy and that he attracted enormous attention in a country full of imitators. Luisetti shot with one hand from all positions, not just set shots but running one-handers. He had the moves and body control to shoot while in the air, pioneering the jump shot, and he even had a jump hook shot in his repertoire.

Success was immediate when Luisetti moved up to the varsity for the 1936 season along with Art Stoefen, Jack Calderwood, and H. B. Lee. They were tall and quick and easily adapted to Bunn's 3–2 zone defense. On offense they broke quickly whenever possible, getting the ball to Luisetti who, at 6 feet 3 inches, was an outstanding dribbler and passer as well as shooter. Failing a quick opening, they settled into a standard single pivot with 6-foot 6-inch Stoefen in the middle. They lost two early games to Washington, but in the championship series at the end of the season whipped the Huskies twice. For the season they were 22–7, All-American Luisetti scoring 416 points. Their reputation reached beyond the region, though their schedule had not, and for the following year an eastern trip was planned.

After three tune-up wins at home they started the tour that was to move the game of basketball into a new era. It was the right time. Luisetti had senior Howell Turner as his running mate at forward, Stoefen at center, and Calderwood teaming with Captain Dinty Moore at guard. Averaging just under 6 feet 4 inches, they were all fast, with shooting ability, and well coordinated both individually and as a team. Reserve strength was there too, with Lee, Heath, and Zonne. They stopped off to beat Central Missouri and then a strong Temple team before 9,000 in the Philadelphia Arena. Twice as many were at the Garden to see the Indians take on the class of the East, Bee's LIU team with Kramer, Hillhouse, Bender, and Merson. The Blackbirds' streak was ended at forty-three as Luisetti's 15 points led a 45–31 Stanford victory. Luisetti not only captivated the fans in that game but was made into a national hero by an attentive press and a publicity campaign that couldn't have been more effective if it had been programmed.

Heading back west, Stanford beat Canisius, Western Reserve, Hamline, and Montana State, and was 14–0 before losing to Southern Cal. They later beat the Trojans three times, while their only loss was to California whom they had also beaten thrice. In the Pacific Coast championship series, they beat Washington State in two close games for their second straight title. Phil Zonne's basket broke a 27–27 tie in the first game, as Stanford won 31–28; and in the second, Stanford clung stubbornly to a a slight lead most of the way, winning 41–40. Luisetti scored

*Hank Luisetti.*

410 points for the season, but it was his all-around play that won him All-American honors again.

Luisetti's last year at Stanford was also Bunn's. Zonne shifted to forward to replace Turner and Lee moved into Moore's slot as Stanford seemed as strong as ever. They had only three games before coming into the Garden and were nearly upset by CCNY. Ahead by 6 at the half, Stanford moved out by 16, with 8 minutes to go, when Stoefen fouled out. Stanford's zone was weakened, and the smaller City team got hot from the outside. Holman's two-handed set-shooters—Bernie Fliegel, Red Paris, Izzy Katz, Lou Lefkowitz, and Ace Goldstein—all scored, and then Fliegel scored again, before Heath hit a one-hander for Stanford. When Paris scored from the corner and Katz converted two free throws, City trailed by only 2 points with less than a minute to go. Pressing, Fliegel fouled Bob Zonne, who put Stanford ahead 45–42. Paris missed a layup, rebounded by Luisetti who dribbled the length of the court only to miss his layup, and Goldstein passed to Katz for a last desperate shot as the game ended.

Two nights later, Stanford faced the only metropolitan team that seemed better than CCNY at that point in the season. LIU had Art Hillhouse, Irving Torgoff, Danny Kaplowitz, John Bromberg, and Dolly King as starters; but Bee's men lost to Bunn's by 14 points. In the two games (along with Minnesota who beat LIU and NYU in the other halves of the double-headers) they drew over 36,000 to the Garden. A few nights later, before another packed house in Philadelphia's Convention Hall, the tired and tense Stanford team lost by 4 points to Temple in a game that probably cost them a claim to the mythical national championship. The score of 35–31 owes as much to the toll of the travel as it does to Jimmy Usilton's defense played by Meyer Bloom, Don Shields, Ed Boyle, and company. In any case, with the pressure off, Stanford loosened up and turned it on against Duquesne on a neutral court in Cleveland. That was the night Luisetti's teammates forced Luisetti to shoot himself instead of passing to the open man. The first of the modern collegiate superstars responded with 50 points in a 92–27 win.

During the rest of the season Stanford lost only to Southern Cal and Cal, and again beat them three times each. In the Pacific Coast championship series they played their toughest opponent, Oregon, who had won twenty-five games and avenged each of their losses at least once. The first game was played at the Civic Auditorium in San Francisco, where 8,000 fans saw Oregon close a 10-point deficit to 4 while Luisetti was out with a slight injury. When Hank came back, he thrilled his hometown supporters by sparking a 13-point spurt that put the game out of reach. He had 20 points altogether, in the 52–39 win. The second game, at Stanford, was even better. Twice in the first half the Indians had to come from behind, but they pulled out by 17 with 5 minutes left. Here Bunn removed his starters one at a time, to great ovations, as Stanford coasted home by 59–51. Luisetti led the scorers with 26; in his three years, Stanford had swept three championship series. His season's total was 465 points. Player of the year for the second time, he would become second choice, behind George Mikan, for player of the half century—and he might have been underrated.

Luisetti's legacy is manifold. He was the first college player to be a matinee idol (though his venture into the movies was ill-chosen). Because of the abundant attention he received in the media, his style of play opened up a brave new world of possibilities. The fast break with a Luisetti on the run could lead to a variety of shots by open men, not just a layup. The ability to shoot on the move led to the development of a rich variety of plays and shots. Those who wished to emulate Luisetti knew they had to excel in every aspect of the game—rebounding, dribbling, passing, and defending, as well as shooting. But most of all it is the one-handed shooting that we remember.

Nat Holman was appalled at the very notion of Luisetti's unorthodox shots. Yet a dozen years later he would eagerly point out that the West wasn't alone in producing great one-hand shooters—and he singled out Tony Lavelli's hook, Paul Arizin's soft jump, and his own Irwin Dambrot's running push. In 1947 Dambrot put in three straight one-handed push shots plus a foul in a 50-second span for a 7-point win over a fine Harold Anderson team from Bowling Green. Holman was delighted with what, in 1937, he had viewed with alarm.

But this regionalism has passed too. One-hand shooting is universally accepted, and doing it off the jump is the prevalent mode of scoring. When Kenny Sailors dazzled Garden audiences with his jump-shooting in the 1943 NIT, they and some of the writers again hailed an innovation from the West to be copied. Few realized—how soon they forget—the direct influence of Luisetti on Sailors and on all the Arizins, Wests, Fulkses, Pettits, Yardleys, Heinsohns, and Robertsons. Legend or not, the story of Hank Luisetti includes many of the elements of contemporary basketball.

# 15

# *Hobson's Choice and the Last Laugh*

HOWARD HOBSON returned to Eugene for his tenth reunion, and he stayed to coach Oregon for twelve years before seeking greener pastures with the Ivy's Blue. He succeeded the coach for whom he had played, another Oregonian, Bill Reinhart, who was to build another dynasty at George Washington. Reinhart had had winning seasons in his first seven, though the conference crown escaped him. Of his players, perhaps only Hugh Latham and Gordon Ridings should be remembered. Four of Reinhart's last six years were losing ones, so that Hobson was coming into a rebuilding situation.

A greatly expanded schedule seemed to help recruiting from the start. Only moderately successful in his first two years (20–11, 19–9), Hobson had nevertheless gotten the Webfeet moving in the right direction. In fact his 1937 team had finished in a three-way tie for the Northern Division lead, losing the playoff to Washington State. Johnny Lewis was the only Reinhart holdover on this team, though all-conference Dave Silver had been recruited by him. Hobson's other three starters were sophomores, 6-foot 8-inch Urgel "Slim" Wintermute, Bob Anet, and Laddie Gale. Another sophomore, Wally Johansen, had beaten out Captain Lewis by the end of the season.

This team came back as a unit to win twenty-five games the following season, win the Northern Division, and go down fighting to the Stanford powerhouse in the championship series. With only Silver to graduate, they were expected to be the best of the West in 1939, and accordingly they scheduled a long eastern road trip. John Dick was the fifth starter alongside Gale at forward, but on defense Dick played up front with Anet and Johansen in a 3–2 zone that looked a lot like Stanford's. Wintermute and Gale were good enough in the back line to allow the other three to gamble, and their ball-hawking caused many turnovers. They would only run on clear opportunities, preferring to hold up and wait to set up in a 2–3 offense with Gale and Dick in the corners.

The system had a few weaknesses, but they could be overcome with superior personnel. Averaging 6 feet 2 inches and with exceptional speed, Oregon should certainly have beaten CCNY in the season's first Garden twinbill. City had a subpar team, but they executed a game plan to perfection against Oregon. They worked patiently against the zone to find free shots from its soft spots, the corners, and that's where Dave Siperstein scored his game-high 14 points on high arcs over Wintermute and Gale. Meanwhile on defense, Al Soupios at 6 feet 3 inches and Babe Adler at 6 feet 1 inch fronted the two big men, effectively keeping the ball from them though spotting them 5 inches each in height. Oregon could not adjust in time and lost 38–36, but that was the low point of the tour and the season.

Before returning home they beat St. Joseph's, Miami, Canisius, Wayne, Western Illinois, and Drake. They lost to Bradley, one of the best five teams in the country, and then at the end of the trip lost to Stanford, but they came on strong thereafter and finished the season with a second straight Northern Division title and a 24–5 record. For the championship series with California, more was at stake than usual. The winner at Eugene would be invited to play in the Western Regionals of the inaugural NCAA Tournament.

Nibs Price, whose Cal teams won over 60 percent of all games throughout his thirty-year tenure, had one of his bigger and better squads at Berkeley, with Bill Ogilvie at center and Ivor Thomas, Bill Biggerstaff, Walt Bickerton, and Captain Chalmers. They had won the Southern Division in a playoff with Southern Cal and took a 24–6 record into the championship series. But the northern expedition and Oregon's zone defense turned the Bears cold, especially after halftime. In the first game, they trailed by 1 point at the half, but Oregon came out blazing after intermission, drew away, and then held off a California rally to win 54–49. Laddie Gale was high man with 18 points. The second game was nearly a repeat of the first, Oregon leading by 2 at the half and winning 53–47, but this time led by Wintermute and Dick with 16 points each.

Two nights later they faced Texas on Treasure Island in San Francisco Bay, the tournament being sponsored by the San Francisco International Exposition. After Oklahoma had beaten Utah State by a comfortable 11-point margin, Oregon did even better, handling Texas 56–41. The following night was even easier, Oregon pulling steadily ahead to win 55–37. Johnny Bunn said that their fast break led by the two guards, their superior front-line height, their zone defense, and their phenomenal one-hand shooting were too much for the Sooners. Bunn also predicted that the NCAA tourney would "develop into the major basketball event of the season." Gale, Anet, and Wintermute were all named to the all-tourney team, and then it was on to Evanston to face the Eastern Regional champions, Ohio State.

With the center jump virtually eliminated from the game, Hobson realized that greater stress would be put on the transitions between offense and defense. His solution was a fast break off the 3–2 zone whenever possible, led by Anet and Johansen who were up front chasing in the zone. But if there was no break, then the guards would hold up and allow the big men to set up in the post and corners. He had the perfect personnel to do this, the balance and the complementary skills. Johansen was a superior ballhandler and Anet one of the greatest dribblers, ranked by Holman with Sailors, Davies, Boudreau, Dick McGuire, and Mac Kinsbrunner. (Oregon's system resembled that of the Wonder Five, where Posnak and Kinsbrunner could stall indefinitely until Begovich, Gerson, and Schuckman set up on offense.) And the weak transition back to defense was compensated for by the speed of the big men and the ability of Dick, Anet, and Johansen to harass the opponent's attack.

Dutch Lonborg, manager of the championship game, called the system unique, but it may have been merely uniquely successful. As pioneers in the elimination of the center jump, the Pacific Coast Conference coaches had been focusing on the related problems much longer than their rivals elsewhere. In the event, however, Hobson had to make a defensive adjustment to hold off Harold Olsen's Buckeyes. Oregon's zone frustrated Ohio State's set offense from the start. Oregon drew out to an early lead, as Ohio State's normally high-percentage shooting was way below par. Finally, near the end of the first half, Jim Hull and Bill Sattler found soft spots in the zone and began to cut into the lead, closing to 21–16 at halftime. Early in the second half, ahead by only 3, Oregon switched to a loose shifting man-to-man defense that simulated their zone setup without weakening the fast-break chances. Ohio State didn't catch on and never caught up. Oregon pulled steadily away to win 46–33. Wintermute was held to two field goals, but Oregon got balanced scoring from Dick (15), Anet (10), Johansen (9), and Gale (8); while for Ohio State, Hull had 12, Lynch and Sattler had 7 each.

As Bunn's remarks implied, the NCAA title did not yet mean a firm claim to a national championship. Yet Hobson's beautifully integrated and conditioned team might very well have become the best by the end of the season. Certainly they peaked late, just before the graduation of four starters. But even though the NIT had a stronger draw, the first NCAA winner was worthy of its historical significance.

The same could be said of the first NIT winner, just a year before. Jim Usilton's Temple team was 20–2 against top-flight competition and then whipped

Bradley, Oklahoma A & M, and Colorado in the tournament. Mike Bloom was the All-American star of the EIC champs, though Ed Boyle was the NIT high scorer and Don Shields the NIT MVP. Howard Black and Don Henderson were the other starters. The next year was Usilton's last at Temple, and he had a losing season for only the second time in a thirteen-year tenure during which he won 72 percent of all games played.

The 1939 NIT stole the spotlight from the NCAA because the finals matched two undefeated powers, LIU and Loyola of Chicago (both of whom are discussed elsewhere herein), but by 1940 the two tournaments were competing on a nearly equal basis for outstanding teams. The NIT had been turned over to a newly formed Metropolitan Intercollegiate Basketball Committee consisting of ten athletic directors. Two of the six NIT teams were also among the eight NCAA entries. One was Duquesne, coached by Chick Davies, whose teams won three out of every four games (314 of 419) over his twenty-one seasons. Led by Paul Widowitz and Moe Becker, the Dukes beat St. John's and Oklahoma A & M before losing in the NIT finals, and beat Western Kentucky before losing to Indiana in the NCAA Eastern Regionals. The other was Colorado, coached by Frosty Cox, a Phog Allen alumnus, and starring Bob Doll and Jack Harvey. The Buffaloes stampeded DePaul and Duquesne to win the NIT but were shot down by Southern Cal in the NCAA.

Allen's drumbeating had brought the Western Regionals and the championship to the Kansas City Municipal Auditorium. There his own Kansas team, with Howard Engleman, Don Ebling, Bobby Allen (the coach's son), Ralph Miller, and Dick Harp (who would eventually succeed the Phog as coach), cooked Rice in the opener, before Sam Barry's Trojans beat Colorado. The regional final was the highlight of the season. In Dale Sears, Ralph Vaughn, Jack Morrison, and Tom McGarvin, Southern Cal had four seniors who gave the team speed, experience, clever ballhandling, and accurate shooting. They dominated the Pacific Coast Conference (though Jackie Robinson of UCLA won the scoring championship) and were generally thought to be the country's best. Though outsized, they outmuscled Colorado to reach the regional championship game with Kansas.

Southern Cal led 21–20 at the half and kept a slim lead until Bobby Allen tied it at 40-all with 2 minutes left. Allen's free throw gave Kansas a lead, but Jack Lippert hit from outside to put SC back in front. They got the ball back and seemed to have the game when Allen intercepted a pass and threw to Engleman in the corner. Engleman's set shot with only 18 seconds left gave the Jayhawks their big upset. Harp's 15 points led the winners, while Sears scored 19 in a losing effort.

The championship game against Indiana was anticlimactic. Kansas was spent by the SC struggle, got off to a 10–4 lead, but were never in the game after Indiana tied them at 14-all. It was 32–19 at the half, 60–42 at the end. Though Lambert's Purdue team, with Beretta and Blanken, had won the Big Ten title by one game, Indiana's "Laughing Boys" had beaten them twice during the season and were chosen by committee for the Eastern Regional berth from District IV. In Branch

McCracken's second year as coach in Bloomington, he had a fast-breaking team featuring Marvin Huffman, Herman Schaefer, Bob Dro, Curly Armstrong, Bill Menke, and Jay McCreary. And he kept them running just as Everett Dean had kept him running for the Hoosiers a decade earlier. Only Duquesne played them reasonably close in the tournament. They ran away with the regionals and the national championship and laughed all the way back to Bloomington.

The NCAA superiority was short-lived. The following year Wisconsin beat Washington State in Kansas City to finish a tournament with little in the way of outstanding play. Meanwhile the NIT was enlarged to eight teams including three from the metropolitan area. A first round loser was Westminster, which had earlier beaten Pitt, an NCAA regional finalist. Duquesne, another first-round NIT loser, had twice beaten North Carolina, a first-round NCAA loser. By and large the NCAA entries had rarely ventured beyond their geographical regions and had sometimes been beaten by teams considered not good enough for the NIT. Limited to eight geographical districts, the NCAA would have to be unusually lucky to get a draw of balanced quality. The NIT, with a cherished right called freedom of choice, could go after the best wherever they might be. Unfortunately other restrictions, in the form of wartime interference with travel and education and everything else, would distort this struggle for basketball-tournament hegemony for several years.

# 16

# *The Kids, Whiz and Blitz*

ONE OF THE major wartime phenomena appearing in college basketball was the emergence of very young teams. With players (and many coaches, too) lost to the armed forces or transferred, sometimes in midseason, it became necessary for many schools to make freshmen eligible for varsity play. Others, especially when travel became as difficult as maintaining personnel, simply canceled or severely curtailed intercollegiate competition.

The first war year did not interfere significantly with sport. The NCAA and NIT lineups were fairly even in strength. Dartmouth, the Eastern Regional winner, had lost to Toledo, an NIT semifinalist; Penn State, first-round loser to Dartmouth, had split with West Virginia, the NIT winner; and Creighton, another NIT semifinalist, had lost to Kansas, first-round loser to Colorado in the Western Regionals.

Stanford was probably the country's best. Everett Dean had moved from Indiana to the Indians four years earlier and had now put together a fine group of one-hand shooters, including Howie Dallmar, Bill Cowden, Don Burness, Ed Voss, Jack Dana, and especially Jim Pollard. They won fairly easily from Rice, Colorado, and Dartmouth in the tournament after winning their berth in a rubber match with Slats Gill's Oregon State team. Dartmouth, with its fifth straight Ivy

*Everett Dean coached Stanford to 1942 NCAA champion-ship with Dallmar and Pollard.*

League championship, was coached by Osborne Cowles, who had played under Dean at Carleton College, but the pupil didn't have the horses to match the master's, even with Pollard out with the flu. Earlier in the tourney, however, Frosty Cox had beaten his mentor, Phog Allen.

West Virginia won three straight upsets to win the NIT. Dyke Raese's Mountaineers beat top-seeded LIU in overtime, then Toledo, and finally Western Kentucky by coming from behind in the final minutes. Even all-star teams from the two tournaments would have been evenly matched. From the NCAA along with Pollard were George Munroe of Dartmouth, Bob Kinney of Rice, Andy Phillip of Illinois, Pete McCloud of Colorado, and Ray Evans of Kansas. From the NIT were Bob Gerber of Toledo, Stutz Modzelewski of Rhode Island, Rudy Baric and Scotty Hamilton of West Virginia, Price Brookfield of West Texas State, and Red Holzman of CCNY.

A year later the war was taking its toll. Both tourneys had to take second choices to complete their draws, but for the first time there would be a test match of the champions. Wyoming, coming from behind to beat Oklahoma, Texas, and Georgetown, survived the NCAA; while St. John's returned the NIT title to New York by beating Rice, Fordham, and Toledo. In a special benefit game for the Red Cross in New York, Kenny Sailors and Milo Komenich led the Cowboys to a 52–47 win over such Redmen as Harry Boykoff and Fuzzy Levane.

But the best team didn't play in either tournament. Under Douglas Mills, Illinois had won all its league games, losing only to a service team in a 17–1 season. They broke all Western Conference scoring records though they played an abbreviated schedule, closing the season by running over Northwestern 86–44 and Chicago 92–25. Run is precisely what they did, but with great coordinated smoothness, and though they shot quickly, it was with remarkable accuracy. These were the Whiz Kids—Andy Phillip, Ken Menke, Gene Vance, Jack Smiley, and Art Mathisen—and they were so good that only a superathlete like Otto Graham of Northwestern could crack the all-conference team that year, instead of Menke, while even such great players as Johnny Kotz of Wisconsin and Eddie Ehlers of Purdue were relegated to second team honors by the Illini. Before the next season they were all gone from Urbana; after the war, all but Menke played some pro ball, but only Phillip, the only Whiz Kid who had been out of his teens when their streak began, became a professional star.

The second bunch of Kids came along the following year, and they made it at least arguable that the NCAA was as strong as the NIT. These were the Blitz Kids from Utah—Arnie Ferrin, Wat Misaka, Fred Sheffield, Herb Wilkinson, Dick Smuin, and Bob Lewis—averaging eighteen and one-half years of age and barely 6 feet in height. Vadal Peterson, in his seventeenth season of running the Redskins, with only four losing seasons in his career, had one of his best teams but nobody and no place to play. The Skyline Conference had suspended play and the Army had appropriated the fieldhouse in Salt Lake City.

*Whiz Kids* (left to right): *Coach Mills, Mathisen, Smiley, Vance, Menke, and Phillip.*

Peterson found a church gym they could use and mostly service teams to play. In twenty games the Utes had won their only three intercollegiate games and had lost only three of the others. Wyoming, the defending NCAA champions, had canceled their schedule, and Utah was offered the District VII bid to the Western Regionals in Kansas City. Unfortunately the bid did not include a guarantee of expenses, so Peterson accepted instead the last opening in the NIT

124

draw. It was perhaps a brash decision because the NIT seemed to have by far the
tougher draw in 1944. The field included powerful teams from Kentucky, St.
John's, Bowling Green, DePaul, and Oklahoma A & M. Canisius, in Allie Seel-
bach's last year as coach, had a solid record including wins over Western Kentucky
and LIU and had won their invitation by beating St. John's in overtime. Muhlenberg, in Doggie Julian's last year there, had given him his best record, including
wins over West Virginia, Penn State, Villanova twice, CCNY twice, and NCAA-
entry Temple twice. And Utah completed that field.

Utah was a team that did a lot of running but not a lot of shooting. They
worked hard to get free for one-hand shots and played sticky, aggressive defense.

*Blitz Kids: Coach Peterson with cup, Misaka behind it, Ferrin kneeling.*

For rebounding they depended on Ferrin, a skinny 6-foot 3-inch freshman, and Fred Sheffield, at 6 feet 1 inch the defending NCAA high-jump champion. Against Kentucky, Utah managed a tie at halftime, mostly on Ferrin's shooting. But with Bob Brannum dominating the boards in the second half and Jack Parkinson leading the hot-shooting Wildcats, Utah could not keep pace, losing 46–38. They may have had a case of Garden jitters in their first visit to the big city—they missed eight of twelve free throws—but good news dispelled their disappointment in the locker room.

Arkansas, with two starters injured in an automobile accident, had withdrawn from the NCAA tournament, and once again Utah was invited to the Western Regionals. This time they required no guarantee, and after two and a half days of train rides (troop movements dominated the rails), arrived in Kansas City to play Missouri. Missouri, not a tournament-caliber team, had been invited for reasons of expedience and proximity. Ferrin's 12 points led Utah's comfortable 45–35 win.

In the Western Regional finals, Iowa State, easy winner over Pepperdine (despite big Nick Buzolich's 22 points), was more of a challenge. One of Lou Menze's best teams, they had won their first Missouri Valley title in a decade, led by Price Brookfield (transferred by the Navy from West Texas State), Jim Meyers, and the Wehde twins. Utah took an early lead, but Iowa State caught them in 8 minutes of the second half. Misaka's two straight field goals put Utah in front for good with 7 minutes left, and they drew out to win 40–31 as Ferrin controlled the ball dribbling with either hand and passing cleverly to the open man. Off in his shooting, Ferrin set up most of his teammates' baskets as Sheffield and Misaka were high in the game at 9 points each.

Meanwhile in the East, Ohio State and Dartmouth had eliminated subpar Temple and outclassed Catholic. For the regional championship, Dartmouth held off several Buckeye comebacks and won 60–53. Earl Brown, who had played for George Keogan at Notre Dame, took over at Hanover from Osborne Cowles and won a seventh straight Ivy title with a squad of Navy and Marine reservists. During the season they had lost only to one service team. Audley Brindley was the captain and star, capably supported by Bob Gale, John Monahan, Joe Vancisin, and Harry Leggat, a Marine transfer from NYU. By tournament time the Navy's V 12 program had given them a bonus in Dick McGuire, St. John's star. Ohio State had been favored, perhaps because of the Green's repeated failures in the tournament, but Brindley outplayed Arnie Risen, outscoring him 28–21, and McGuire shackled high-scoring Don Grate.

The championship game shaped up as a good one. Utah, now known as the Blitz Kids, was returning to the Garden with confidence and determined to justify all the travel. Dartmouth was used to being in town again, but it was the Utes that did the running. Peterson's plan was to double-team Brindley and Gale with the ball, gambling that the other men would be reluctant to shoot. The strategy worked, though Utah could never pull away by more than 4 points. They went into a freeze with 4 minutes left and a 36–32 lead. Dartmouth pressed and fouled, but twice Utah waived the free throw to keep the ball. With less than 2 minutes to play, the hometown boys struck back. McGuire stole the ball and fed Leggat. Ferrin got it back for Utah, but Gale tipped in a rebound for Dartmouth. Again Utah could not maintain a freeze, Dartmouth recovered a loose ball, and McGuire hit a set shot at the buzzer to send it into overtime. Four free throws by Ferrin kept the game tied, and then with 3 seconds on the clock Herb Wilkinson's one-hander from the circle gave Utah the NCAA title 42–40.

The Blitz Kids then took on the giant-killers from St. John's in the Red Cross Classic between the two tournament champions. Again tight team defense and Ferrin's all-around brilliance won for Utah. Lapchick's big three—Hy Gotkin, Bill Kotsores, and Ray Wertis—were held to 26 points, while Ferrin (17), Wilkinson (11), and Lewis (8) matched the whole St. John's output in the 43–36 win. A burst of 7 straight points in the middle of the second half to establish their longest lead at 35–26 was the blitz that won it for the Utah Kids. Kotsores, a freshman Redman, was the NIT MVP, but he was no match for the NCAA MVP, freshman Ferrin. The NIT may have been stronger throughout the draw, but at the top there was room reserved for the Runnin' Redskins from Utah.

# 17

# Iba and the Coming
# of the Giants

IN 1937 Phog Allen surveyed the entire college basketball scene and found "at least thirty-three" players who were 6 feet 5 inches or taller. Allen, like Hank Iba, lamented the notion that their sport was a game for goons. Yet it was obviously true that the elevated goal made height an advantage, and often tall boys who had no other athletic attribute performed to the best of their limited but elevated ability on the court. What happened was that in the course of a few decades, the country grew up, physically, if in no other way. The best basketball players in 1920, the game being what it was then, were all around 5 feet 10 inches, which seemed to be optimum size for maximum coordination. By 1940 athletes of 6 feet 3 inches and 6 feet 4 inches had attained that level of coordination in great numbers, and by 1970 the same could be said of 6-foot 9-inch and 6-foot 10-inch players.

Few big men had played the game effectively before 1937. Aside from Matty Begovich at 6 feet 5 inches and Joe Lapchick at 6 feet 4 inches, it is hard to find one with more than specialized skills. Allen had a 7-footer enrolled at Kansas, but he drowned accidentally before ever playing a varsity game. Keaney had his son to rebound and initiate the fast break at Rhode Island, but Warner did little else at either end of the court. The man who devised a system to make full use of a big man was Leonard Sachs, for twenty years coach at Loyola of Illinois, and the man who made the system work was Mike Novak.

Novak on defense, with his size (6 feet 9 inches, 220 pounds) and timing, was a demon goaltender. And because he had Novak back there knocking away shots, Sachs could deploy his other men in a variety of zone alignments. On offense Novak's size and agility allowed Loyola to run plays off the pivot that were refinements of Horse Haggerty's Celtic maneuvers. Novak set screens for his teammates that were all the more effective because he was a threat to turn either way to drive or shoot. During Novak's years at the Chicago school, Loyola won close to 80 percent of their games. It took a special defense, like the one devised by Bill Reinhart at George Washington, to stop him. And in 1939 it took unique shooting instructions from Clair Bee to LIU for the Blackbirds to beat the Ramblers in the NIT finals, ruining a perfect season for Loyola.

Novak was the culmination of the old-style pivot man, though his goaltending was a glimpse ahead. Another forward look was Oregon's Slim Wintermute with his one-hand shooting touch. In the decade of the Forties, so many outstanding big men played with the complete skills of coordinated athletes that it was difficult to find a major team without one. Harry Boykoff of St. John's, Arnie Risen of Ohio State, and Don Otten of Bowling Green have already been mentioned. Charlie Share, who followed Otten at Bowling Green, was even bigger. An exemplary list might include the following in the East—Frank Crossin at Penn, Ed Peterson at Cornell, John Mahnken at Georgtown, and Larry Foust at La Salle; in the West—Bill Roberts at Wyoming Red Rocha at Oregon State, and Jack Nichols at Washington; and in between—Tom King at Michigan, John Mills at Western Kentucky, John Pritchard at Drake, Milton Schoon at Valparaiso, and Ralph Siewert at North Dakota State. Of course even among these awesome figures two contemporary giants stood out, competition only for each other as king of the mountains—Bob Kurland and George Mikan.

When Kurland arrived in Stillwater, Hank Iba had been in charge for eight seasons. Oklahoma A & M's ascendancy began with Iba, as he installed his extraordinarily deliberate system on the theory that it's not bad to lose occasionally as long as you never lose bad. And the Cowboys had done too much losing, never having won a Missouri Conference championship. Iba's first year produced a .500 record, the school's best in a decade but the worst their new coach would have for twenty years. In 1936, with Merle Rousey and Taylor Little, they tied for the title, and then they won it four straight years with such stars as R. C. Cox, Richard Krueger, Merle Scheffler, Jesse Renick, Harvey Slade, and Howard Doyle. They had gone to the NIT semifinals in 1938 (beating NYU for third place in the consolation game) and 1940 (again taking third place by beating DePaul 23–22). In 1941, with Eugene Smelser, Vernon Yates, and Lonnie Eggleston, they slipped to second behind Ed Hickey's Creighton team, and then the two tied in 1942.

Through eight years Iba's record was 153–47, a .765 winning percentage, and he had never had a leading scorer. Defense and ball control were what he taught; eliminating mistakes was the cherished goal. His defensive system was man-to-man but loose away from the ball, a "swinging gate" theory that applies zone principles to man-to-man assignments. On offense his team ran set plays off constantly repeated patterns, and no one dared show impatience. Kurland fit in perfectly with this system, and it is a good thing he did because Iba was not about to change even with or for a well-coordinated 7-foot prodigy.

Kurland was not a natural shooter, but he worked hard to develop a variety of shots to go with the dunk that did come naturally. Obviously he was a natural rebounder, though he may have lacked the instinctive sense of timing of an Alex Groza (Rupp remembers Tennessee fans pleading with the Vols not to shoot because Groza would be sure to get the ball). But when it came to defense, Kurland did have the timing to knock shots away before they reached the basket. His lack of speed was no problem; the Cowboys would run their weave till the cows came home, waiting for the big man to set up in the post. In his freshman year he was used sparingly by Iba as the team finished second to Creighton again, but in 1944, while the league suspended its official schedule, Kurland was not only a regular but an All-American. Oklahoma A & M was 26–4 that year, losing only to service teams, to earn another trip to the NIT. There, after beating Canisius, they lost to DePaul and then in the consolation to Kentucky.

In the following season, with the league still inoperative and a new goaltending rule in effect, Kurland and Iba and Oklahoma A & M came back stronger. The rule change made Kurland a better, more complete player, Iba thought, and he had a strong supporting cast as well—Cecil Hankins, Weldon Kern, Doyle Parrack, and Blake Williams. With a 23–4 record during the season, they beat Utah, Arkansas, and a splendid NYU team to win the NCAA championship and then beat NIT champs DePaul in the Red Cross benefit game.

With the resumption of league play for 1946, Iba's team played fewer service teams and wound up with an even better record, 28–2, winning all twelve conference games. They went on to win a second straight NCAA championship, beating Baylor, California, and North Carolina. Even Iba could not keep down the scoring on that squad. The starters, Kern, Williams, Sam Aubrey, and J. L. Parks, all made the all-conference first team along with Kurland who was a three-time All-American. He scored 58 against St. Louis and led the nation with 643 points, nearly 20 a game. The team averaged about 50 points a game, and it is likely that Kurland contributed as many assists as baskets.

With Kurland gone, Iba didn't change a hair, nor the part down the middle

*Hank Iba.*

130

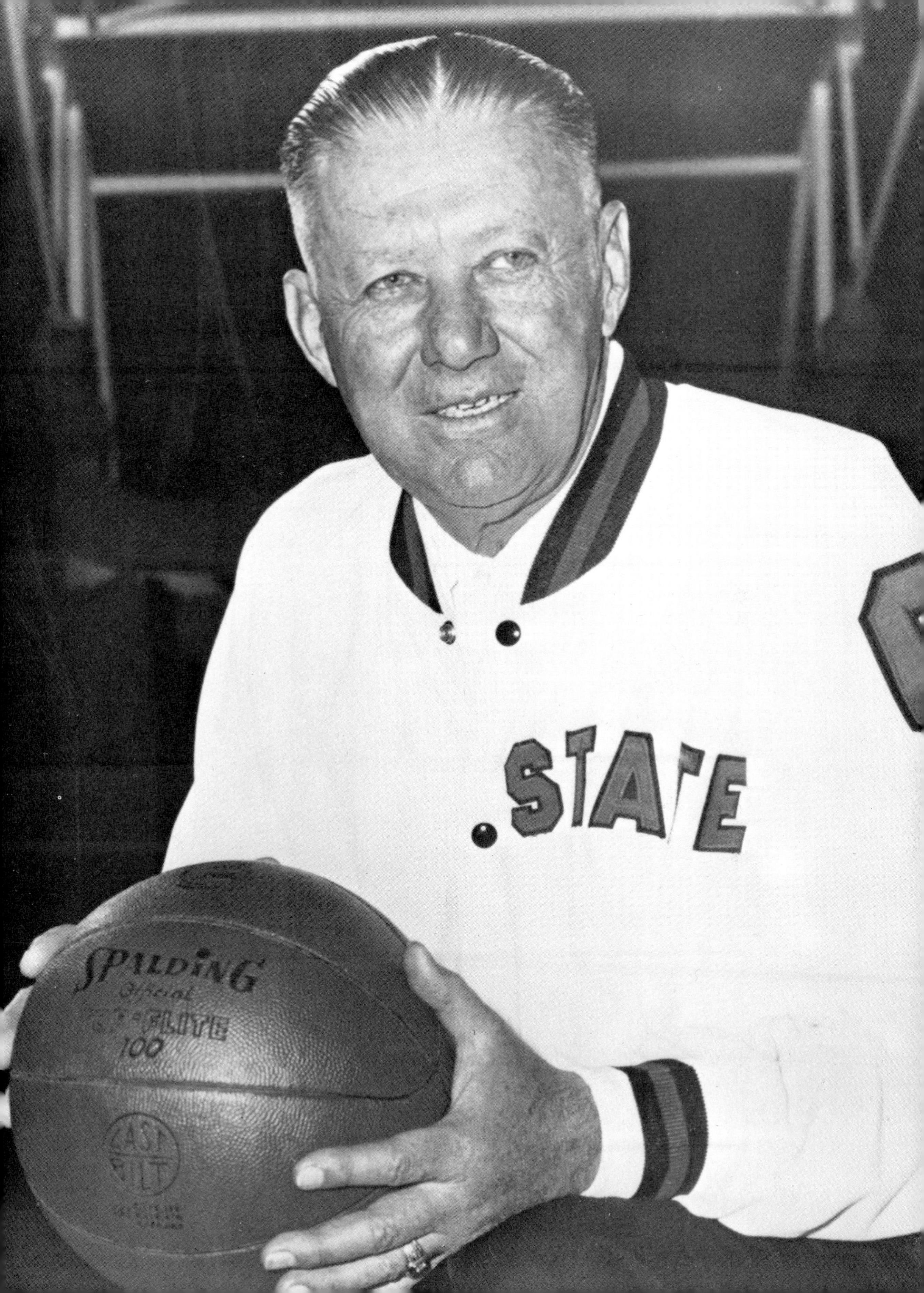

STATE
SPALDING
Official
100

of his head. And his slowdown tactics continued to infuriate fans and opponents alike as he went on winning. In the eleven years they remained in the Missouri Valley Conference, they won the title five more times, going to the NCAA finals in 1949, the Western Regional finals in 1951, the Midwest Regional finals in 1953 and 1954, and the NIT in 1956. As Oklahoma State they went to the Midwest Regional finals in 1958, but once they became part of the Big Eight, the championship years were over for Iba. Not that his teams were playing in a stronger league; it was a matter of the game having passed him by.

At his retirement in 1970, Iba had a record of 741–313, third on the all-time winners list. It is difficult to argue with such consistently impressive success, yet Iba is likely to be remembered as the coach under whom the Olympic winning streak was broken. The U.S. Olympic Committee, itself a notorious anachronism, chose Iba as coach in 1964. With Bill Bradley, Walt Hazzard, and Lucious Jackson, he won the gold medals in Tokyo, running up big scores despite the emphasis on defense and control. Again in 1968 Iba won at Mexico City, with Spencer Haywood, Jo Jo White, and Charley Scott performing brilliantly despite the shackles of the system.

But in Munich, with both the system and the coach past retirement age, the frustrations first of selections and then of training and finally playing were too much for another talented team. The 51–50 loss to Russia in the finals owed a great deal to Olympic politics and international officiating, but the point is that no American team in 1972 should have been involved in a game in which 50 points could win. In Helsinki in 1952, Russia had held the ball against Kurland and Lovellette to produce a 36–25 score, but even in London in 1948 Kurland and Groza had led a 65–21 rout of France.

It was Kurland who had brought Iba-style basketball to its peak in 1945 and 1946, but it was Mikan with his aggressive moves and versatile shots who presaged the new day of the big man. At 6 feet 10 inches George Mikan did not have the agility or coordination of 7-foot Kurland, and he had the additional handicap of having to wear thick glasses, but he weighed as much and had a ton of determination. Perhaps his biggest break came in his freshman year at DePaul when he auditioned for George Keogan, hoping to play varsity ball at Notre Dame. Rejected and disappointed, he only worked harder when he returned to DePaul, playing in the CYO league (where he faced a strong black youngster named Sweetwater Clifton) as well as for the freshmen. Then Ray Meyer, who had been Keogan's assistant, took over at DePaul. The combination produced eighty-one wins in ninety-eight games over the next four years.

Meyer realized the potential in Mikan and helped him fulfill it. He directed the big boy's energies, working him long hours in drills to develop coordination— jumping rope, boxing—and then forcing him to learn a hook shot. Mikan did not just learn it, he perfected it, and he became in time an effective and tenacious player in every phase of the game. He even had the good hands usually associated with little men. (Meyer once credited Mikan's years of piano lessons with developing his fingers to the point where he could control a basketball on their tips.)

Meyer built his approach to the game (and his reputation as well) on the presence of Mikan in his lineup. The screen-switch defense, learned as both player and assistant from Keogan at Notre Dame, was perfect for DePaul to keep Mikan close to the basket. And he designed an offense around the big man in the single pivot, saying years later that the "big center is the essential I must have to field a winning team."

Everything clicked into place in their first year together. During the season they were 18–4 including two losses to the Camp Grant team that gave the Illini Whiz Kids their only loss. The other losses were to Duquesne and, disappointingly, to Notre Dame, shortly before Coach Keogan's sudden death. Nevertheless they won the District IV invitation to the NCAA, where they beat Dartmouth in the first round while Ozzie Cowles cried "goaltender, goaltender." But in the regional finals, Elmer Ripley's Georgetown team, with Mahnken neutralizing Mikan, beat them 53–49. Still, Nat Holman called George "the greatest basketball center ever seen in Madison Square Garden," presaging his later recognition as the player of the half century.

Mikan's junior year started off with thirteen straight wins before Valparaiso upset DePaul. They got revenge later in the season, by 31 points, and finished 20–3, losing to Marquette and Illinois. They beat Ohio State 61–49 as Mikan, playing on a bad ankle, bested Arnie Risen, but when the Buckeyes got the NCAA bid, the Blue Demons came to the Garden for the NIT. They beat Muhlenberg by 23 points and Oklahoma A & M by 3 before losing to an inspired St. John's team in the finals. Mikan was not dominant in the tournament, though he led all scorers with 49 points. His supporting cast, including Dick Triptow, Gene Stump, Jack Dean, and Whitey Kachan, helped considerably to bring them this far.

Mikan was improving every year. As with Kurland, the goaltending rule only forced him to be more of a fully rounded player. Through a twenty-game season DePaul lost only to the Great Lakes Navy team and in a split series with Illinois. The NIT was a romp—West Virginia 76–52, Rhode Island 97–53, and Bowling Green 71–54—as Mikan scored 33, 53 (equaling the whole opposition), and 34 to win MVP honors unanimously. But in the Red Cross game Mikan fouled out in the first half; Stump, Kachan, Ernie DiBenedetto, and brother Ed Mikan could not keep up with Iba's boys; and DePaul lost their best shot at a national title. Mikan had finished his season with 558 points, leading the country with a 23.3 average.

Mikan played another year for DePaul, his fifth in school but only his fourth on the varsity with extended eligibility rules. The record was 19–5, including split series with Notre Dame (Vince Boryla, Billy Hassett, Leo Klier) and Oklahoma A

& M, the eventual NCAA champion. Mikan scored 25 against his future team-mate Vern Mikkelsen of Hamline (Howie Schultz had given him more trouble the year before). He scored 555, again leading the nation with a 23.1 average, and he completed four years with 1,870 points in ninety-eight games.

Mikan went on to greater heights of achievement as a pro, and so did Kurland as a two-time Olympian and perennial AAU all-star, but there is no doubt that the two brought a new dimension to college basketball. In those terms it is hard to separate the two. Between them they produced a single overwhelming impact, providing the second (after Luisetti's shooting) of what I consider the five major elements in contemporary college basketball.

Five times in their college careers Mikan and Kurland played against each other. DePaul won three of those games, by a total of 9 points, and lost two by 8 points each time. Of the postseason games, Oklahoma A & M won two of three. Only once in the five titanic struggles did either score more than his average—Kurland in the first 1946 meeting—and DePaul won the game. Kurland out-scored Mikan slightly in their meetings, and Mikan had the edge in rebounds. If there was a perceptible difference, it was a matter of maturity: in the big Red Cross game, Kurland's baiting drew Mikan into fouls and he didn't last 14 minutes of play. Yet there may be a deceptive factor in that comparison. Kurland played in a system that suited him perfectly; Mikan would not find his appropriate style until he personally made the NBA a profitable operation. This history will make no judgment between the two as collegiate performers. Together they put the coordinated big man into the center of skilled contemporary basketball operations.

*Duel of giants; Bob Kurland* (left) *and George Mikan.*

# 18

# *The Blue's Baron in Brown*

THE GOLDEN era of basketball in Lexington began in the fall of 1944, at the beginning of Adolph Rupp's fifteenth season as the Wildcat coach. This may be difficult to accept when the first fourteen years are examined. During that time Kentucky had won 233 games and lost only 59, a winning percentage of .798. In the twelve years of the SEC's existence, Kentucky had won the league tournament six out of eleven times, tied for the title the year there was no tournament, and had the league's best record in three of the years they did not win the tournament.

In his first two years, Rupp's team was in the old Southern Conference. In 1931, Kentucky started the season with ten straight wins but ended with a 2-point loss to Maryland in the championship game when Bosey Berger scored twice in the last minute. A year later they lost only two games, both by 1 point, to Vanderbilt in the final season game and to North Carolina in the Southern Conference semis. When the SEC was formed, Kentucky was the first champion. In its second year they entered the tournament undefeated and heavily favored. For the first round Kentucky drew Ole Miss, but the Rebels had to withdraw because of flu and were replaced by a Florida team with a poor record. Florida promptly upset Kentucky, and Rupp argued thereafter that season records should decide league championships.

*No justice in the Baron's court; the Baron is not amused.*

The win–loss records, impressive as they are, are not the measure of Kentucky's and Rupp's contributions during those years. Nor are the outstanding players who earned national recognition: Carey Spicer, Aggie Sale, Frenchy De-Moisey, Ellis Johnson, LeRoy Edwards, Bernie Opper, Mickey Rouse, Lee Huber, Bob Brannum. Their greatest value lay in the way they helped move basketball toward a truly national game. Rupp, who had played under Phog Allen on the undefeated 1923 Kansas team and later coached the Freeport, Illinois, high school teams (over 80 percent victories), brought fast-breaking ideas to Lexington, where Johnny Mauer had been teaching a deliberate, ball-control game. Over the years Rupp demonstrated that he could adapt his style to his personnel, that versatility is a great virtue, and that his teams would still be identifiably his.

Most important, Kentucky under Rupp sought to play the best teams from all sections. Most SEC schools scheduled mostly southern opponents, but outside of league play Kentucky looked for bigger game. They played Notre Dame regularly; as early as 1933 they took on the Missouri Valley champions; they scheduled Big Ten powerhouses; and they took on New York's best at Madison Square Garden. In 1935 they took a brutal beating from NYU, losing by a point on a last-minute foul. Kentucky's plays were repeatedly whistled for blocking, while Slim Terjesen and King Kong Klein were muscling LeRoy Edwards at the other end. (Keogan, whose Notre Dame team had lost to NYU earlier, had warned

Rupp that he better bring his own officials if he wanted a fair shake.) Edwards was nevertheless acclaimed by the New York sportwriters, and the agitation over the roughness of that game strongly influenced the forthcoming 3-second legislation.

Rupp was dismayed over the beating, but he continued to advocate a postseason tournament with representatives from across the country to decide a national champion. Meanwhile he went on with his ambitious intersectional scheduling. LIU's Torgoff gave the Wildcats a shooting lesson in the Garden in 1939; in 1940 Kentucky beat Ohio State for the Sugar Bowl championship, but Athletic Director Shively would not allow his SEC champs to entertain an NCAA bid because the team had been weakened by the flu. The following year, Kentucky lost in the Sugar Bowl to the reigning NCAA champions from Indiana, though Lee Huber won a place on the all-time Sugar Bowl team along with Bob Cousy, Paul Arizin, Bob Davies, and Ed Macauley.

In 1942 as SEC champions Kentucky entered the fourth renewal of the tournament Rupp had proposed years earlier. In the first round they upset Illinois in New Orleans, one of the greatest victories in Rupp's career over a team that was just a year away from national prominence as the Whiz Kids. But the Wildcats were spent and the next night were badly beaten by Dartmouth. The next year reinforced Rupp's objection to conference tournaments when Kentucky lost the SEC championship to Tennessee after beating the Vols twice during the season. In 1944, the Big Blue from the Bluegrass may have been the country's best. During the season they lost only to Illinois while winning the SEC regular schedule and the tournament and all other intersectional games, including a return match with Illinois and a Garden party with St. John's. For postseason play they came back to New York to challenge the country's best in the NIT.

Kentucky drew Utah in the first round and beat them by 8 points. In the semis they lost to St. John's by 3 in the last minute. Then in the consolation game they whipped Oklahoma A & M by 16 even though Kurland shut out Brannum. The Kentucky center had to be satisfied with passing off to teammates who banked shots over Iba's goaltender. Meanwhile St. John's went on to win the tournament by beating DePaul, and Utah, given a last-minute invitation to replace injury-ridden Arkansas, went on to win the NCAA title. Utah completed their turn-around by beating St. John's in the Red Cross benefit game, but Kentucky after all had beaten them both and Oklahoma A & M to boot.

All these heroics notwithstanding, Kentucky began its rise toward true preeminence in the 1945 season. Not much was different. Coach Rupp was as crusty as ever. No one had yet accused him of mellowing. He was tough, outspoken, critical even in victory, dour and ironic in defeat, and if anything more colorful than ever despite the constant brown suit. His players were driven hard in practice to cut down on technical errors. They were drilled on basic offensive plays and man-to-man defense, but they were always encouraged to develop individual skills and styles. Success was what pleased the Baron, but mistakes would mean immediate substitution and usually a tongue-lashing. Rupp's plays were designed to do two things: establish the defensive pattern of the opposition and give his offense comfortable and familiar areas for shots. Above all, Kentucky players were supposed to be able to shoot whenever open, and Rupp reasoned that they should try to get open at those places on the floor where they shot best. The ambitious schedule had the added benefit of keeping Rupp abreast of all the current developments, and he made use of whatever the situations demanded. He and the Wildcats grew with the game.

The personnel had changed very little from the previous season. Of the starters only Brannum, who had gone into the service, was missing. Tingle, Schu, Parkinson, and Moseley were all back, but the latter was dismissed for missing a practice. The real difference, of course, was the freshman from Martin's Ferry who was to take Brannum's place at center. He was Alex Groza, 6 feet 5 inches and 167 pounds, and he had come to Lexington disappointed that he had received no scholarship offer from Ohio State where his brother Lou had been a football star. Kentucky won its first eleven games, including wins over Wyoming, Temple, Indiana, and LIU, all on the road. The most satisfying win was against Ohio State in Lexington, with Groza matching bigger, stronger, more experienced Arnie Risen in rebounds and points.

After Groza reported for army duty, Kentucky lost some games—to Tennessee and Notre Dame by 1 and to Michigan State by 16 (with Groza they had beaten the Spartans by 31). Two games later, on February 19 at Ohio University, the win put Rupp's record over 80 percent, and it never again fell below though another twenty-eight seasons were to come. Still, even without Groza in 1945, they managed to win the SEC by getting revenge on Tennessee in the finals, when freshman Johnny Stough held Paul Walther to a single field goal. But in the NCAA, Ohio State got its revenge, eliminating Kentucky 45–37. The consolation win over Tufts completed a good season, but it was best as a promise of better things to come.

Three freshmen starters were among those betters for 1946. Wah Wah Jones was the center, Ralph Beard was a guard opposite captain Jack Parkinson, and at forward opposite junior Jack Tingle was Joe Holland who beat out senior Wilbur Schu. They won seven straight, including a 14-point win over St. John's in the Garden, despite Harry Boykoff's 27 points while holding Jones to 7. Three nights later the streak ended in Philadelphia when Temple won 53–45. Six more wins followed before the annual meeting with Notre Dame in Louisville. Elmer Ripley had a strong team, with Billy Hassett, Frank Gilhooly, Leo Klier, Johnny Dee, and Vince Boryla. Boryla outscored Jones 18–16 in the pivot, and Beard, playing before his hometown crowd, was shut out by Dee. Kentucky lost 56–47, but it was the last loss of the season. They swept through seven remaining games on their regular schedule and the four games of the SEC tournament without being seriously challenged, then beat Temple in a postseason rematch. In the NIT they drew Arizona with high-scoring Link Richmond in a battle of Wildcats, but Fred Enke's team was no match for them; even Stewart Udall couldn't conserve more than a 77–53 beating.

The semis against West Virginia were tough, but Kentucky's tighter defense preserved a 59–51 win over Lee Patton's young Mountaineers who had beaten St. John's in the first round. The finals figured to be a great scoring battle against a Rhode Island team that averaged 83 points per game. Doggie Julian's Muhlenberg team had held them to 59 but lost by 10 in the semis; but Rupp believed that he had been shown the way to win. Their fast break would have to be shut off. He told his team they would have to hold the Rams to 45 points to win.

*The balance of a bureaucrat, the hands of a pol—Stewart Udall, here, was preceded on Wildcat five by cousin Calvin, followed by brother Morris, who went on to the pros and the House.*

This was a classic Keaney team led by Ernie Calverley. In the first round, against Bowling Green and big Don Otten, Calverley had saved the day with a 58-foot shot in the final seconds, tying the score at 74-all, then leading an 82–79 overtime win against Harold Anderson's stunned Falcons. In the championship game Beard held Calverley to two field goals and 8 points while leading Kentucky with 13. Rupp's plan was good, the team's execution sound, and the coach's prescience remarkable. Rhode Island was held to 45 points and Kentucky won with 46. In the final minute Beard drew a foul on Calverley and sank the winning free throw. Kentucky had its first national title.

For the next season they figured to be even stronger. Tingle, Holland, Jones, and Beard would be back from the NIT champions; and Groza, Brannum, Campbell, Rollins, and Barker would be back from service, along with Jim Jordan, an All-American at North Carolina during the war. Entering freshmen were still eligible too, and among them Al Cummins, Dale Barnstable, and Jim Line looked very good. All this proved an embarrassment of riches for Rupp and assistant Harry Lancaster. At first the starters were Tingle, Holland, Beard, Rollins, and Groza, who had grown to 6 feet 7 inches and filled out to 220 pounds. In their first eleven games they simply overwhelmed tall opposition, extending Kentucky's winning streak to 26. They averaged better than 73 points a game and held opponents to under 37, almost a two-to-one ratio. Against the best teams during this streak, DePaul and St. John's, they won by 20 points. The closest game was against Miami of Ohio, when Blue Foster's deliberate game plan kept the score down to 62–49.

But it was a troubled team, with All-Americans riding the bench, and the trouble caught up with them in New Orleans. There, in the Sugar Bowl game, the patient slowdown of Oklahoma A & M brought off a 37–31 upset. Rupp's reappraisal resulted in one major change—the election of Kenny Rollins as captain, instead of Tingle, to provide floor leadership—and somewhat freer use of substitutions. But the starting lineup remained the same, with Jones playing behind Groza at center and Barker getting an occasional start over Tingle or Holland.

Ten wins followed, including a 60–30 trouncing of Notre Dame, led by Kevin O'Shea and Johnny Brennan. Beard redeemed himself in Louisville, scoring 17 and holding the Irish star O'Shea to 2. Then, in a return match with DePaul in Chicago, Ray Meyer's slowdown plus cold shooting by everyone but Groza added up to a 53–47 loss. The six remaining games on the schedule were easy wins (by an average margin of 32 points), and then Rupp had to pick a ten-man squad for the SEC tourney. Former All-Americans Brannum and Jordan were left behind, and Brannum transferred to Michigan State in time to be eligible for the next season. That tournament was so easy (including 98–29 and 84–18 wins over Vanderbilt and Auburn) that the all-tournament team was Jones, Beard, Rollins, Tingle, and Holland. Groza played only briefly because of a back injury.

Kentucky tuned up for their NIT defense against Temple, and Jones for the first time started at forward. The experiment was such a success that that's where he stayed for most of his career. His overhead shot from the corner won the first-round game against LIU, and Kentucky survived Everett Case's North Carolina State slowdown. But in the finals, Utah executed Vadal Peterson's deliberate attack even better, and along with a tenacious defense it ended another Kentucky streak. Arnie Ferrin and Wat Misaka were back from the 1944 NCAA champs that Kentucky had eliminated from the NIT, and they exacted a sweet, slow, deliberate revenge. Misaka bulldogged Beard so thoroughly that neither scored from the floor. Ferrin bearded Groza and played him even. It was Vern Gardner who made the difference, with 15 points in the 49–45 game. Gardner was named MVP, though paradoxically Beard was voted the outstanding player of the year in the Garden.

The Fabulous Five came into being in game twelve of the following season, after much experimentation by Coach Rupp with another talented squad. The early part of the season was marked by injuries, by Jones's slow return to form after the football season, and by seven straight wins by a total score of 523–240. In Philadelphia they lost to Temple 60–59, with Beard and Jones out with injuries; but in the Garden three nights later Jones led them back against St. John's, along with good performances from Rollins and Jim Line. After three more wins, they headed for Michigan State where Bob Brannum was waiting for his day on court. On the evidence he made his case, outscoring Groza 23–10 and inspiring the Spartans to hold vastly superior Kentucky to a 47–45 edge. That was only the second game for the starting lineup of Groza, Beard, Jones, Barker, and Rollins, but Coach Rupp was convinced he had found the right combination of complementary skills.

Six games later, five of them on the road, they took their 18–1 record to South Bend and returned to Lexington stewing over the Irish upset. Whatever the home-court advantage is worth, it seems to be worth twice as much at Notre Dame. Kentucky suffered no further embarrassment that season. Nine wins took them through the regular schedule, including revenge on Temple, and four more in the SEC tournament took them to New York for the NCAA. They roared past the Columbia Lions by 23 and faced the defending champions from Holy Cross in the regional finals. Doggie Julian's Crusaders had been carried to an eighteen-game streak that season on the shoulders of George Kaftan and the arms of Bob Cousy.

Rollins drew the assignment on Cousy, who didn't get a field goal until Kenny had left the game. Meanwhile Groza had some advantage in his duel with Kaftan and Jones had a solid game as Kentucky's balanced scoring gave them an 8-point victory. The championship game was anticlimactic, the Western Regionals having had a comparatively weak draw, and Kentucky blew Baylor out by 16 points, though they seemed let down from the pressure game with Holy Cross.

*Beard shoots over Groza's (15) screen, Jones (27) at left.*

The season was far from over. In that Olympic year, a tournament of college and AAU teams was held in New York. Unfortunately, St. Louis, the NIT champions, declined the invitation. They were probably the only college team that could rival Kentucky, who routed Louisville, the NAIA champions, 91–57, and then were sharp in a rematch with Baylor, winning 77–59. In the finals Kentucky would face the AAU champion Oilers, led by Bob Kurland. The day before the game, the Baron put his team through a brisk half-hour workout in the Garden, followed by their basic drill on fundamentals. Doggie Julian later told Rupp, "That was the finest exhibition of ballhandling that I have ever seen."

Rupp's strategy for the game was for Groza to move away from the basket, drawing Kurland out on defense, and setting up Beard and the others. In the event, Groza scored only 4 points but had several assists. Kentucky was hurt when Barker went out in the first half with a broken nose and Jones went out on fouls with 11 minutes to play. Their effectiveness on the fast break and on the boards was thus diminished. Still they stayed close to the pro-level Oilers, losing 53–49 as Kurland scored 20 points. The Olympic committee chose the five starters from each team, and Rupp was named assistant to the Oiler coach, Bud Browning. In three subsequent exhibition games, the Kentucky five beat the Oiler five in one double-overtime game and lost by 6 and 8 in the other two. Of course this squad swept through the eight Olympic games in London, beating France 65–21 in the finals, with only Argentina playing them close.

143

Actually the "Fabulous Five" is a misnomer because this great team had great depth. No fewer than fourteen players put in some time in competition, with Holland, Barnstable, Line, and Johnny Stough playing a lot. With Rollins and Holland out of eligibility, Barnstable became the fifth starter for the following season. Through eight games they were confidently unbeaten but in the finals of the Sugar Bowl Tournament came up against the defending NIT champions from St. Louis. This shaped up as a classic match-up between two high-scoring teams, with two great centers, Groza and Macauley, going one on one. It turned out to be a defensive struggle; Groza and Macauley held each other to 12 and 13 points, Marv Schatzman held Wah Wah Jones to a single field goal, and Ed Hickey's Billikens squeezed it out 42–40 on Lou Lehman's 7 points in the last 5 minutes.

The Baron was not amused. The loss brought him to the realization that he was not getting the best possible results from his talented team. As good as they were, they prided themselves on teamwork and balanced scoring. Rupp ordered a simple change that had tremendous impact. He moved Barnstable to forward and put Barker at guard with one instruction: feed Groza. From this point on Kentucky was a pivot-oriented team. In the previous season Groza had outscored Beard by only 12 points, with Jones not far behind. This year he would outscore the two of them combined, though the all-around play of everyone on the team seemed to benefit from the change.

Seventeen straight wins took them through the regular season, and they swept through four games of the SEC tournament without being challenged. Coach Rupp then set out to do what no team had done—win both the NIT and the NCAA. But 1949 was the year of NIT upsets. Top-seeded Kentucky went out with the other three seeds in the quarterfinals when Jack Kerris played the game of his life for Loyola, outscoring Groza 23–12. A less cocky, more determined Wildcat team went about their business in the NCAA. Against Villanova and Paul Arizin, Groza scored 30, 27 against Illinois in a 29-point win, and 25 against Bob Harris and Oklahoma A & M. In the finals Kentucky got out to an early 10-point lead, and then Rupp had them loosen up and drop back on defense. But Iba's disciplined team never varied their deliberate patterns, never opened up on offense, and never got close in the game.

It was fitting that Kentucky's second straight NCAA was earned against Oklahoma A & M, the only other team to have repeated as champions. Kentucky was ranked number one by the AP poll in its first year, and Groza, Beard, and Jones were all All-Americans. They graduated directly into the pros as the Indianapolis Olympians, leaving Barnstable the only returning starter. But only one phase of the golden era had ended. Jim Line and Walt Hirsch were experienced forwards, and up from an undefeated freshman team were Bobby Watson, Skippy Whitaker, C. M. Newton, and the big man Rupp thought might be even better than Groza, Bill Spivey.

144

Kentucky lost only to St. John's in their first five games and came to New Orleans to face an unusually strong Sugar Bowl field. They beat Villanova by 1 point in overtime and then Bradley, with Unruh and Melchiorre, by 5. But this championship, over the country's first-ranked team, was the high point of the season. Kentucky won sixteen of the next nineteen games and then their seventh straight SEC tournament (including rubber-match wins over Georgia and Tennessee), but North Carolina State got the NCAA district bid. Kentucky went to the NIT as second choice behind Bradley but were humiliated in the first round by CCNY, who would win the tournament as Rupp predicted. The Baron, after suffering the worst defeat of his career, 89–50, thanked his team after the game for two things, getting him named coach of the year by the Metropolitan Basketball Writers and embarrassing the hell out of him.

In the 1951 season Kentucky regained the top ranking and the NCAA championship. Spivey, Watson, Hirsch, and Shelby Linville were joined by sophomores Frank Ramsey, Cliff Hagan, and Lou Tsioropoulos on this team, whose 32–2 record matched that of the 1949 team. The two losses were similar, too: the first to St. Louis in the Sugar Bowl semis by 1 point in overtime and the second by 4 to Vanderbilt, whom they had already beaten twice, in the SEC finals. But they won the number one ranking in the fifth game of the season, beating Kansas 68–39 as Spivey bested Clyde Lovellette, and they maintained that position all season, finishing with a 10-point win over Kansas State for the NCAA championship. Kentucky was the first school to win it three times.

Part of Rupp's success was based on discipline. On his first road trip in his first year as coach, he had put an end to overly casual dress and such practices as card games on trains and stealing towels from hotels. "We are not packing around a bunch of tramps, gamblers, and thieves." Now, after twenty-one seasons, when the point-shaving scandals were breaking in New York, he said, "The gamblers couldn't touch my boys with a ten-foot pole." But within months he discovered that they had been touched: Beard, Groza, Barnstable, Line, and Hirsch were all implicated. The NIT loss to Loyola and the recent Sugar Bowl loss to St. Louis were among games in which Kentucky players had agreed to shave points. Rupp refused to dwell on the dismaying revelations, consoled himself with thinking about the forthcoming season with Spivey, Hagan, Ramsey, Tsioropoulos, Watson, and Linville back. But this rationalization was undermined when Spivey was also implicated.

Spivey fought the charges, denying his guilt under oath and polygraph, but he never played another game for Kentucky. And like the Olympians he was banned from the NBA. No doubt he never took part in a fix, but he had been approached by fixers, had been aware that teammates were involved, and had never reported any of this. To be coldly objective about it, one should be impressed that these Kentucky teams were so good that they could run up the record they did

and be controlling the margin of victory at the same time. As good as they had seemed to be, they had pretended to be not quite as good as they were. But basketball is an emotional game anyway, and no one could be purely objective. The glory of the golden years was tarnished by the revelation of these brazen acts, and Rupp's wry manner took on a new bitterness that made the color of his tone seem sarcastic to many.

Under the strained circumstances the performance of the team that year was remarkable. They lost only twice during the season, once to Minnesota when big Ed Kalafat had a big night with Hagan and Ramsey in foul trouble, and once to their old nemesis in the Sugar Bowl championship when St. Louis won by a point in the final seconds. The winning streak went to twenty-two games in the SEC finals, as Tsioropoulos's layup beat LSU by a point, though Bob Pettit outscored Hagan 25–19. The streak ended at 23 in the NCAA Eastern Regional finals at Raleigh, when St. John's, whom they had earlier beaten by 41 points, upset them by 7. For the second straight year both polls ranked Kentucky number one.

The point-shaving led to investigation of other irregularities—scholastic, recruiting, and subsidizing. Kentucky was the natural focus of attention, worthy by its eminence to be the scapegoat. Suspended by the NCAA and the SEC, Kentucky played no intercollegiate schedule in 1953. Rupp and Lancaster stayed on, however, and so did the players. They drilled, practiced, played some intrasquad games, and waited till next year. And when the next year came they simply won every game. Xavier came within 6 points and no one else closer than 12 through twenty-four games. This was the first year of the Kentucky Invitational Tournament (KIT) during Christmas break, and unlike most similar, subsequent events, Kentucky has always tried to invite the best teams. In that first KIT, second-ranked La Salle with Tom Gola was the losing finalist.

The SEC tournament had been discontinued, but to determine the NCAA representative, Kentucky went to Nashville to play LSU, also undefeated in conference play. Hagan and Pettit played each other to a 17-point deadlock, but Ramsey's 30 points were the difference. Kentucky was trailing by 4 in the second half when Rupp suffered heart spasms, but both the coach and his team came back. Kentucky didn't play in the NCAA after all. Hagan, Ramsey, and Tsioropoulos were ruled ineligible. Though they retained a year's eligibility during the suspension, they had all stayed in school and had enough credits to graduate before the season was over; they were all technically graduate students. Even after beating LSU, then, Kentucky yielded its place to Harry Rabenhorst's team. The tournament was won by La Salle, a 13-point loser to Kentucky, so that the Wildcats probably deserved their number one rating in the AP poll.

*Easy score for Spivey (77) over Melchiorre; Watson (38) in foreground.*

*Ramsey (left) and Hagan, cocaptains 1954.*

Other championships and other top rankings would come to Rupp in his eighteen remaining seasons in Lexington—and he never had a losing one—but the golden decade was over when Ramsey, Hagan, and Tsioropoulos graduated to the pros. It is perhaps the greatest tribute to the Baron that pro coaches say that his players are better prepared than anyone else's to play professional basketball. Like Iba's boys they are always well-conditioned athletes, like Wooden's they have the habit of winning, like Holman's they have the ability to adapt instantly to free-lance situations, and like Dean Smith's they are always well-schooled in fundamentals. It may be that those who have played in the blue uniform for the man in the brown suit have developed a perception of the color of the game that goes beyond these definable basics and provides the special, extra element in the product.

# 19

# *See How They Run*

FAST-BREAK basketball goes all the way back to the origins of the game, and it is probably no exaggeration to say that Keaney's breakneck style of the Thirties was close to what Naismith had in mind at the beginning. But the modern fast break is a carefully worked out approach to the game, and we must look elsewhere than to Keaney or to Lambert for its origins. And when it comes to the matter of its spread, we will see a further breaking down of regional distinctions.

Several coaches besides Lambert and Keaney have been considered influential in the development and refinement of the fast break. Adolph Rupp deserves some credit, and Ed Diddle, Branch McCracken, Ed Hickey, Jack Gardner, and John McLendon also rate some mention here. But according to Red Auerbach, whose credentials as fast-break expert are considerable, credit should go to his college coach at George Washington, Bill Reinhart. Reinhart's accomplishments don't show up in statistics, though his teams won 475 games in thirty-three years. Throughout his career at Oregon and George Washington his ingenuity was called upon to overcome weaknesses in personnel, and his recruiting at GW was hampered by limitations of facilities and the program at large. But Reinhart's players learned solid fundamentals, the values of conditioning and discipline, and above

*Fast-break architect Bill Reinhart.*

all the importance of strategy and intelligence—basketball as a thinking man's game.

One of Reinhart's good GW teams was promised an NIT bid if they beat Loyola in 1938. He devised a special defense to stop Mike Novak, beat Sachs's charges twice, but got no invitation for the effort. It was his scientific approach to the fast break, however, that put Reinhart, as Auerbach put it, twenty-five years ahead of his time. The idea was to take a rebound and whip a pitchout to gain a quick numerical advantage downcourt. Three on two was the most likely combination, and the classic attack had three men coming down the lanes at full speed with the ball going back and forth among them without any dribbling. This remains the dominant fast-break strategy, except that the man in the middle generally dribbles now, handling the ball until the defense commits itself.

Assuming this situation to be the most productive, Reinhart examined many approaches toward attaining it. First the defense has to be set up for quick conversion to offense, either by zoning or switching man-to-man to have the big men rebounding and the fast men breaking. Getting the third man (generally a forward to join the two backcourt men) up into the pattern is a major problem. Another is establishing passing lanes for the outlet pass so that the rebounder knows just where to look to initiate the break. Then, should the defense recover, checking back to equalize the numbers, the idea is to have a fourth man, a trailer, get downcourt into position for an open shot, usually off the shoulder of the man in the middle lane, while the break still has its momentum. Reinhart's solutions to these problems provided a blueprint for the modern fast break.

Often, as was the case with most of Keaney's teams, the fast break will compensate for lack of size. But when speed and size work together, the attack can be devastating, as it was with Ed Hickey's championship team at St. Louis. Hickey had played at Creighton under Arthur Schabinger in the days of their North Central Conference championship with All-American James Lovely. Returning to his alma mater as coach in 1937, he found his team usually chasing Oklahoma A & M in the Missouri Valley Conference and usually playing Iba's style of ball control. But in 1941, 1942, and 1943, he led them to league titles and had them doing some running, led by Brownie Jaquay, Ralph Langer, Ed Beisser, and Ward Gibson. In the 1941 NCAA tournament they were outrun by John Friel's Washington State team in the first round. In the other two years, Creighton went to the NIT, losing a semifinal match to Western Kentucky (Ed Diddle's Hilltoppers outran them) and a first-round upset to Washington and Jefferson.

Hickey left Creighton in 1947 with a 132–62 record and moved over to St. Louis, which had just won the conference title under John Flanigan, and he did even better there. With the Billikens, from the outset, he really had the horses to run. Ed Macauley and Marv Schatzman played a backline zone on defense, while up front combinations of Dan Miller, D. C. Wilcutt, Lou Lehman, Bob Schmidt, and Joe Ossola played a switching man-to-man—the pattern originated by George Keogan. From this defense they converted brilliantly to a fast-break offense with Macauley becoming the best ballhandling and shooting-off-the-break big man in the history of the game, at least until Elgin Baylor and Tommy Heinsohn and Sidney Wicks.

Second to Iba again in 1948, Hickey took St. Louis to the NIT, while Oklahoma A & M (Bob Harris, Ambrose Bennett, Joe Bradley, J. L. Parks, Vernon Yates) waited in vain for an NCAA bid. And the Billikens ran away with the tournament, averaging 65 points a game in wins over Bowling Green, Western Kentucky, and NYU. Macauley was MVP, with Wilcutt second in the balloting. This was Hickey's high-water mark, though in eleven years at St. Louis, his 212–89 record included three conference, one Cotton Bowl, and two Sugar Bowl titles, six other NIT appearances, and two NCAA entries. From 1959 to 1964, his teams at Marquette added another seventy-two wins to his record, two more NCAA tries, and an NIT third place in 1963. But Hickey's offense had notably slowed by then, and when Providence raced by them in the Garden, he must have been reminded of Creighton days two decades earlier.

Ed Diddle's win over Hickey in the 1942 NIT was perhaps the most satisfying of all his 759 wins. The most disappointing loss followed immediately, when two West Virginia free throws in the last 20 seconds beat Western Kentucky for the championship. Over a period of forty-two years, Diddle's Hilltoppers ran and shot whenever they could, scored over 100 points in more than a score of games, and earned their coach a lifelong winning percentage of .715 in over a thousand games, while he cheered them on with his ever-present towel, which was chewed, waved, and thrown at the action, the crowd, and the officials.

Branch McCracken, on the other hand, viewed the constantly quickening play with apparent aplomb. McCracken is a good case in point for the passing of regional distinctions from college basketball and the significance of the coach rather than the area to the style of play. He had played himself under Everett Dean at Indiana. The Dean heritage goes straight back through *his* coaches to Doc

Meanwell and the Wisconsin system of patterns and ball control. Indiana played ball-control basketball under Dean, though McCracken set a league scoring record in his All-American senior year despite the system. Two years after Bill Reinhart brought his fast-break thinking from the Pacific Coast to the Atlantic, Dean brought his patterned offense from Bloomington to Palo Alto. His predecessor, John Bunn, also a heartland product, had learned to let loose with Luisetti and company, but Dean retained his system.

To be fair and accurate, Dean by no means advocated a rigid ball-control offense. Indeed he encouraged a lot of free-lance variations off a four-man weave around a single pivot. Perhaps more than any other Big Ten or Pacific Coast coach

*Coach Diddle did more with a red towel than old Hiram's goat.*

during his time, he had his teams playing a style that resembled what once was called "eastern style." And he won with it, three Big Ten championships in fourteen years, two Pacific Coast crowns in eleven years, 378 wins altogether for a .639 percentage. His big team was the NCAA champion in 1942, averaging over 6 feet 3 inches, starring Jim Pollard, who played almost without substitution through thirty games as did teammates Don Burness, Ed Voss, Bill Cowden, and Howie Dallmar (later coach at Penn and Stanford). Pollard caught the flu before the title game, but Jack Dana replaced him as the Indians from the coast beat the Indians from the plains of Hanover 53–38. No one had come close to Stanford in the rather mediocre field, and while Dallmar won the MVP award, Pollard's 43 points in two games were high for the tournament.

Dean's student, McCracken, upon replacing his mentor at IU for the 1939 season, immediately retooled the offensive machinery for the fast break. And ironically he beat Dean to an NCAA championship by two years. That was the "Laughing Boys" team—Marv Huffman (the first NCAA MVP), Bill Menke, Bob Dro, Jay McCreary, Herman Schaefer, and Curly Armstrong—and their attitude demonstrates one of the greatest virtues of the fast-break style, that it is as much fun to play as to watch. IU lost the Big Ten to Purdue that year but won the bid by beating the Boilermakers twice. It wasn't until 1953 that they finally won the Big Ten and that year they also won another NCAA title, winning through a difficult draw over DePaul, Notre Dame, LSU, and Kansas, and earning their number one ranking in both polls. Don Schlundt was their big rebounder, initiating the fast break with outlet passes to Dick Farley and All-American Bob Leonard. Through twenty-five seasons at Indiana after eight at Ball State, McCracken's teams ran his record to 451 wins in 728 starts.

*Schlundt (left) and Leonard, backbone and medulla of Indiana's fast break.*

Only three teams beat Indiana in McCracken's second championship season. Two of them, Notre Dame and Minnesota, also lost to Indiana, but the third, Kansas State, never got a second chance. This was one of Jack Gardner's best teams in ten years at Manhattan, and not long after he had begun to adjust his offensive thinking toward the fast break after being brought up in the deliberate style of Sam Barry. Barry was another Doc Meanwell product who went from Wisconsin into coaching and eventually brought his ball-control offense to the West Coast—Southern Cal by way of Knox College (1919–1922) and Iowa (1923–1929). His standard attack called for the guards to handle the ball, waiting for the forwards to run picks off the pivot. His record at SC included at least a share of the conference title eight times, and his 1940 team with Ralph Vaughn, Dale Sears, and Tom McGarvin was considered by some the country's best, despite a 1-point loss to Kansas in the Western Regional finals of the NCAA. At his death in 1950, Barry's record through seventeen seasons at SC was an impressive 260–142, and he will also be remembered for his contributions toward eliminating the center jump and establishing the 10-second rule.

Gardner came to Kansas State for the 1940 season determined to change the Wildcats' image from also-rans to winners. The change was slow in coming as the war thwarted all rebuilding efforts. But in 1948, in the newly formed Big Seven Conference, they were first, and for five more seasons until Gardner left, they were never worse than one game out of the league lead. According to Forddy Anderson, Gardner believes that basketball equals mathematics as a pure science; and this may explain the expansion of his system to embrace the fast break. I say expansion rather than changeover because Gardner always demanded that his teams discipline themselves to hold the ball whenever appropriate.

Gardner made up elaborate checklists to anticipate what would happen and elaborate charts to study what had happened. But preparations could often be misleading and adjustments inadequate, as Gardner himself is fond of recalling. Several examples during his ten seasons at Kansas State (147–81) will illustrate this. In 1949 in Madison Square Garden Gardner deployed a set offense against LIU. In the second half Clair Bee sprang his 1–3–1 zone to nullify the screening patterns, Kansas State could not adjust, and LIU came back to win. In 1950 Bruce Drake mixed up the Kansas State defense with his Sooner Shuffle, and Oklahoma beat them in the Big Seven Tournament. For the next season, Gardner studied the shuffle offense and prepared a defense for it, only to lose 49–46 to Oklahoma. Then, for the rematch, he figured he had concentrated too much on defense; he concentrated this time on offense and ran away to an 87–48 win.

The planning paid off more often than not. Kansas, with Phog Allen's set offense, was always a challenge. Once Gardner almost upset them by playing a four-man box and a basket-hanger. And it wasn't until Lovellette's senior year that he played on a Kansas team that beat Kansas State. Gardner had noticed big Clyde's habit of looking up while running back down the floor, so he coached

154

his players to stand in his way and draw fouls. In Clyde's junior year, Gardner noticed he was out of shape for their second meeting, so he coached his center Lew Hitch to do a lot of running. He did, Lovellette ran out of gas in the first half, and Kansas State won 65–51.

In 1949 Nebraska, led by Duke Retherford, was leading the conference when they played a rubber match with Kansas State. But in the previous game Gardner had picked up the Cornhuskers' hand signals. He designed a defense to cut off the passing lanes on all the called plays, and Kansas State won 53–28, knocking Nebraska down into a tie for the league. In that 1953 victory over national champion Indiana, Gardner interrupted the flow of Indiana's fast break off missed free throws. McCracken had Schlundt tapping the ball out to Leonard or Farley, but Gardner drilled his team to cut these off, and the strategy accounted for the edge in an 82–80 game.

Gardner's best year at Manhattan was 1951 when he lost only four games, by 1 point to LIU in the season opener, by 6 to Indiana, by 3 to Oklahoma whom they beat twice, and by 10 to Kentucky in the NCAA finals. Against the great Wildcat team (Spivey, Ramsey, Hagan) Gardner had a 6-foot 1-inch leaper named Eddie Head, whose perfect timing enabled him to rebound with 6-foot 5-inch and 6-foot 6-inch centers. Gardner had proven this scientifically with the "jump-reach" tests which he originated in 1947. But Head and Ernie Barrett, Lew Hitch, and Jack Stone were no match for the Baron's boys.

When he moved to Utah for the 1954 season, Gardner was committed to the fast break as his primary offense. In Salt Lake City that is what they were used to through most of Vadal Peterson's twenty-six years. Gardner's ten-year mark at Kansas State had been a .647 winning percentage, and he improved on that through eighteen years at Utah, having a losing season only in his first. That was the year that Colorado State beat them with a press in their first meeting. Gardner naturally drilled the Redskins in preparation for the rematch, showing Bob Fulton how easy it was for a center to score against a press. Trailing by 5 with 2 minutes left, Colorado State went into the press, Fulton came back to help out, drove in and dunked it—but then it is always easy for a center to score for the other team. But better times were ahead for the Utes.

They became under Gardner one of the best run-and-gun teams ever, and they consistently played a challenging schedule. In ten of eleven years they played the eventual national champions. They played in the Sugar Bowl, the Far West Classic, the KIT twice, the Dixie Classic twice, the Holiday Festival three times, the NIT twice, and the NCAA five times. In the 1954 KIT, having just beaten La Salle, defending NCAA champions, Utah faced Kentucky determined to take over the Wildcats' number one ranking. With 2 minutes left they led by 5 points and Gardner ordered a stall. But Utah's sophomores, Curtis Jensen, De Lyle Condie, and Ted Burner could not control it. As Kentucky got hot the Redskins lost their poise and tempo and sharpness and eventually the game by 5 points.

Gardner still wonders about losing that one but reports that Coach Rupp was more upset than he: the Baron drove to a postgame party for the visiting coaches and left his car double-parked on a busy Lexington street with the motor running and the lights on.

Among the memorable games for Gardner's Runnin' Redskins were the 1960 victory over top-ranked Ohio State by 97–92 and the whole NCAA tournament of 1961. Utah won the Far West Regionals by beating Loyola of California 91–75 and Arizona State 88–80. In the semis they lost to eventual champion Cincinnati 82–67, and then played four overtimes in the consolation game against St. Joseph's before winning 127–120 on 32 points by Billy McGill.

One more running story about Gardner. He was a compulsive drinker of milk during games, believing in its nerve-calming properties (that St. Joseph's game was a 4-quart affair). In the final regular season game against Utah State, with the conference title already clinched (and a loss to eventual champion California in the offing), his boys added some Milk of Magnesia to his bottle. He had, he says, "a very interesting evening."

By the end of the Forties the classic confrontation in basketball was no longer East vs. West; it was now fast break against ball control. When two set offenses went against each other, the result was likely to be tedious. In the 1950 NCAA consolation game, for example, North Carolina State under Everett Case and Baylor under Bill Henderson ran patterns that were all too familiar to each other. Raggedly and poorly played, the game dragged on with NC State winning 53–41 in a battle of attrition. On the other hand, two fast-breaking teams could completely abandon defense, resulting in a boring exchange of long passes and layups. In the 1949 NIT, Bradley's 95–86 quarterfinal win over Western Kentucky was a game like that. But in the next game Loyola played defense and beat Bradley 55–50.

If a team were allowed to execute the fast break, there was little that could be done to stop it. But a deliberate offense keeps the ball away from a fast-breaking team, and good rebounding can slow up the start of the break. The two finalists in the 1949 NIT, San Francisco and Loyola of Chicago, were both masters of this strategy. Between them they had beaten almost every ranking running team in the country—Kentucky, Bradley, Manhattan, Utah, CCNY, and Bowling Green. The finals went to San Francisco 48–47 as Pete Newell's zone press provided a slight edge. But if ball control and deliberate patterns were sometimes the answers to Kentucky and St. Louis and the other running champions, the Iba-Newell system did not always prevail. Three more chapters in this section will highlight other prominent champions who succeeded with the fast break.

156

# 20

# *New England Renaissance*

IT IS ONLY 50 miles from Springfield to Worcester, yet it was fifty years from the Penn-Yale game in 1897 to the time when Holy Cross could bring a national championship to New England. Indeed, until Doggie Julian's triumph in 1947, the NCAA title had gone east of the Mississippi only once, to Indiana in 1940.

For decades New England basketball had been colored Big Green. Under Lew Wachter, Dolly Stark, and Osborne Cowles, Dartmouth had been the dominant basketball power in the Ivy League for over twenty years. Beginning in 1938, Cowles's second season as coach, they won the conference eight out of nine years, including seven in a row. Their successive stars, Gus Broberg, Audley Brindley, and Ed Leede, also dominated the area. Seven times through 1946, the District I berth in the NCAA went to New England, and four of those seven teams came from Hanover. The others—Brown, Tufts, and Harvard—never survived the first round, but twice Dartmouth went to the finals, losing to Stanford in 1942 and by just 2 points to Utah in 1944.

Despite this record, that is, because the record was compiled primarily in the basketball backwaters of New England, Cowles's reputation is based on his subsequent eleven years at Minnesota. There, close to the scene of his undergraduate days at Carleton, Cowles became known as an excellent teacher of the jump shot, with shooters like Whitey Skoog, Dick Garmaker, Chuck Mencel, and Ed Kalafat --but he never won another title.

Rarely had any other school challenged Dartmouth's preeminence during those years, but rarely did anyone seem to care, so little was the sport emphasized. Providence College, during Albert McClellan's tenure as coach (1928–1938), won almost 70 percent of their games, but against Dartmouth they were two wins and six losses. A good example of relative strength: in 1932 the Friars won nineteen games while losing to only three college teams, Dartmouth, St. John's twice, and CCNY.

The City team came to Providence on a day in February when Chinese artillery was shelling Japanese troops outside of Shanghai, when George Bernard Shaw was injured in a car wreck in South Africa, and when King Levinsky was outboxing Jack Dempsey in a Chicago four-round exhibition. The Providence *Journal* called the Beavers the "best college quintet to ever hit this town" after they embarrassed the Friars 37–20. Joe Davidoff had 15 points and Moe Spahn 11, but CCNY really won the game before it started. Holman's men dribbled onto the court one at a time and took a two-hand set shot just inside the midcourt line. So many went in that the vision seemed to awe the Dominicans who were described as "bewildered by the excellent passing and fast play." Perhaps even more bewildering was the way Nat Holman, against the existing rules, coached his team from the sidelines like a ventriloquist without moving his lips and never getting caught by the suspicious officials.

Down the road in Kingston, Frank Keaney had begun a twenty-eight-year reign (1921–1948) at Rhode Island during which they won over four hundred games for a .770 percentage. Keaney's teams with their running and long lead passes were exciting, but their schedule was not. It wasn't until 1938 that they began to win over Providence, and they never played Dartmouth. In 1941 they were first-round NIT victims of Seton Hall; in 1945 they survived the first round against Tennessee but were humiliated by DePaul 97–53 with Mikan himself equaling the Rams' whole point total; and in 1946 they had their best success in the tournament.

Rhode Island's small, fast-breaking team was led by Ernie Calverley who, at 5 feet 11 inches and 145 pounds, lined up at center against Bowling Green's 6-foot 11-inch Don Otten. With only seconds to play, Calverley's shot from 58 feet tied the score at 74 and sent the game into overtime, with Harold Anderson's stunned Falcons falling 82–79. Rhode Island went on to beat Muhlenberg in the semis, but Kentucky shut off the fast break and edged them in the finals 46–45 on Beard's free throw. Calverley, held to 8 points by the Wildcats, nevertheless was the tournament's high scorer and MVP.

While Rhode Island was beating Muhlenberg, the Mules' former coach was looking ahead to his second year at Holy Cross, the year that would finally bring a champion to New England. Doggie Julian was a Pennsylvania product, a graduate of Bucknell and coach at Albright as well as Muhlenberg before moving to Worcester. And his basic style of play was similar to that of Duquesne, the dominant basketball power in western Pennsylvania. On defense they played tight, aggressive man-to-man with zoning alternatives when necessary. On offense they played a variation of the double post.

Double-post offenses had been popular since the late Twenties, though many coaches saw the weakness of clogging the middle for the three other players. Defending against a double-post attack was a fairly simple coaching procedure. Still, with mobile and versatile players like Ohio State's Dick Schnittker and Bobby Donham under Tippy Dye in 1949 and 1950, it could prove very successful (the Buckeyes had come closest to beating CCNY during the tournament sweep). Everett Case had worked out one patterned variation of the double post at North Carolina State, where any of the other players could interchange with the men in the pivot positions.

At Duquesne the variation was even more effective. In twenty-one seasons (1925–1948), Chick Davies, a Duquesne man himself, had won three of every four games. His successor, Dudey Moore, who played for him for four seasons (1931–1934), did almost as well through ten years and with even higher rankings. At its best, as in 1949 and 1950, the Dukes' moving-pivot pattern had the two big men, Chuck Cooper and Ed Dahler, moving toward the corners to provide picks off the weave for the other three, Farrell, Dougherty, and Skendrovich, to drive down the opened middle.

This was the kind of pattern that Julian installed at Holy Cross, and it was successful from the start. His first season in Worcester produced a 12–3 record even though all games were played on the road. The Crusaders had no facilities of their own at home. Two of the losses came late in the season, to Valparaiso and Yale, but the one that made the biggest impression was the first, to Rhode Island in the Boston Garden. For one thing, the house was sold out—13,900 seats—ten days in advance, which showed that New England was finally ready to support the game it had birthed and the rest of the country had nurtured. And for another, the game itself taught Julian the value of a fast break for a winning performance as well as an exciting show for the crowd. Despite Julian's dogged defense, the Rams broke away often enough to win 65–58.

That championship season began rather inauspiciously. The Crusaders beat three New England opponents and then Toledo but lost the next three on a Christmas swing against North Carolina State, Duquesne, and Wyoming (three good teams, the first two going on to the NIT and the third to the NCAA). Ev Case's Wolfpack and Dudey Moore's Dukes had no trouble figuring out Julian's offense, and though Holy Cross held all three under 60 points, they had not put together a varied enough attack. They started to run some against Wyoming, losing 58–57, and began to put it all together in the next game against Toledo. In the next three games they averaged 77 points and went on through a twenty-three-game streak to the NCAA championship.

None of the regulars was over 6 feet 4 inches. George Kaftan was the star rebounder and scorer, and the other starters were Joe Mullaney, Dermie O'Connell, Ken Haggerty, and Frank Oftring. On the bench were Bob Curran, Bob McMullan, and a freshman who thought he should be playing much more, Bob Cousy. Like many great teams, this squad had several future successful coaches, and it is the fairly common geographical irony that a Pennsylvania coach took a lot of greater New York area players to a title in New England. But it was neither the Duquesne pattern nor the City style that won for Holy Cross; it was, ultimately, their ability to run a cohesive fast break whenever there was an opportunity.

In the tournament they came from behind to beat Navy 55–47, came from behind to beat CCNY 60–45, and several times came from behind to beat Oklahoma 58–47. Julian was always proud of the defensive efforts that those scores indicate. In later years (following two calamitous years with the Boston Celtics, he coached seventeen seasons at Dartmouth until his death in 1967), he continued to stress defense. He had limited success in these years, except for the Rudy LaRusso teams, but he was proudest of a defensive specialist, Gene Booth, who held both Chet Forte of Columbia and Hot Rod Hundley of West Virginia to 12 points in 1956, when they were both averaging 28.

The NCAA championship was a fine accomplishment, though the NIT draw was stronger (Kentucky losing to Utah in the finals, with Duquesne, LIU, North Carolina State, Bradley, West Virginia, and St. John's also-rans). But it was not the be-all and end-all of New England's basketball renaissance. Two other factors were of far greater importance, and Holy Cross was the major contributor of both. One was the establishment of the sport as a primary fan attraction in the area; and the other was the contribution of the third of the five major elements in modern basketball: the triple-threat backcourt man with his tricky dribbling, clever passing, and outside shooting. The one provided the impetus for emphasizing or reemphasizing basketball in many New England schools: Providence, Boston College, Yale, and Connecticut among others have drawn national attention since, and dozens of colleges have drawn enthusiastic crowds. (The Boston professional team, of course, has been one of the most successful franchises of all.) The other added to the figure of Hank Luisetti (the first element—the modern shooter) and the configuration of Mikan and Kurland (the second element—the modern big man) the unique form of Bob Cousy.

It has often been pointed out that Cousy was far from a dominating player in his collegiate days, even on his own team, that he matured as a professional, and

*Seein' is believin'—Cousy's magic.*

that he attained his peak skills only after Bill Russell joined the Celtics. Indeed, the Celtics were reluctant to take a chance on him, after other New England college stars had fizzled, including his teammates Kaftan, Mullaney, and O'Connell, and Harvard's Saul Mariaschin and Wyndol Gray. Even Yale's Tony Lavelli, whose graceful sweeping hook shot and delicate touch at the free-throw line had made him an all-time high scorer and three-time All-American, failed in the pro game. And there is some truth in this view of Cousy, who certainly did improve as he perfected and adapted his skills against the best competition.

It has also been pointed out that most if not all of Cousy's passing and dribbling wizardry had been anticipated by players like Bob Davies and Bobby Wanzer from Seton Hall and Dick McGuire from St. John's. And there is some truth in that too. But the point is that it was Cousy who captured the fancy of the fans. It was Cousy whose dazzling passes were cheered even when they produced turnovers, Cousy who electrified the crowds by dribbling behind his back, Cousy who became the big draw and the people's choice even when he was not his coach's. So it was Cousy who made basketball promotions pay off as never before and who aroused generations of imitators after.

In his freshman year, Cousy had difficulty breaking into Julian's starting lineup. Even though he had contributed to the championship effort (though even more to the team's crowd appeal), he wrote to Joe Lapchick at St. John's about a transfer. Lapchick advised him against it, saying in part, "Doggie Julian is one of the finest basketball coaches in America, and some day you'll be proud you've played for him." Cousy began his sophomore season as a starter and ended it as a starter, but there were some problems along the way. Doggie was nervous on the bench, especially when his team was running. The more Cousy played, the more they ran. And one day, the Cooz missed a practice, unintentionally, but with no communication between coach and player, discipline had to prevail over speed.

The season had started like the last, three road losses in the first eight games, followed by a winning streak. It was during the streak that Cousy was benched, but when Loyola threatened to end it at twelve, Julian sent him in to save the game. The silence between them persisted, but Cousy started the rest of the games. The streak went to nineteen through the season and then twenty as Holy Cross beat Michigan in the NCAA. Groza, Beard, and Jones were too much for the Crusaders in their quest for a second championship, as Cousy shot one for fourteen in the Eastern Regional finals. The consolation win over Washington was little consolation for Cousy who had another off night.

In the following year Julian replaced Honey Russell as coach of the struggling Celtics, and he was replaced in Worcester by Buster Sheary. But if the departure of the coach didn't hurt Cousy, the departure of Kaftan and O'Connell sorely hurt the team. With Cousy in control on the floor, they ran more, scored almost as much, but won much less. The 19–8 mark earned no postseason invitation, though they had beaten three of the NIT entrants. One of these, the losing finalists from

Loyola of Illinois, they had beaten by a point in Boston Garden when Cousy first dribbled behind his back. Rudy Klaerich (or Gerry Nagel—there is conflict of testimony among the eye-witnesses) overplayed him to the right as he went downcourt on a break. With no one open for a pass, the Cooz bounced it behind him with that long arm and without breaking stride continued the dribble with the other huge hand, on in for a score. The crowds have loved it ever since.

His senior year was the best in many ways—scoring, the team averaged just under 74 a game; winning, they were 27–4; streaking, they had twenty-six in a row. But it ended dismally. There were late season losses to Columbia and Yale, and in the NCAA they lost in the first round to North Carolina State. Sam Ranzino and Dick Dickey were hot, Cousy, Laska, and McLarnon were not, although Formon kept Holy Cross in it early. In the consolation game with Ohio State, Formon turned cold along with the others, and Ohio State, with Schnittker, Donham, Jacobs, Taylor, and Burkholder all scoring in double figures, beat the deflated Crusaders 72–52.

The quest for another title had been turned back, but Cousy and Holy Cross had put New England back in bold face on the basketball map. Even with erratic play at times, they had shown their class with flashes of brilliance and a new quality of surprise and excitement in the game. Bob Cousy, perhaps as no other college player since Luisetti, had become a public idol, and it had nothing to do with just another pretty face.

*Doggie rides victorious Crusaders:* (from left) *Mullaney, Cousy, Kaftan, O'Connell, McMullan, and Oftring.*

# 21

# McLendon and
# the Mighty Mites

TO TALK ABOUT the fast break without talking about John McLendon is like talking about the interpretation of dreams without talking about Freud. McLendon's book, *Fast Break Basketball*, is a primary text for any coach interested in developing the kind of attack that has won over six hundred games and nearly 80 percent for its author. He has expressed thanks to Dr. Naismith, under whom he studied at Kansas, and attributes the fundamental soundness of his basketball training to his luck at having attended school in Kansas, a state "known for its excellent basketball, early one-hand shooting, rugged boardwork, and a general dedication to the game."

McLendon's Kansas-bred version of heartland basketball has been carried through his career to North Carolina College in Durham, to Hampton Institute in Hampton, Virginia, to Tennessee State in Nashville, to Kentucky State in Frankfort, to Cleveland State and the Cleveland Pipers, and to Denver and the Rockets. Under his vigorous training, all of his teams have run, whatever their size, and under his vigorous teaching they have run the classic patterns, filling the lanes, finding the trailers, and converting to offense from any possible situation.

His proudest moments came over a dozen years apart. In 1960 his Cleveland

Pipers—a year later the AAU champions—beat the Olympic team with Robertson, West, Dischinger, Boozer, Lucas, Bellamy, and Imhoff. This squad, called the greatest amateur team ever assembled, was outrun by McLendon's Pipers in a brilliant 103–96 exhibition of offensive efficiency. Back in 1947, North Carolina College won the Central Intercollegiate Athletic Association tournament, winning the finals in triple overtime. McLendon's Eagles had four men 5 feet 7 inches and under, including three starters, and these mighty mites worked so well together that no member of the championship team could be singled out by the sportswriters who chose the all-conference team.

McLendon later won three consecutive NAIA titles at Tennessee State in the heyday of Dick Barnett, Jim Barnhill, and Ben Warley, a good indication that he didn't go out of his way to find little men to play his running game. But probably his best college player was one he left behind at Durham for his successor, Roy Brown. That was Sam Jones, the greatest carom shooter courtside of the Knoxville Bear. Jones personified McLendon basketball: when he came to the NBA he was, in Bob Cousy's words, "the fastest human I'd ever seen on a basketball floor." The scouting report from Bones McKinney said that he was lightning fast and had all the moves and all the shots. Sam himself, with no false modesty, says that for eight of his twelve years with the Celtics he could beat anyone on the team running up and down the court.

The story of how a player at a small black college could be a first-round draft choice for the NBA champions in 1956 is an instructive one. Sam Jones went to prep school in North Carolina at Laurinberg Institute, which sent Jimmy Walker and Charley Scott among others on to basketball fame, and the decision to go to college in Durham was not an easy one. He had been interested in CCNY until the scandals broke and also in Notre Dame, but he shopped mainly for a baseball scholarship because at the time that seemed a better long-range prospect. He discovered that colleges with emphasis on baseball were reluctant to sign him because they thought he'd play basketball anyway, and then he settled on a school with no baseball program at all. There was none of the pressure of big-time competition and none of the added pressure of black athletes in white establishments, but the basketball was good and fast and competitive. Jones says that there were others with equal skills at North Carolina College and at the other schools in their conference, but that he was lucky to be noticed. It happened during his tour of duty in the army, when he played against Frank Ramsey, Frank Selvy, and Bobby Leonard, establishing a reputation with players who had come to the pros through established big-time basketball schools.

By the Sixties it was no longer possible for the pros to neglect small-college players. The NAIA tournament, for one thing, is the biggest and best showcase for basketball talent. The tournament originated in Kansas City in 1937 as a replacement for the national AAU tourney that had moved to Denver. In its second year it established the thirty-two-team draw that is its present format as it draws the winners of regional competition from over five hundred schools throughout the country. In 1957, the NCAA also began a national tournament, another thirty-two-team format in eight regionals, for its College Division members, over four hundred schools, many of them also NAIA members. The first College Division tournament was won by Wheaton College, a championship that came some fifty-three years after Wheaton, along with Latter Day Saints University (now Brigham Young), lost the "Olympic college championship" series to Hiram College at the World's Fair in St. Louis.

Small-college basketball deserves a volume to itself, and it is barely possible to name some outstanding names here. In keeping with the McLendon philosophy, the NAIA schools have produced many prolific scorers. In Kentucky alone, one finds career scoring records for the state not among Rupp's performers at Lexington, but at Kentucky State where Travis Grant scored over 4,000 points for a 33.4 average in four years and at Georgetown where Dick Vories (2,968) and Cecil Tuttle (2,340) both contributed to the success of Coach Robert M. Davis's "Aggressive Basketball" style along with twice Little All-American Charlie Grote. It was Grote who scored 28 points in the 1959 opener, an upset win against Louisville, a major basketball power that went on to the NCAA semifinals that year.

It was during the Tennessee State dynasty (1957–1959) that Georgetown played Texas Southern in the NAIA consolation game, a game that stands out as

*Travis Grant in the process of breaking all-time career scoring record.*

exemplary of small-college offensive productivity. Against Bennie Swain, a 7-foot pivot man, Davis elected to try a controlled offense, but though Georgetown shot 50 percent, the Texans had run over them to establish a 102–82 lead with 10 minutes left. When they slowed it down, Davis went to a half-court press and closed to 104–96 with 3 minutes to go. Texas Southern decided to run again and in the final flurry ran out to a 121–109 score. The teams had scored a point every 6 seconds at the end. Tired—the ten players had played five games in five nights—they never did let up on offense.

Earl the Pearl Monroe put on the greatest one-man one-season performance in college history in 1967, not only scoring 1,329 points but single-handedly carrying Winston-Salem to the College Division championship. Under Coach Clarence Big House Gaines, the Rams ran up a 31–1 record, with Monroe shooting better than 60 percent from the floor and averaging 41.5 a game. In the Mideast Regional finals, Monroe scored 49 in the 88–80 win over Akron. At Evansville, Winston-Salem eliminated LIU and then the defending champions from Kentucky Wesleyan. Against the defensive pressure of the Panthers, Monroe scored only 24 but fed Gene Smiley and Bill English for 49 points in a dazzling display of one-on-two ball-handling and passing. In the title game the Pearl cautiously scored 40 points in the 77–74 win over Southwest Missouri.

Monroe's records removed some of the dubious statistics of Bevo Francis from the books. Back in 1953, big Bevo had made little Rio Grande College of Ohio a household word. As a freshman, 6-foot 9-inch Francis averaged over 50 points a game, had 1,954 for the season and 116 against Ashland Junior College, and led his school to thirty-nine straight wins in which they averaged over 100 points a game. But so many of their opponents were jackleg schools that the records were disallowed. Rio Grande went nowhere in the NAIA tourney. But on a revised and nominally acceptable schedule in 1954, Rio Grande won twenty-seven games with Francis scoring 1,254 for a 46.5 average. The best win was 89–87 over a mediocre Providence College team, and Bevo's high was 113 against Hillsdale.

Despite these heroics, it would not be accurate to describe small-college basketball as strictly offense-minded, fast-breaking, and high-scoring. Many other styles of play have been bred and refined in the NAIA and College Division schools. Bill Healey's "Rotation Offense," for example, is a disciplined pattern, developed at Eastern Illinois, that took him to a 388–188 record, including six conference, five state college, and two NAIA Holiday Tournament championships. Garland Pinholster's "Wheel Offense," for another, is a continuity off a disguised 1–3–1 that has taught the virtue of patience to many teams at Oglethorpe College. Dayton Spaulding at Plymouth State devised a "Destroyer Offense" to beat a full-court press, and it too requires precise discipline to execute. Ray Mears's philosophy of controlled patterns was developed at Wittenberg before he took it into the big time. Perhaps best known is the deliberate system that Buzz Ridl employed with great success at Westminster in Pennsylvania, a school rich in basketball tradition.

Ridl used combinations of man-to-man and zone defenses similar to those of Temple and Villanova under Litwack and Kraft. And on offense, Westminster was a model of deliberation that agonized fan and foe alike. In 1959, their first year under Ridl's discipline, Westminster won the Pennsylvania NAIA playoffs to qualify for the trip to Kansas City. They lost by 3 points to Southwest Texas State in the second round, though 5-foot 10-inch Chuckie Davis made the all-tourney team, but they bettered that showing the next three years in a row. In 1960 they knocked off Maryland State, Whittier, and Hamline before taking on three-time champion Tennessee State in the semis. McLendon and Barnett were gone, but Tennessee State was riding high on an eighteen-game tournament streak.

Westminster simply held the ball and Davis kept them in the game. With 3 minutes left and down by 38–37 they decided to play for one shot. The play called was Ridl's "middle-clear-through pattern" (which had been in Rupp's playbook for decades), and with 6 seconds left Ron Galbreath shot and missed. But Don McCaig rebounded and scored for the tiny Titans' gigantic upset. Unfortunately, Southwest Texas dominated them in the finals.

A year later they were back to their own tricks, holding the ball against Winston-Salem, led by Cleo Hill with a 28-point average. Westminster led 15–9 at halftime—Hill had never gotten his hands on the ball—and the Titans kept it out of reach all the way. In the semis they went up against what was probably Fred Hobdy's finest Grambling team. They had 6-foot 8-inch Charlie Hardnett and 6-foot 9-inch Willis Reed up front, while Herschel West and Rex Tippitt between them average almost 40 points a game from the outside; the Titans' starters averaged 6 feet 1 inch. They held the ball, ran their patterns, and shot brilliantly. At the half they led 28–25 with 13 for 15 from the floor. At the end they had shot 75 percent but lost on Tippitt's shot, 45–44, after Reed had kept Grambling close by hitting nine of ten shots from the top of the key. Grambling easily beat Georgetown for the title.

Ridl's best chance at the championship came in 1962 when Westminster was the top-ranked small college team in both polls. With left-hander Warren Sallade at the high post, 6-foot 6-inch Lou Skurcenski inside, Ron Galbreath and the Douds twins outside, Westminster had the ideal material to run or walk their patterns. Galbreath's hot shooting over screens set up by a moving pivot, and Sallade's uncanny passing that allowed Skurcenski to score at will, led them to the finals again. But another group of Texans, this time from Prairie View A & M, upset them 62–53, when no degree of control was sufficient to stop Zelmo Beaty.

Beaty of course went on to star in the pros, and so did the leader of the following year's NAIA champions, Lucious Jackson from Pan American. In the NBA draft in 1964, when Jackson and Reed were both eligible, the Knicks' first choice was Jim "Bad News" Barnes from Texas Western, a school that was pushing toward big-time prominence under Don Haskins and with eager recruiting of black

*Pan American's Lucious Jackson always got a kick out of the game.*

*Arad McCutchan making use of a time-out at Evansville.*

players. Sam Jones passed along the tip from his old coach, Roy Brown, to the Celtics that they should draft Reed. But instead he went to the Knickerbockers on the second round. Being black was no longer a handicap in this business, but playing at a black school away from the big time and the centers of publicity still was. Reed, like Jones, had been able to develop his skills against good competition, but without the exposure and the press-agentry, he could still be second choice to Barnes as Jones had been to Hundley.

The scouts seem to be wiser now, especially under the pressure of competition between pro leagues. Nobody would miss an NAIA or College Division tournament where the play and the players might be the best to be seen in a given year. "Now *there's* a tournament," says Red Holzman of the Kansas City affair. And Evansville can be just as exciting if not as saturating.

The host school, Evansville College, has won the College Division tournament five times in its first sixteen years. This Indiana school, coached by Arad Mc-

*Help till it hurts, says Jerry Sloan (52); he and Larry Humes (50) block out so teammate Herb Williams (30) can get rebound.*

*Pre-Clyde Frazier led Salukis to NIT title.*

Cutchan, exemplifies the best of what small-college basketball has to offer. And Jerry Sloan, from his championship teams of 1964–1965, may well be taken as an exemplar of what that is. Away from the external pressures of the big schools and the mass media, the concentration on the game can be even more intense. The play is rough, with hard-nosed aggressive defense and constantly attacking offense. Any open shot must be considered a good percentage shot and no man fails to help his teammates scrapping for the loose ball, for the rebound, or with the other team. Sloan, a wiry 6 feet 6 inches, plays any position at either end of the court. Team offense and team defense are both produced by the dedicated concentration of each individual's play. You learn to help out or you don't make it.

In 1965, Evansville went undefeated through the twenty-nine games of the season and the tournament. The finals were against SIU, whom the Aces had beaten twice by 1 point during the season. Tied at 74 in regulation, Evansville won by 3 in overtime. MVP Sloan in the final three games had 69 points and seventy-six rebounds, but it was his assists and defensive plays at crucial points that won the games and the honors over teammate Larry Humes and the Salukis' Walt Frazier. During the season Evansville had beaten eight University Division teams, and the following year SIU made the transition so well that they won the the NIT. It was clear that class could not be classified by arbitrary divisions.

# 22

# *After the Fall*

NEW YORK CITY basketball did not dry up and die under the glare of District Attorney Hogan's investigation or the provincial backlash that made the Garden a forbidden pleasure dome for many schools. The metropolitan area in the early Fifties had outstanding teams at Columbia, NYU, St. John's, and Seton Hall.

In the Ivy League, after years of languishing mediocrity since Danny Meehan's championship teams of 1930 and 1931, led by Lou Bender, and the 1936 champions coached by Paul Mooney, an NYU classmate of Howard Cann, Columbia had returned to the fore. In his first year as coach, 1947, Gordon Ridings, an Oregon product of Bill Reinhart and Red Auerbach's first college coach at Seth Low, brought them a league title. They had the scoring leader, too, in Walt Budko, despite the presence of Lavelli, Leede, and Mariaschin in the conference. Columbia repeated in 1948, Budko getting good support from Sherry Marshall and Al Vogel again, though they were overmatched against Kentucky in the NCAA first round.

Ridings's other two years with the Lions were somewhat less than roaring successes, though they never fell lower than a second-place tie. Just before the start of the 1951 season, Ridings suffered a heart attack and was replaced by Lou Rossini, the freshman coach, who had played on the 1947 champions. Rossini duplicated

*Lou Rossini roaring to his Lions.*

Ridings's feat with a league title in his own first year as head coach. John Azary was his captain and star, with Bob Reiss, Tom Powers, and Al Stein as dependable starters. But the Lions' main threat was sophomore Jack Molinas who showed occasional brilliance in every aspect of the game. A strong rebounder and shooter, Molinas also had the speed, ballhandling, and moves to make Columbia's fast break overpowering. They scored 90 points or more five times during the season in which they went undefeated both in and out of the conference.

But in the NCAA Columbia ran afoul of the strong Illinois team that gave champion Kentucky their only serious challenge. The aggressive team rebounding of Don Sunderlage, Bob Peterson, Rod Fletcher, Irv Bemoras, Ted Beach, and Clive Follmer stifled the Lion fast break, as Coach Harry Combes had thought it should, and the Illini won by 8 points. Columbia nevertheless retained third and fifth rankings in the wire-service polls, while their interborough rivals at St. John's, ranked only ninth, went a round further in the tournament.

Molinas played out his career at Columbia under the shadow of Penn's Ernie Beck, who dominated scoring and All-American notice for the league. Yet Molinas was the better rebounder and all-around player; during their first year in the NBA, he easily showed his superiority over Beck. Then he fell under another shadow, admitted betting on his own team, and had his pro career ended abruptly and prematurely by Commissioner Podoloff's edict. Ironically he was not involved in any dumping or point-shaving as a pro (though he says many others in the league were), but as a junior and senior at Columbia—as a leading scorer and rebounder—he was single-handedly fixing games, was never caught, was never even investigated. That's how good he was. A decade later he was a key figure in the 1961 scandals, the chief liaison between the gamblers and the players, and he served four years in prison for it.

It would have taken a St. John's–Columbia match to determine a metropolitan champion for 1951. LIU at 20–4 and CCNY at 12–7 had canceled their remaining games in mid-February, and Manhattan at 16–6 and NYU at 13–4 had played weaker schedules and both lost to St. John's. It was the fourth season for Frank McGuire as the coach of the Redmen. He had played for Buck Freeman, and when he succeeded Joe Lapchick, he brought Freeman back as his assistant. Freeman's own devotion to the welfare of his players had its reward in McGuire's subsequent success. Unable to retain a head coaching job but always a skillful scout despite his problem (or his pleasure), Freeman went along on McGuire's staff, to North Carolina, and eventually to South Carolina until his retirement.

McGuire's style maintained the eastern pro tradition that Lapchick had nurtured at St. John's, and after a mediocre first season he took the Redmen to post-season tournaments his other four years as their coach. In 1949 they were first-round NIT victims of third-place Bowling Green; in 1950 they were semifinalist losers to runner-up Bradley, winning third place in the NIT over Duquesne; and in 1951 they tried both tourneys, taking third in the NIT over Seton Hall after losing to runner-up Dayton in the semis, and then losing to champion Kentucky in the Eastern Regional semis. This was the first year of a sixteen-team NCAA draw, and St. John's beat two teams in it, Hugh Greer's UConn Huskies in the first round and North Carolina State in the Eastern Regional consolation. The latter, over a fine Everett Case team, was the second of McGuire's many clashes with Atlantic Coast Conference teams. In the first, only his sixth game as a varsity coach, Case's Wolfpack had whipped him by 20 points—a score he settled many times over.

St. John's had big Zeke Zawoluk in the pivot with Al McGuire (brother of Dick, nothing but player to Frank), Jack McMahon, Ray Dombrosky, and Ronnie MacGilvray roaming around him. A year later, a deep squad more than made up for the loss of Dombrosky and Al McGuire, and again they tried both tourneys. La Salle, the eventual winner, knocked them out of the NIT, but in the NCAA they went all the way to the finals. Duquesne and Dayton also tried both tournaments; it was the last time this was allowed, preserving CCNY's 1950 sweep as unique.

St. John's began the Eastern Regionals by beating North Carolina State at Raleigh and then stunned everyone by knocking off the country's top-ranked team, Kentucky. They repeatedly drew fouls from the aggressive Wildcats, shut off their fast break with alert defense, and beat them by shooting 45 percent as a team, Zawoluk accounting for 32 and McMahon 18 of their 64 points. In the championship round in Seattle, McGuire showed how well he could defense a big man by holding down Illinois' Johnny Kerr. St. John's outrebounded the Illini by a big margin and sent Harry Combes back to Champaign with his second-straight third-place finish.

In the finals the Redmen had an even bigger defensive problem, Clyde Lovellette of Kansas. They worked him over to the limits of the law but couldn't stop him. Phog Allen's giant had his finest hour, scoring 33 points though he had Zawoluk and one or two others on him whenever he had the ball, and holding Zawoluk to 6 in the first half. Kansas led all the way, winning 80–63, and shooting 44 percent from the floor. St. John's shot 46 percent, got fine floorplay and rebounding from McMahon and especially MacGilvray, but could not match Lovellette.

St. John's would come back again, in Lapchick's second tour of duty after the pro wars. And McGuire would come back, too, finding a way to stop an even more impressive big man from Kansas, Wilt Chamberlain, and win an NCAA title for North Carolina. But in 1952, if there was any man in the country who was a match for Lovellette, it was Walter Dukes of Seton Hall.

Honey Russell returned to South Orange for the 1950 season, and it didn't take him long to build another powerhouse. After one losing season, along came his 7-footer, and Honey said, "With Dukes we'd still be tough even if the other four were from Singer's Midgets." In 1951, wins over Beloit and North Carolina State carried them to the NIT semifinals before they lost to Brigham Young. The consolation loss to St. John's, by 2 points, finished a 24–7 season, but the way Dukes had come along under Russell's tutelage suggested better things to come in the future. A coach who had actually gotten some good games out of Chuck Connors as center for the Boston Celtics was likely to make an All-American of the awesome raw material he found in Dukes.

In 1952 Dukes was an All-American, and Seton Hall ran through a season with twenty-five wins in twenty-seven starts. It could just as easily have been a perfect season, with a 3-point loss to Siena in the thirteenth game and a 3-point loss to Loyola of Illinois in the twenty-fourth, both looking inexplicable on paper and suspicious on court. Even the 4-point loss to La Salle in the NIT's first round looked like Seton Hall could have won it. Actually they played the eventual champs closer than anyone else (including St. John's) in the tournament, but all they had to show for it was a hope for next year.

The 1953 season could also have been a perfect one. The Pirates won twenty-seven straight games as Dukes and Richie Regan, both seniors, had formed the outstanding big man/little-man combination that is the backbone of most great teams. Harry Brooks, Mickey Hannon, Arnold Ring, and Richie Nathanic were supporting players on a team that averaged about 80 points a game, committed less than sixteen fouls a game, and shot almost 43 percent from the floor. Yet the streak was ended with successive 6-point losses to Dayton and Louisville, both of whom they had beaten before. In the NIT, this time, they went all the way.

The first victim was Niagara, one of the best of Taps Gallagher's twenty-nine Purple Eagle teams. This was the team that had gone six overtimes to beat Siena in the longest game on record, ending at 12:17 A.M. Larry Costello played all 70 minutes, but it was Eddie Fleming who stole the show, playing 69 minutes and, during a time-out near midnight, having to piss in a bucket while his teammates gathered around him. Frank Layden, later a coach, had a 12-point college career and scored 8 of them in this 88–81 game. Niagara beat Brigham Young in overtime in the first round before losing by 5 to Seton Hall. (Niagara has continued to produce fine teams and players, for example, Calvin Murphy and Manny Leaks.)

Next came Manhattan, and they were one of Ken Norton's highest-scoring teams. Seton Hall played defense and beat them 74–56. In the finals, against St. John's, they ruined Al DeStefano's first year as coach by shutting off the Redmen's

*Dukes and Regan (opposite) teamed to bring NIT championship to Seton Hall for Coach Russell.*

attack completely and keeping a safe lead all the way to win 58–46. Dukes, with 70 points in three games, was the MVP; Regan was second in the balloting. Dukes maneuvered his 220-pound body so well that he drew an amazing number of fouls. In his three years he converted 611 free throws, a statistic even more impressive than his career total of 1,779 points or his 734 rebounds as a senior. He could do it all, and for two years whenever he did Seton Hall won. On those unaccountable nights when he did not play his game, the Pirates usually were scuttled.

It is unfortunate that the year of Seton Hall's triumph was 1953, the first year of the NCAA's clear dominance in the crowning of the national champion. The NIT came to be known as the Catholic tournament and the runner-up tournament, and though many fine teams have emerged through its draw, there is no doubt that the expanded NCAA with NIT entrants excluded has been stronger down the line. But in 1952 and especially in 1953, there can be little doubt that Honey Russell's Seton Hall team with Dukes and Regan was a great team that would have been competitive with any team of its era.

# 23

# *The Guns of Morgantown*

THE EPITOME of the Kentuckiana style was reached at the end of the Fifties in West Virginia, when in other areas the influences of the playground game and the full-scale recruitment of black players had already altered that style considerably. In Morgantown the basketball tradition extended back to 1904, and in other parts of the state some distinction had been attained by oher schools, including Davis and Elkins, Salem, West Virginia Wesleyan, Morris Harvey, West Virginia State, and Marshall. At West Virginia University (WVU) they looked back with pride to a high-scoring forward, Sleepy Glenn, in 1929, and to their NIT teams in the Forties.

In 1942 they were the surprise winners of the tournament, led by Scotty Hamilton and MVP Rudy Baric. The following year they had an outstanding player in Joe Walthall but were not invited to defend their title. In 1945–1947 they were eliminated each time by the eventual winners—DePaul, Kentucky, and Utah. Coach Lee Patton's record over five years (1946–1950) was 91–26, and his stars Leland Byrd and Fred Schaus received some All-American notice. But West Virginia was still an independent, and though they often ambitiously challenged major schools, the bulk of their schedule was weak.

A new era began under Red Brown in 1951 when they became the seventeenth member of the Southern Conference, which still included six of the present ACC schools and had been dominated for four years by North Carolina State. The Mountaineers could not quite break that domination; in the clumsy schedule they didn't even get to play the Wolfpack for three years. They ranked second in 1951 but were eliminated from the league tournament by William and Mary. In 1952, led by All-American Mark Workman, they finished first, earning a number nine national ranking in the AP poll, but were upset by Duke in the tournament, 90–88, and NC State won it again. In 1953 West Virginia got its shot at the Wolfpack in the tournament, got shot down 85–80, and got no consolation when Wake Forest won the title. In 1954 the league was down to a manageable ten teams, the new ACC accounting for the secessions, but West Virginia could not manage to win it.

That was the year that George Washington, under Bill Reinhart, won the title and the tournament, though most of the attention went to second-place Furman. Frank Selvy, a Kentuckiana gunner if there ever was one, was closing his career in style: 2,538 points (32.5 average) for three years, 1,209 (41.7 average) for his senior year, including 100 against Newberry. It was also the last year as coach for Brown. He had won 72 of 103 games against major competition, and as he moved up to the athletic directorship, he left the basketball team a legacy that would enrich them further: a coach named Fred Schaus and a player named Rod Hundley.

Over a hundred schools had tried to recruit Hundley, a sensational shooter and passer with a gift for publicity ever since his junior high school days. He played the game fast and loose, just the way he did everything else, and his talent for basketball was second only to his capacity for startling and delighting a crowd. His choice was North Carolina State, though he delayed making it official because he so thoroughly enjoyed being entertained on a grand tour of campuses. Hundley liked Everett Case, liked the way he'd say, "Hey, boy, how you doin'? If you ain't doin' right, Old Joe Hays gonna get you." And Hundley liked the way NC State played fast and loose with NCAA rules for recruiting and subsidizing players. But before he could sign to go to Raleigh, the ACC and NCAA announced sanctions against NC State for recruiting violations and that their investigations were continuing. Hundley called Case, who advised him that his career might be jeopardized if he came to Raleigh after all and that his home state university would probably be best. Red Brown signed Hundley and even became his legal guardian.

Brown chose Fred Schaus as his successor because he "thought he'd be a good coach for Rod." Hundley was the kind of player and person who preferred never to try to fulfill his potential than ever to discover his limitations. His freshman year did little to sharpen his skills against mediocre opposition, but it did confirm his propensity to clown on the court. Scoring was secondary to the fancy pass or tricky dribble, and winning the game meant less than winning the crowd with outrageous antics. He had the talent to do it all on court and the nature and wit to enlarge his arena to the whole of his life for the role he chose to play.

Hundley's rewards—tangible as well as psychological—came from achievements attained despite self-imposed handicaps. As a sophomore he led West Virginia to nineteen wins and their first Southern Conference title. He scored 711 points, a national record for sophomores at the time, and led his team in assists. He rebounded well as a forward and even played defense when he had a mind to, shutting off a hot-shooting Corky Devlin of George Washington, for example. He was MVP in the conference tourney, scoring 30 points in the 58–48 overtime final. But in the NCAA La Salle eliminated them in the first round by 34 points, and Hundley finally saw a player he could acknowledge as his superior, Tom Gola.

His junior year, 1956, was even better. He scored 798 points as West Virginia won the Orange Bowl Classic and the Southern Conference. In the league tourney Hundley was MVP again. Against Furman in the semis he completely outclassed Darrell Floyd, Selvy's successor as the national scoring champion, scoring 32 (Floyd's average) in the first half. Against Richmond in the finals he broke away from a double-teaming defense in the last seconds to score the winning basket. But again they were first-round losers in the NCAA, this time 61–59 in overtime to Dartmouth as Doggie Julian devised a defensive game plan to thwart Hundley along with Lloyd Sharrar and Clayce Kishbaugh.

As a senior Hundley scored less but enjoyed it more. West Virginia won twenty-five of thirty games, including the Birmingham Classic and a third straight conference title. It was during this season that they beat North Carolina State 107–79 after Hundley told Everett Case, "Old Joe Hays gonna get your ass tonight." Again MVP in the league tourney, Hot Rod finally won All-American honors, his publicity usually comparing him to both Bob Cousy and Houdini, as Bill Libby points out in *Clown*, the story of the Hot Rod, "Number 33 in your program, number 1 in your heart." WVU had moved up to number seven in the AP rankings, but again they lost in the Eastern Regional first round, to Canisius 64–56. Hundley, however, won the highest accolade for a college player: he was first-round choice in the NBA draft. Len Rosenbluth, college player of the year from Chapel Hill, went first; but the NBA's best rookie the following season was Woody Sauldsberry of Texas Southern.

While the Mountaineer varsity was winning most of their games in 1957, the freshmen were winning them all. Jerry West, a skinny 6 feet 3 inches, averaged 19 points and seventeen rebounds a game. He had been wooed as ardently as Hundley had been, but West was won for different reasons. There was an element of loyalty to his home state and to other West Virginia high school stars, Willie Akers and Butch Goode. He received about sixty scholarship offers, many of which embarrassed him by going beyond allowed limits. Of them all, Maryland and Texas A & M had impressed him, but Schaus's soft-sell and Hundley's

*Hundley, West, and Thorn, the Guns of Morgantown.*

flattering attention reinforced the decision made years before, and West came to Morgantown.

West was Hundley's opposite—a serious, intense, introspective loner. He was probably a better natural shooter but worked constantly to improve other aspects of the game where he may have lacked Hundley's instinctive gifts. And he hated to lose, which made all the difference. Hundley could joke it off; West brooded. Hundley had flair; West had determination. Hundley would win a crowd's heart with his charm; West would impress everyone with the greatness of his own heart. West suffered not at all by following Hundley immediately at West Virginia; his reputation suffered only because his career exactly coincided with that of Oscar Robertson at Cincinnati.

In West's sophomore year the Mountaineers won top national ranking in both polls. They beat Kentucky and NC State to win the KIT and finished the regular season 23–1, losing only to Duke by 4 in Durham. The Southern Conference tourney was easy, and with twenty-six wins they went into the NCAA as favorites only to stumble in the Garden to Manhattan. Kentucky, beaten by WVU in Lexington, won the title.

West was the star of the team, the MVP in the league tournament, but not a prolific scorer on an experienced team. Sharrar was back at center, and Bob Smith and Don Vincent were steady players. Akers and Goode were up from the freshmen along with West. Schaus, who had prepared to coach by playing pro ball for five years, had them playing a wide-open style, aggressively gambling on defense, aggressively attacking on offense. He was not a tough disciplinarian or fundamentalist (Hundley had broken any such tendencies he might have had), but West gives him credit for a brilliant basketball mind and a special gift for preparing teams for particular opponents. And the fans gave him credit for directing the Kentuckiana extravaganza that West Virginia basketball had become.

In 1959 the team was somewhat weaker and smaller, but they scored more and went further, all the way to the NCAA finals. Clousson and Ritchie alternated at center where Sharrar was missed. Akers started with West at forward, Smith and Bucky Bolyard were the guards, and Lee Patrone the key substitute. The season's record was 22–4, with losses to Virginia, Kentucky in the KIT finals, Northwestern in double overtime, and NYU in double overtime in the Garden on a memorable performance by Tom Sanders. Among the big wins were a 101–63 revenge against Duke, a dramatic comeback against Holy Cross on national TV, and a rough football-like match against Tennessee with Gene Tormohlen in Knoxville. In the conference tourney West was again MVP. In the finals he held Art Musselman of the Citadel to 7 points while contributing 27 points, nineteen rebounds, and six assists himself.

This time they beat the first-round NCAA jinx. Unhappy at their low ranking, number ten in the AP, they had something to prove in a tournament in which they were decided underdogs against Kansas State with Bob Boozer, Cincinnati with Robertson, Kentucky with Johnny Cox, and California with Darrall Imhoff. Finally, they survived an Eastern Regional. With Akers bottling up Rudy LaRusso, they beat Dartmouth 82–68. Then, against St. Joseph's, they made one of the most remarkable comebacks in the tournament's history. With 13 minutes to play they were trailing by 18 points, and nothing seemed to be going right. Schaus moved West into the pivot, and with his teammates feeding him each time down the floor he turned it around with 14 points in under 4 minutes. With a minute to play West stole the ball and went all the way to put West Virginia in front by a point, then added two free throws for a 36-point total in a 95–92 win.

The regional final against Boston University was a letdown. West scored 20 in the second half for an 86–82 win against a team that wasn't really in their class. And then it was on to Louisville and the showdown in Freedom Hall. Louisville had eliminated Kentucky and Michigan State to become the Cinderella favorites of the hometown crowd. Cincinnati had survived its shoot-out with top-ranked Kansas State. And California had come through easily in the West. A Robertson-West showdown was a good possibility, but it never happened. Disciplined California under Pete Newell shut down the free-wheeling Cincinnati attack, while West Virginia gunned down the U of L Cardinals as West's 38 points led the way.

In the finals, defense won, and defense almost won. With Imhoff controlling the boards and Cal controlling the ball, Newell's strategy worked so well that West Virginia fell way behind. Their fast break was contained, and they were frustrated in getting the ball because of Cal's discipline. Then Schaus ordered the Mountaineers into a half-court zone press, and they began to come back. The bigger, more-disciplined team began to crack as the quicker West Virginians forced turnovers. West, playing with four personals, led the gambling press and converted Cal errors, scoring 28 points. The last time he got his hands on the ball it was too late to shoot; West Virginia lost the game and the championship 71–70. With 160 points in five games West was the tournament MVP, but a very unhappy runner-up. He'd beaten Hundley's season record with 903 points, shot almost 52 percent from the floor, and led the team with over four hundred rebounds.

Schaus took West and Robertson to the Pan-American Games and inevitable gold medals, and they all looked ahead to 1960—to another shot at an NCAA championship, to the Olympics, and to pro careers. West Virginia won ten in a row to start the season, including another KIT championship over Kentucky with West scoring 33 while playing with a bleeding broken nose. The first loss came in the finals of the Los Angeles Classic, a convincing demonstration by California, 65–46, that their NCAA championship had been no fluke.

Back home WVU won their next six, including an 89–81 win over undefeated and highly ranked Villanova. West received a lot of publicity because before that game he shook hands with and put his arm around George Raveling in a spontaneous gesture of goodwill—Raveling was supposed to have been the first black to play on West Virginia's home court. West doesn't make anything of the incident, and neither does Rod Hundley, who remembers playing against Penn State's Jesse Arnelle on the same court five years earlier. Indeed, he remembers Penn State's tough zone press that beat West Virginia in overtime and that Arnelle outscored him 28–11. The fact is that Arnelle played in Morgantown two years before that, scoring 16 in a losing effort in 1953.

The 1960 season was marred again by a loss to William and Mary, WVU's first in the conference since before West's arrival, and later by losses to St. John's (Tony Jackson and Leroy Ellis) and George Washington. But they went on to win the league tournament, beating top-ranked VPI in the finals. West was once more the MVP, and the NCAA was once more a disappointment. They beat Navy but lost in overtime to NYU as West's last-second shot bounced off the rim. Yet another MVP honor was given to West, as his team outran St. Joseph's 106–100 in the Eastern Regional consolation. With Robertson, Imhoff, Bellamy, Boozer, Lucas, Dischinger, and Adrian Smith, West played for Pete Newell on one of the greatest of all Olympic squads. Like Robertson he went on to a great pro career and eventually a world championship (when they each teamed with a great center, Chamberlain and Abdul-Jabbar), but like Robertson he always regretted the NCAA crowns that escaped them.

When Schaus and West left Morgantown for the Lakers, newly removed to Los Angeles, West Virginia was not left without resources. A new star had arrived in Rod Thorn, who had been declared a state treasure by the legislature so that he wouldn't leave West Virginia. And as his coach, Red Brown hired George King, like Schaus an experienced pro, and like Hundley and West a great collegiate scorer when he played at Morris Harvey College, down the road in Charleston. But though they have cracked the top ten and braved the postseason tournaments since, the Mountaineers have never regained the eminence of the Schaus years. It is as if the Kentuckiana age had passed without the news coming to Morgantown.

# Part 5

# Black Is Beautiful

IF THEIR NAMES are not household words for all basketball fans, they are at least inscribed and pictured together at the Basketball Hall of Fame: Pop Gates, Wee Willie Smith, Tarzan Cooper, Speed Isaacs, Puggy Bell, Bruiser Saitch, Zack Clayton, Fats Jenkins, Pappy Ricks, Bill Yancey, Casey Holt. They were stars of one of the greatest teams in history, the New York Rens, or officially the Renaissance Big Five after the Harlem ballroom where they played. Founded by Bob Douglas in 1922, they won over 2,300 games in twenty-two years. In the four seasons 1933–1937 they were 473 and 49, including a streak of eighty-eight wins in their best year, 127–7 in 1934. They played anyone who would play them, anywhere they could get a game. And they won what was called a world's pro championship in 1939, at the end of a decade when there was no better team. But often as they barnstormed they had to sleep in their own bus because accommodations were denied them.

In the second city another ballroom was the original home of another black team, organized by Abe Saperstein in 1926. Neither Savoy nor Chicago got into their name, however, as the Harlem Globetrotters became internationally acclaimed entertainers. They weren't always clowns. They toured like the Celtics, like the Rens, and like them they beat most of the teams they played. Saperstein

*Black is beautiful.*

*Dr. J.*

*Mike Maloy.*

*Bob Lanier.*

*Ken Durett.*

Dr. J.

Jim McDaniels and
Artis Gilmore.

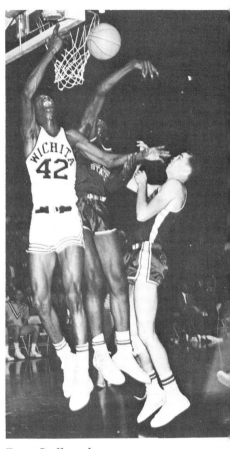

Dave Stallworth.

Manny Leaks and
Calvin Murphy.

Jo Jo White.

had a knack for recognizing talent, and by 1940 he had assembled a team that replaced the Rens as pro champions. Even in the postwar years of clowning with Tatum, Haynes, and Lemon, there were spells of good basketball to show off the talents of temporary acquisitions like Clifton, Dukes, Chamberlain, and Hawkins. Often playing against college teams, they might have to go all out and play it straight to win—and sometimes they didn't. But it's been a long time since the Globetrotters were denied accommodations. Black basketball has come a long way, baby, but then basketball has come a long way because of the black.

As late as 1962, Mississippi State won the SEC championship and with not so rare presence of mindlessness refused to play in the racially integrated NCAA tournament. It was a gesture as archaic as it was inane, one of the last gasps of a lily-white sports establishment that could only jokingly use the word supremacy. The decade of the Fifties had already seen a racial revolution in college basketball that has permanently changed the complexion of the game. When Don Barksdale was an All-American at UCLA in 1947, he was as much of a freak as Kurland and Mikan had been in 1944. But a decade later an All-American squad would have to include Bill Russell, K. C. Jones, Willie Naulls, and Sihugo Green (1956), or Elgin Baylor, Wilt Chamberlain, Guy Rodgers, and Oscar Robertson (1958). The change was not merely one of dominant pigmentation. Patterns of shooting, rebounding, floorplay, ballhandling, and defense also changed along with patterns of recruitment.

A black player prominent in college basketball had been rare before this time, but a couple are worthy of note. Jackie Robinson, hand-picked by Branch Rickey to break the color line in Major League baseball, starred in basketball as well as football at UCLA, where he led the Pacific Coast Conference in scoring in 1940. At Yale, Jay Swift first played in December of 1944, and within five years the Elis were not only giving a long cheer for Captain Levi Jackson's men in the Bowl but were also cheering Jackson on in the Payne Whitney Gym. Jackson had earlier played on the New England champion Hillhouse High School team, but many outstanding black schoolboy players were not recruited at all. Champion high school teams would see their black starters get no major college offers and either go to small black schools or not continue their education at all.

In the postwar years of the late Forties, when some slight progress was made, it happened at schools in the large urban centers, often at the Catholic schools. In December 1946, on a day when Jack Kramer and Ted Shroeder were winning the Davis Cup from John Bromwich and Adrian Quist, returning it to the United States from Australia for the first time since 1939, Tennessee was refusing to play its scheduled game with Duquesne without a guarantee that black freshman Chuck Cooper would not see action. And speaking of action, it was the same week that the Negro National League filed suit against Branch Rickey over the signing of Robinson. Before 1950, Floyd Layne, Joe Galiber, and Ed Warner had come to CCNY, Walter Dukes to Seton Hall, and Sherman White to LIU.

188

In my judgment the most important single development in this anguished struggle toward equal opportunity came during the off-season in 1950 when Walter Brown drafted Duquesne's Cooper for the Boston Celtics. Washington then drafted Earl Lloyd of West Virginia State, and shortly thereafter the Knicks acquired the services of Sweetwater Clifton from the Globetrotters. From this point on there was no way for the best black players to be kept from the highest level of basketball in the NBA. Indeed they have come to dominate the league to such an extent that Dan Jenkins's sarcastic definition in *Semi-Tough* can have some point: "Every twenty-four seconds ten niggers jump up in the air." Clearly, when the pros look to places like Grambling, Tennessee State, Winston-Salem, and Prairie View A & M for high draft choices, then colleges that aspire to titles are missing out on good material. So the college recruiters have learned from the pro scouts to seek prospects from the black schools as well as blacks from integrated schools.

Despite the changes, many blacks still prefer to go to black schools. San Francisco, Cincinnati, Texas Western, and Loyola of Illinois may have won their championships with black players, and blacks may have helped make such schools as Jacksonville, Marquette, North Carolina, and Michigan basketball powers, but the schools themselves have not necessarily returned any favors. This section will look at some of the biggest basketball stories in an era of social change and examine finally some of the remaining problems.

# 24

# *The Dons and the Impossible Dream*

IN FOUR YEARS at the University of San Francisco (USF), Pete Newell gave the Dons a taste of prominence, the heady feeling of winning a national tournament in the 1949 NIT. He also gave them a system of tight, aggressive defense and disciplined, patterned offense. This was the first year of the AP poll; San Francisco was ranked eighth, and four others in the top ten were in the NIT including number one Kentucky. In the first round the four local teams, St. John's, NYU, CCNY, and Manhattan, were eliminated by Bowling Green, Bradley, Loyola of Illinois, and San Francisco in what some papers called the Metropolitan Massacre. The same four then eliminated the four seeded teams, St. Louis, Western Kentucky, Kentucky (consoled later by the NCAA championship), and Utah. San Francisco then held Harold Anderson's high-scoring Bowling Green team to 39 points and beat them by 10, while Loyola knocked off Bradley. The final was a squeaker, 48–47, with Don Lofgran scoring 20 in winning the game and the MVP award, despite tapping in 2 points for Loyola as well.

The effectiveness of Newell's teaching can be measured in other ways than that championship or the national title he brought to Berkeley ten years later. The point is the influence he worked and the way his players carried it on. From that 1949 team, John Benington, Rene Herrerias, and Ross Giudice carried New-ell's successful methods on into their own coaching careers. Moreover, and even more to the point, his successor at San Francisco, Phil Woolpert, kept up the tradition of Newell's style. This was the prevailing style on the West Coast, and its pedigree traces back to Loyola at Los Angeles, where Woolpert played for Scotty McDonald and where both McDonald and Newell too played for James Needles.

When K. C. Jones graduated from Commerce High School in 1951, only one black had ever played basketball for the Dons, Carl Lawson. K. C. had broken the San Francisco AAA prep-league scoring record that year, but he was thinking more about getting a job, maybe in the post office, and buying a car than going to college. There were no scholarship offers until a friendly reporter did a feature on K. C., saying he had many schools after him, including Stanford, Cal, UCLA,

*Coach Needles's most influential squad at Loyola included future Coaches Mc-Donald (eyes half-closed) and (directly under the coach's wings) Woolpert and Newell.*

and Washington. Phil Woolpert took the bait, visited K. C., offered him a scholarship to USF, and was promptly accepted.

Jones's first year, under Ross Giudice, was memorable for two bits of bravado by Harold DeJulio, alumnus and basketball fan *extraordinaire* at San Francisco. First he amused the team by telling them that if they won the championship that year (1952) they could go on to the Olympics. Then he went out across the Bay to Oakland and recruited Bill Russell, who also had no other college offers. Nevertheless, the team had their third straight losing season, Woolpert's second. The next year, with Russell working hard and developing his skills under Giudice, Jones led the Dons to within a game of a .500 season. They had turned the corner, the new recruiting practices had begun to pay off, and they were optimistic about Woolpert's fourth year.

They all worked very hard. Woolpert's emphasis was on defense, yet they drilled for hours on play patterns until their timing was precise. The opening game was against Newell's Cal team at Berkeley. When Russell blocked the first shot taken by Cal's big center, Bob McKeen, Coach Newell was heard to say, "Now where in the world did he come from?" Whether he meant the rejection or the recruitment, the fact was that he had seen a basktball precedent established before his astonished eyes. Russell blocked twelve more that night, held McKeen to 14 points, and scored 23 himself. The win was exhilarating, but the wind was taken out of the Dons' sails before their second game when K. C. Jones suffered a ruptured appendix and was lost to the team for the year. The league voted to extend K. C.'s eligibility through the regular season play of 1956. Meanwhile the team went through their schedule with a commendable 14–7 record, and DeJulio's vision began to seem less quixotic.

The 1955 opener against Chico State was easy, with a 6-foot 1-inch center trying to play Russell. That weekend brought back-to-back games in Los Angeles. Friday night, while they beat Loyola, UCLA was trouncing Santa Clara 75–35. The Broncos had a fine basketball tradition of their own, in which George Barsi had produced excellent teams and players like Bruce Hale and Bob Feerick who had gone on to pro careers and then to coaching; indeed, Feerick was now back at his alma mater, and they had gone to three straight Western Regional finals led by Kenny Sears. No wonder that, as K. C. says, there was no thought of any championship among the Dons when they heard that score, just fear about playing the eighth-ranked team in the country. "We went in there expecting to be beaten by 20 or 25," he says, "there" being the pre–Pauley Pavilion sweatbox in Westwood. But instead it was a close game. Russell, "playing like hell and getting pushed and shoved all over the place," outplayed Willie Naulls, and K. C. collared All-American Maury Taft, whom he calls next to Gola the toughest man he ever had to guard in college, who "shot the eyes out of that jump shot."

That loss turned everything around for the Dons. Woolpert came out of that game with two new starters at a guard and a forward slot and with a team that believed in itself. Losing on the road 47–40 to UCLA showed them that they could beat anyone. Woolpert made no adjustments in strategy for the rematch a week later; but now the team's own confidence matched that of the coach. K. C. and Hal Perry, his new running mate at guard, had a bet on who would get the first shot off. The winner of the bet is not on record, but San Francisco won the game. After another win they traveled to Oklahoma City for the All-College Tournament, drawing top-seeded Wichita State in the first round. San Francisco by this time had six black players on the team, and the day before the tournament they attracted a lot of attention in the workouts. The floor was raised like a stage, with seats below, and spectators were jeering them as "Globetrotters" and throwing pennies. Russell picked them all up, telling the coach to keep them for him, and that may have been the toughest part of the tournament for the cool Dons. The next night, Wichita's touted tenacious defense was blown out in the first minutes 25–3, and Oklahoma City and George Washington were never close in the subsequent games. Russell was unanimous MVP.

Another sixteen straight wins followed. Loose and confident, they never felt the pressure. Russell demoralized everyone on defense, taking away layups and stopping up the middle. Jones and Perry harassed the ball from end to end. If the opposing guards crossed, they switched; if someone got by one, the other would pick him up; and if someone went to the hoop past them, there was Russell. They could fast break because Russell would go to the board and get the release pass out, or if necessary they could run the disciplined patterns that Woolpert had drilled into them. So with a 23–1 record, they went to the NCAA Western Regionals, first winning a preliminary round easily from West Texas State 89–66. The semis brought them Jack Gardner's fast-breaking Utah team led by Art Bunte. San Francisco held them 20 points under their average, winning 78–59.

The regional final against Oregon State was San Francisco's most difficult game in the two championship years. K. C. remembers the pregame as setting another historical precedent: Russell's famous upchucks. Swede Halbrook, 7 feet 3 inches, was expected to be a match for Russell, and he was helped out by a 6-foot 6-inch forward, Tony Vlastelica. At the beginning of the game, these two double-teamed Russell in the middle, leaving 6-foot 4-inch Stan Buchanan open about 12 feet from the basket. Buchanan, who joined Jerry Mullen as starting forwards after the UCLA game, did whatever was required—run, rebound, defend, or go up into the stands for a loose ball—but he couldn't shoot. The Dons would pass the ball into Buchanan and he'd throw it back out again; when this had happened several times, they called time-out and Woolpert insisted that he had to take the open shot and keep taking it. Twice down the floor they gave the ball to Buchanan at 12 feet, and twice he shot and missed. But then he hit three in a row, and Oregon State called time-out. Slats Gill switched them back to straight man-to-man, and the game stayed close right to the end.

With 13 seconds left and San Francisco leading by 2 points, Jim O'Toole

*The Dons en route to NCAA finals: Bill Russell's first experience with long distance.*

made a great defensive play during a time-out. Jones had broken from the huddle and gone back out on the floor before the time-out was over, but Woolpert called him back for a final word. O'Toole, who had shadowed Jones all night, jumped in front of him to block his move to the bench; Jones tried to go around him and O'Toole blocked him again; so Jones pushed him out of the way and was on his way to his coach when he saw the referee up in the air signaling a technical foul. Oregon State got the point and the ball at midcourt, trailing now by one. The ball was passed crosscourt and then down into the corner, the favorite spot for little Ron Robins's two-hander. The ball hit the back of the rim, went straight up in the air, and came down in the hands of 7-foot 3-inch Halbrook and 6-foot Jones. Halbrook won the tap, but it was Hal Perry who grabbed the ball. Then it was a wild scene as Perry, scrambling to get the ball past the time line, was swarmed under by all the Beavers. But by the time they wrestled the ball away and went in for the layup that would have won the game, the final whistle had blown, virtually unheard in the melee, and the 57–56 score remained.

After that, the championship tournament in Kansas City was easy. Colorado was held in check 62–50 in the semis, and then came the defending champions, Ken Loeffler's La Salle team led by Tom Gola, the great all-around player who had totaled 114 points in five games to win MVP honors in the 1954 NCAA playoffs. The Dons were sitting around nice and loose during their pregame meeting, when Woolpert said, "K. C., you've got Gola"; and K. C. says, "That just blew my whole dinner." Everyone had expected Russell to be on Gola, but Woolpert's idea was not to let Gola's versatility outside draw Russell away from the hoop. Then, of course, should Gola take Jones inside, Russell would be there as always to help out and take away the layups. The strategy worked. K. C. was giving away half a foot in height, but Gola was held to six field goals and 16 points; Jones himself got 24; Russell's 23 gave him 118 for the tournament and sewed up another MVP award. The final score was a comfortable 77–63.

Not only were the Dons played against during time-out, they were attacked during the off-season. Much legislation was proposed, with Russell in mind, to tighten the restrictions against offensive goaltending and defensive goaltending; but only one "Russell rule" was passed, widening the foul lane from 6 to 12 feet. Nevertheless, San Francisco came back stronger for the next season, a better shooting team, with Mike Farmer, Carl Boldt, and Gene Brown joining Russell, Jones, and Perry. Even as defending champions they were not thinking championship or streak or perfect season. Their schedule was harder, which was a blessing, because, in K. C.'s words again, "Every game was like a war, every loose ball a battle; and

*Russell with ultimate penetration on offense.*

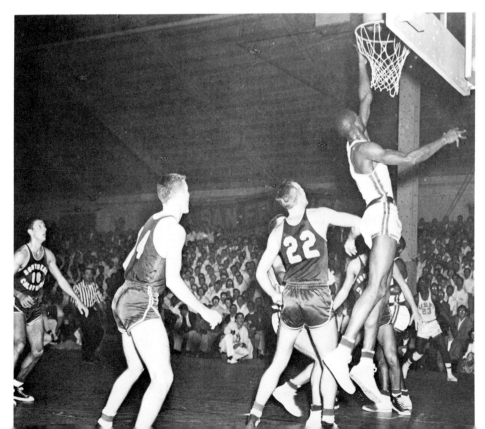

you're trying to stop a man from shooting; you get the ball, you run—there's no time for thinking about the end of the year."

After seven wins the Dons came east to tilt against a stacked draw in the Holiday Festival Tournament. The opener was a rematch with La Salle, but Gola was gone and so was Coach Loeffler. Still, under Jim Pollard, the Explorers stayed close for most of the game. Four minutes into the second half they had a 45–43 lead, sparked by Alonzo Lewis's shooting, but the Dons tightened up their defense and moved Russell closer in on offense. They dominated the rest of the game, pulling away to a 79–62 score, as Russell blocked twelve shots, scored 26 points, and pulled down twenty-two rebounds.

The semis were especially tough, with Holy Cross, the crowd favorite, led by Tommy Heinsohn. They led the Dons at halftime by 32–29, but with Russell (24 points, twenty-four rebounds) holding Heinsohn to 12 points and Bill Mallen coming off the bench for five second-half field goals, San Francisco turned it around, won going away 67–51. In the finals UCLA and Willie Naulls went down 70–53. Russell was MVP almost as a matter of course (although Jones got a vote after holding Maury Taft to 13 points); Frank McGuire said that he'd never seen anyone quite like him; and Joe Lapchick said that San Francisco had the best college basketball team he'd ever seen.

They were awesome: the sequence—pressure the ball, block the shot, rebound, and run—repeated over and over simply devastated all opposition. Two parts of the whole sequence were Bill Russell by himself. He brought the fourth major element of modern basketball to the game; he was the intimidator of inside shooters,

*Russell (6) with defensive rebound.*

*Jones (4) to Perry (23) on the break.*

the rejecter of shots, and the quick releaser of outlet passes to trigger fast breaks after rebounding. And now the Dons closed in on the major college winning streak of thirty-nine. LIU had set it from 1935–1937 until beaten by Stanford, and Seton Hall had tied it from 1939–1941 until LIU ended it to preserve their own share of the record. Both teams had actually won forty-three straight, but four for each had been against noncollegiate teams (including their own alumni). Standing in the way of a new record were the California Bears of Berkeley, where Phil Woolpert was to get a new lesson from his old tutor and friend, Pete Newell.

California stationed Joe Hagler, a substitute center, at the point out near midcourt, and he just held the ball under his arm. The idea was to draw Russell out and open up the middle, but he came out to the foul line and no farther, so Cal just held the ball, at one stretch for 8 minutes. This was the only time during the streak that San Francisco faced a stall, but the effect was merely to hold down the score. The Dons won 33–24 when they pressed all over the court for the last 7 minutes during which they outscored the Bears 17–3 with Jones getting 8 himself. They laughingly accepted the tactic without complaint as an assist to their top-ranked defense. Each game the rest of the way lengthened the streak until the perfect season and K. C. Jones's career were completed. In the regionals at Corvallis they faced a familiar foe but held Naulls to six field goals and beat UCLA by 11. Russell was outscored only by Gene Brown, starting in K. C.'s place. Utah, led by Art Bunte's 23 points, scored an unusually high 77 against San Francisco, but the Dons won by 15. Russell, high man with 27, added yet another MVP award.

In the final round at Evanston several streaks were on the line. Doc Hayes had probably his best SMU team with Jim Krebs, Joel Krog, and Larry Showalter, but the Dons ended their wins at nineteen in a row by a convincing 86–68 score. Meanwhile Iowa was winning its seventeenth in a row, beating Harry Litwack's fine Temple team by 7 as Bill Logan outscored Hal Lear 38–32. Bucky O'Connor's Hawkeyes were high-scoring but also well-disciplined, and they had a brilliant scorer and floor leader in Carl "Sugar" Cain, who had 34 in the 89–77 Mideast Regional final against Kentucky. At the start of the game, K. C. Jones looked on from the bench in utter frustration as Cain, his future brother-in-law, went back-door several times to open up a 15–4 lead against San Francisco. Woolpert made an obvious defensive adjustment, putting Brown instead of Boldt on Cain, and from that point on it was all the Dons. They caught Iowa at 24–23, led 38–33 at the half, and won 83–71. Russell had twelve blocked shots, 26 points, and twenty-seven rebounds.

In a shocking reversal of form the MVP trophy went to Lear, presumably for his record 160 points in five games. This broke Russell's streak at five straight tournament MVP awards, and it may have been a dubious tribute to San Francisco's team play. Their fifty-five consecutive wins tied the all-college record set by Peru State Teachers of Nebraska from 1921–1926. The Dons extended the record to sixty at the beginning of the following season until Illinois stopped them. It was a record that few thought would ever be broken, as they had made DeJulio's impossible dream a reality. Russell and Jones both went on to lead their country to an easy gold medal in the Olympics (in eight games, the smallest margin of victory was 30 points) and then of course to the championship Boston Celtics teams. Russell, as remarkable a sportsman as he was an athlete, made the Olympic team as a high jumper along with Charlie Dumas but then withdrew so that both Phil Reavis and Val Wilson could go to Melbourne. Perhaps the best tribute of all paid to that unbeaten San Francisco team was the fact that Dayton and Louisville, both ranked among the top six or seven teams in the country, declined to challenge the Dons in the NCAA tournament and went on to the NIT finals.

# 25

# *After the Big O Comes Number One*

THE SEASONS from 1958 to 1963 are the Cincinnati era in college basketball: three years of Oscar Robertson, two years of national championship teams, and a year of number one ranking as NCAA runner-up. Looking back to those six seasons, one can find a great deal of other matters worthy of some attention. Most obvious is that fact that Jerry West's career at West Virginia coincided with Robertson's at Cincinnati. West played in Robertson's shadow because the Southern Conference offered weaker competition, yet he took West Virginia just as far. Pete Newell's disciplined California teams and Fred Taylor's high-scoring Ohio State teams were also very prominent throughout this period.

Others worthy of note were the NYU teams with Tom Sanders, the Dartmouth teams with Rudy LaRusso, Jack Gardner's Runnin' Redskins from Utah, Dayton's NIT finalists with three Bockhorn brothers, Providence's perennial NIT entrants, the Kansas State teams with Bob Boozer, St. Bonaventure with Tom Stith, Bradley with Chet Walker, and some routinely excellent Kentucky teams. Among small colleges, Tennessee State was outstanding with Dick Barnett; Buzz Ridl led Westminster to renewed prominence; and Fred Hodby's Grambling team was prodigious, with Willis Reed, Charlie Hardnett, Herschel West, Rex Tippitt, and Bobby Ricks. Other leading players included Chamberlain, Elgin Baylor, Bailey Howell, Dave DeBusschere, Terry Dischinger, Len Chappell, and Art Heyman. Almost lost in the crowd was the remarkable performance of Hersch Carl, who broke Mikan's scoring record at DePaul and made the Catholic All-American team, a couple of neat tricks for a 5-foot 9-inch Jewish boy.

Yet with all this, the names of Robertson and Cincinnati dominated basketball awareness during the period. The argument about the greatest college basketball player ever usually resolves into a simple either/or proposition, either Oscar Robertson or someone else. The strongest camps for someone else are supporters of Hank Luisetti, Tom Gola, Jerry West, and Bill Bradley. There are supporters, too, of Elgin Baylor, Julius Erving, and Earl Monroe, but weaker competition or abbreviated careers make these claimants weaker. Currently, David Thompson is gaining new support with every game. The big-man theory can argue for Mikan, Kurland, Russell, Chamberlain, Abdul-Jabbar, and Walton. And the given-night theory can produce a thousand candidates including Elvin Hayes, Austin Carr, Sidney Wicks, Ron Widby, Dick Groat, Frank Selvy, Ernie Calverley, and any one of twenty Kentucky Wildcats. But the other side of the equation must remain Oscar Robertson.

Jerry West says simply that Oscar is the greatest all-around player he ever saw. Bob Cousy agrees and expands on that thesis, concluding that Oscar could call out all his moves in advance and still be unstoppable. Pete Newell recalls that his California team made the mistake of scoring over Oscar with 6 seconds left in a first half, so that Oscar got the ball, got through the whole Cal team, and got the basket back at the buzzer. He had, to put it boldly, all the basketball skill and all the basketball sense that can be imagined in one person. Strong, fast, quick, agile, accurate—and all superlatively. Defending, rebounding on both boards, shotmaking, playmaking—all superlative. The ability to see what is happening, to anticipate what will happen, to know what should be done, to adjust instantly to get it done— all superlatively. All the moves, all the shots, and all performed with a grace and timing that allowed no wasted motion. Even as a high school player at Crispus Attucks in Indianapolis, Robertson had put it all together. He embodied the fifth of the five major elements in contemporary basketball, the one that makes the others cohere. Oscar was uniquely the soul of the game, the blend of all the individual playground moves with the sense of all the team patterns.

When Robertson came to Cincinnati, the basketball program was progressing well under Coach George Smith. In five years Smith's teams had won seventy-five, lost forty-seven. In 1955, as an independent team led by Jack Twyman, they went to the NIT semifinals where they lost to fifth-ranked Duquesne with Dick Ricketts

*Always on balance, always on target: the Big O (12).*

200

and Sihugo Green, but they beat St. Francis with Maurice Stokes 96–91 in the consolation game. Still, they had never been highly ranked nationally, nor had they ever recruited a black player. Oscar Robertson, of course, made all the difference.

To the varsity for the 1958 season, along with Robertson, came Ralph Davis and Larry Willey. In their careers the one would score over 1,100 points and the other set a Missouri Conference record for field goal percentage—both tributes to Robertson's playmaking, while Oscar himself was setting all kinds of scoring records. Their first varsity year they won Cincinnati's first conference title, losing to Kansas State in the Midwest Regionals to close out a 25–3 season, and were second-ranked nationally. Oscar won the national scoring title by averaging over 35 points a game and far outscoring everyone else, even Baylor and Chamberlain. In the junior year his scoring average fell 2½ points but still led the country; the team ranking and record fell to fourth and 26–4, but they still led the conference; and they won the Midwest Regionals only to fall to champion California in the NCAA semifinals. Finally in 1960 they were 28–2 and top-ranked by the AP, and again they won the Missouri Valley Conference and the Midwest Regionals only to fall once again to California in the semis. Oscar won his third national scoring title, totaling a record 2,973 points and 1,338 rebounds in his three years, and graduated with thirteen other NCAA records, including seven assists a game in eighty-eight games.

George Smith's job was easy during those three years. Robertson controlled every game he played, and it would have been foolhardy for a coach to impose a system that would hamper the free-wheeling style of his superstar. Cincinnati didn't lose at home during Oscar's career, were 79–9, and were never out of the top five in the national rankings. Recruitment was no problem at all any more, including a new-found ability to attract blacks to a school that had previously been classified as northern redneck. George Smith, now with an enviable eight-year record of 154–56, stepped aside (or up) to athletic director and left the post–Robertson syndrome for his former assistant Ed Jucker to treat.

The enormity of Jucker's problem became clear in an early game against Seton Hall. Cincinnati lost to a team that three years earlier Robertson himself had outscored 56–54 in a 118–54 romp in Madison Square Garden. The three blacks on the starting team, Paul Hogue, Tom Thacker, and Tony Yates—part of Oscar's legacy to Cincinnati—along with Bob Wiesenhahn and Carl Bouldin seemed to be vying for All-American notice, all trying to wear the mantle of the big O. Jucker tried to get through to them that they had to be a complete team and forget trying to emulate a nonpareil. Slowly the disciplined pattern offense began to make sense

*The Cincinnati Kid (12) deals a tough hand.*

*Jucker's juggernaut brought two titles to Cincinnati after Robertson graduated.*

*Newell (left), with Imhoff (center) and Dick Doughty on the bench: Cal was NCAA champion in 1959, runner-up in 1960.*

to them, and to jell, and the tight defense began to take hold. Or perhaps they were shocked into it by successive conference defeats (the first such in Cincinnati's history) by St. Louis and Bradley that left their record at 5–3. Whatever, nearly halfway in the Dayton game and down by 11 points, Cincinnati came together as a team and the pieces of Jucker's pattern all fell into place. They won the game by 10, and twenty-one games later they were NCAA champions.

Jucker credits his defensive thinking to Hank Iba: assigned man-to-man with zone principles. That is, defenders away from the ball drop off their men to help out against the ball, to shut off passing lanes, and to rebound. On offense, Cincinnati featured backdoor plays attributed by Jucker to Pete Newell's Cal teams that beat Cincinnati in the 1959 and 1960 NCAA tournaments, plus variations that he developed or borrowed from such opponents as Miami of Ohio, St. Louis, and Ohio State. In other words, whatever worked against them could be made to work for them. And with the goals of perfectly balanced scoring and minimal individuality, they progressed toward a unique team style of great cohesiveness.

The Missouri Valley Conference had emerged in these years as perhaps the nation's strongest. In 1957, while tenth-ranked St. Louis with Bob Ferry went to the Midwest Regionals, Bradley, with Barney Cable, Shelly McMillon, and Bobby Joe Mason, won the NIT over Memphis State and Win Wilfong. In 1959 and 1960, while Oscar took the Bearcats to the NCAA, both St. Louis and Bradley went to the NIT, the latter to the finals twice and the championship the second time. Now, in 1961, it was John Benington's Billikens, 21–9, who were the NIT finalists, while Bradley with Chet Walker was 21–5 and sixth-ranked by the AP, and Wichita State was 18–8. Cincinnati came from this league to handle Texas Tech easily in the Midwest Regionals. Fourth-ranked Kansas State was tougher in the regional finals but went down by five. In the semis at Kansas City they drew Jack Gardner's high-scoring Utah team, held them to 67 points, and beat them by 15.

The championship game was a classic. Fred Taylor's Ohio State team, top-ranked and defending champions, had most of the 1960 team back, including Jerry Lucas, John Havlicek, Mel Nowell, and Larry Siegfried, one of the greatest-shooting and highest-scoring teams in college history. But Cincinnati was nearly flawless. The scoring was balanced (17 for Wiesenhahn, 16 for Bouldin, 15 for Thacker, 13 for Yates, and 9 for Hogue), and they committed only three turnovers. On defense they were superb. Lucas got his 27 and Siegfried 14, but Havlicek only 4; Ohio State shot 50 percent from the floor but was held to an amazingly low fifty shots. Cincinnati committed only three fouls in the second half despite the tenacious defense, and Jucker says that the turning point came on a defensive play when Yates, doubling back after a basket to steal the inbounds pass, tapped the ball to Thacker who stuffed it. The final score was 70–65.

The following season, Cincinnati actually improved its 27–3 record to 29–2. Wiesenhahn and Bouldin were gone, but they were replaced by Ron Bonham and

George Wilson, the fourth black starter. The two losses came early in the season, by a total of 3 points, but they stuck to their system. The highest point total against them was 71 by Wisconsin in the Holiday Festival Tournament in the Garden, but they got 101. The conference championship came in a playoff with fifth-ranked Bradley, but to get there they had to salvage a near loss to Drake. Down 9 points with 4 minutes to play, Cincinnati used a full-court press that produced a series of traps and steals that allowed them to win by a point. In the regionals, Hogue and Wilson blocked Paul Silas's first three shots for Creighton, and Cincinnati went on to win comfortably by 20. Eighth-ranked Colorado was even easier, 73–46. But at Louisville in the semis, in shapes of things to come, there was a scare from UCLA.

Wooden's team, led by Johnny Green, dropped all five men back for defensive rebounding and then exploded up floor in a five-man fast break. Cincinnati countered by picking men up quickly in backcourt to slow them down. Still UCLA stayed in the game till the last 6 seconds by very accurate shooting despite the Bearcats' pressure. The finals were very nearly anticlimactic, although once again the opposition was Ohio State, and again the Buckeyes were top-ranked, averaging 85 points a game. The starting lineups for both teams were 60 percent the same.

But Jucker shifted defensive strategy this time, with Thacker dropping off Nowell to help Hogue out on Lucas. Meanwhile on offense, Bonham moved outside to keep Havlicek away from the boards and slow down the Ohio State fast break. Both moves worked. Lucas had only 11, while Hogue scored 22 and Thacker 21; Bonham's 10 was way under par, but Havlicek had only 11, and the fast break was effectively stalled. Cincinnati drew out by 12, 71–59.

The following season, with only Paul Hogue gone from the five starters, Cincinnati did not suffer its second loss until the last game, the NCAA championship game with Loyola of Illinois. Again they had won the Missouri Valley title, again led the country in defense, and again featured the deliberate, patterned team play taught by Jucker. They beat Texas, Colorado, and Oregon State to get to the finals, and for most of that game they led by holding down the fast-breaking, high-scoring team from Chicago. But with Bonham, Thacker, Wilson, and Yates all getting into foul trouble, Loyola caught them and in overtime beat them 60–58. Ironically it was the first time in this six-year period that they achieved the number one ranking in both polls. Loyola, a Catholic school with a fine basketball tradition, twice NIT finalists, won the NCAA championship with four black starters, as their opponents had done before them.

*Ohio State 1961, a dream come true: in front are Joe Roberts (31), Doug McDonald (12), Richie Hoyt (13), Mel Nowell (3), Larry Siegfried (21), Jerry Lucas (11), John Havlicek (5), Bobby Knight (24), Gary Gearheart (4), and Dick Reasebeck (10). In second row are Coach Fred Taylor* (far left) *and Gary Bradds* (behind Lucas).

# 26

# Team Tokenism Triumphant

DAVE DEBUSSCHERE describes Adam Clayton Powell as having been the self-appointed chaplain of the Knicks, who blessed the team with invocations such as "Sock it to me, baby" and "Let it all hang out." Mac Davis tells another Powell story. On a visit to a famous mid-American university, the Congressman was told that the enrollment was 19,000. How many blacks, he asked. Nine, he was told. Why, that's nothing but tokenism, the indignant dignitary said, whereupon the basketball coach rushed forward with the words of truth: "That's not tokenism, that's my championship basketball team plus four substitutes."

The joke chronicles an inevitable development. If a black star could help a team win, a whole team of black stars could bring a winning team to a school. Many black colleges, including Morehouse, Howard, and Muskingum, had a basketball tradition dating back to near the turn of the century, but the basketball establishment took no notice. The Colored Intercollegiate Athletic Association had its first official champion in 1912, but not until 1940 was it, along with four black conferences (SIAC, EIAC, SWC, and MWC), reported in the Spalding *Guide* in a section called "The Colored Colleges." (Once before, in 1932, the *Guide* had reported on the Middle Atlantic A.A., an association of seven small black schools in New Jersey, Maryland, Delaware, and West Virginia.) In 1952 the section was

208

changed to "Negro Colleges," but it was dropped shortly thereafter. By then, the profound social changes had begun to take effect, and a pragmatic ethic in education had started to replace the arrant hypocrisy of separate but equal. Expediency's gain was principle's loss, however dishonorable or archaic the principle.

In the large urban centers, particularly at the Catholic schools, the recruitment of black players became a matter of course. At San Francisco, the sophistication of the environment was such that K. C. Jones says he had no awareness of racial factors in the assembling of the Dons' championship teams. Bill Russell, one of the most sensitive and articulate observers of the society, had to go on the road to have his racial consciousness raised. But the San Francisco lesson didn't have the effect that the Cincinnati prominence did. As a phenomenon, the Russell-Jones team could be viewed as an occurrence rather unique than instructive. At Cincinnati, however, Robertson's greatness paved the way for Jucker's assembling of champions. That Cincinnati won consistently with team play—a substantially black team—made all the difference, as opposed to the teams that sometimes won with a single black star—Kansas with Chamberlain, Kansas State with Boozer, Seattle with Baylor, St. Bonaventure with Tom Stith. The point was particularly well made when Cincinnati broke the domination of predominantly white basketball powers at Ohio State, California, Kentucky, and North Carolina.

In 1963 top-ranked Cincinnati had its own title lifted in an overtime struggle with Loyola of Illinois. George Ireland, after weathering several lean years during the Fifties had put together a team with four black starters, and these Ramblers from Chicago ran with the best. In 1962 they led the country in scoring, averaging over 90 points a game, won twenty-three games, and didn't lose their fourth until champion Dayton eliminated them in the NIT semis. A year later they were scoring even more and losing even less. Jerry Harkness was the biggest gun, and with his running mates John Egan, Les Hunter, Ron Miller, and Vic Rouse took a 24–2 record into the NCAA. There they broke records in the first-round win over Tennessee Tech by 111–42 and came through the regionals with wins over Mississippi State (Babe McCarthy's last winning Maroon team, led by W. D. Stroud) and Illinois (Harry Combes's first Big Ten champions, led by Dave Downey, since Johnny Kerr's sophomore year in 1952). Then in the semis they ran past Vic Bubas's second-ranked Duke team, led by MVP Art Heyman and Jeff Mullins, by a 94–75 score, to set up the meeting with Cincinnati.

The Bearcats dominated the game from the start. Jucker's disciplined attack was run with methodical ease by Bonham, Thacker, Wilson, Yates, and Shingleton, while Loyola chafed with impatience to get the ball and run. Cincinnati's defense, the best in the country, broke the rhythm of Loyola's fast break; their tenacious concentration made Loyola's shooters tentative. But Cincinnati paid a price in fouls for not permitting the Ramblers to run and shoot. With four Bearcat starters in foul trouble, Loyola's shooters got loose to score and came from behind to tie the game, then win it in overtime, 60–58.

Once again an urban Catholic school with a largely black team had won the NCAA title. If the same combination has not clicked since, it is not for lack of trying. La Salle, Detroit, Villanova, St. John's, Duquesne, and Boston College are a few who have tried that proven path. The best example is Marquette, where Al McGuire has brought many a star black player from New York to Milwaukee to challenge the UCLA supremacy. But by this time competition for the player comes from all kinds of institutions in all areas. Small Catholic campuses in comparatively small towns—Niagara, St. Bonaventure, Notre Dame—compete with their urban sisters for black brothers from Watts, D.C., Bedford-Stuyvesant, and Roxbury. And of course other schools—the great state and land-grant universities, the nonsectarian colleges, the exclusive private schools, and other denominational institutions—have all long since caught on.

Red Auerbach once said that the real change was not social in nature but dietary. Whereas in the Thirties a tall white boy could have the strength and coordination to play basketball, a black boy of equivalent height would probably have rickets. By the Fifties this was no longer true, and in the Sixties the good big man was more likely to be black than not. Perhaps the best example is upstart Jacksonville, who extended UCLA in the NCAA finals largely on the strength of two black 7-footers, Artis Gilmore and Pembrook Burrows, who had led Joe Williams's Dolphins to twenty-seven wins and a team average of over 100 points a game.

Probably the best example of the triumph of team tokenism came in 1966, the only time between 1964 and 1973 that a team other than UCLA won the NCAA. Texas Western (now University of Texas, El Paso) was the school that performed that feat, coached by Don Haskins, and it may have been the inspiration for the piece of Powell apocrypha that began this chapter. Ranked third in the country by virtue of their 23–1 record going into the tournament, the Miners came through with five wins, including upsets over seventh-ranked Cincinnati, fourth-ranked Kansas, and top-ranked Kentucky in the championship game.

Haskins had brought more blacks to El Paso than they were used to seeing in the whole student body, including Dave "Big Daddy" Lattin, Bobby Joe Hill, Wille Cager, Orsten Artis, Neville Shed, and Willie Worsley. Lattin at 6 feet 7 inches was the big man of the team, Worsley at 5 feet 10 inches the smallest, but they could all run and shoot and play one-on-one defense. Moreover, as a team they could also play a strikingly quick zone defense and a fancy-passing set offense. There was nothing flukey about their record or their tournament wins, though they did have several psychological factors going for them in the finals.

The game against Ted Owens's Kansas team in the Midwest Regionals was the toughest, and it was team play that won it 81–80, as the Miners could not match big Walt Wesley underneath or Jo Jo White outside. Meanwhile in the Mideast, Kentucky eliminated Dayton with big Henry Finkel and then put Michigan out 84–77. This was Cazzie Russell's senior year, and again Coach Dave Strack had prevailed in the Big Ten over John Kundla's fine Minnesota team with Lou Hudson and Archie Clark.

In the finals at College Park, Texas Western drew Utah, the class of the West, while Kentucky shot it out with second-ranked Duke. Again the Miners had no one to match Jack Gardner's star, Jerry Chambers, who won the MVP trophy though his team finished fourth. And again Texas Western's team play won for them as they outran a team famous for its fast break by an 85–78 count. The other semis were supposed to produce the champion. Vic Bubas's Blue Devils had lost only three games on an arduous schedule, thanks to two fine 6-foot 7-inch shooters, Jack Marin and Mike Lewis, along with Bob Verga and Steve Vacendak. Rupp's Runts—Thad Jaracz, Tom Kron, Larry Conley, Pat Riley, and Louie Dampier— had nobody over 6 feet 5 inches, but they were the Baron's pride and joy, deadly but unselfish shooters, aggressive rebounders and defenders, and proud competitors who had lost only in Knoxville to Tennessee in twenty-seven games. It was a brilliant match, worthy of a championship, marred only because Verga and Conley were both sick and played little. Marin and Lewis scored 50 points for Duke, but Kentucky, with more balanced scoring down the lineup after Dampier's 23 and Riley's 19, won 83–79.

Kentucky's fair-haired boys went into the finals heavily favored, but they had left their championship play behind them in the semis at Cole Field House. Texas Western, on the other hand, were still running as if they had something to prove. Kentucky slowed the pace considerably, working for open shots from medium range in the first 5 minutes. The shots came but they weren't falling, and the Miners tightened up on defense. Bobby Joe Hill made successive steals from Kron and Dampier for easy layups, and Texas Western never trailed. Gaining confidence on offense and aggressiveness on defense, they controlled the game without breaking it open. Kentucky had many more shots from the floor but seemed always to be forcing them, winding up shooting under 40 percent for the first time all year. Don Haskins's cool recruits, however, calmly won the game at the free-throw line with twenty-eight of thirty-four. There was little in the way of social rewards for them in El Paso, none of them was ever awarded a degree from Texas Western, and they feel that they have lived out the full meaning of exploitation. But they had finally gotten a lesson across to the SEC, the ACC, and the world: since that time no pretender to basketball eminence has ever drawn a color line in its recruiting.

# 27

# *Overcoming Hardship*

A SMILING Ronnie Hogue, talking about his four years as a basketball star at the University of Georgia, says that he never met any serious problems because of his constant "attitude of cool." Recruited by Ken Rosemond out of McKinley High School in D.C., Hogue was the first black player at Athens, and during his career he turned the hoots and jeers in places like Starkville and Oxford to appreciative cheers; the attention turned from the racial anomaly to the basketball prodigy. The Southeastern Conference, along with the Southern the last bastion of resistance to integrated athletics, had discovered that traditions of competitiveness in sports outweighed certain others. In a dozen years the University of Alabama moved from the image of Governor Wallace standing in the doorway to block black matriculation to the image of a basketball team with five black starters and high national ranking.

Years of accommodation and accomplishment they have been, but grave problems remain. The black athletes have found acceptance much easier in the fieldhouse than in other parts of the campus. Like some of their white brothers, many black players complete their eligibility but not their degrees. An egregious example

212

of a pluralistic society, the black player labors in a tight, closed little system that tends toward the monolithic and considers conformity a virtue. The sense of being exploited as a commodity is much more acute for a player who has no normal social life on a campus where he cannot find someone to date or to cut his hair. Thus defections have been neither uncommon nor unexpected.

Two of the greatest went together, Baylor and Chamberlain, after the 1958 season when they both averaged over 30 points a game to finish second and third to Oscar Robertson. Elgin Baylor had carried John Castellani's Seattle team all the way to the NCAA finals, beating San Francisco, California, and Kansas State along the way. Baylor's 35-foot jump shot with 2 seconds to play ended the Dons' twenty-game winning streak, and his 135 points won him the MVP trophy for the tournament. For Baylor there was little point in playing another year at Seattle. He was eligible for the NBA draft because he had transferred from Idaho and his original class was graduating. He would be twenty-four years old before the next season started, and his game was already mature beyond his years and his collegiate competition. Seattle could hardly hope to come this far again, and there was to be another coaching turnover. The offer to Baylor from Bob Short was a good one, and Elgin went to the Lakers in Minneapolis, starting his remarkable pro career early but not prematurely and saving the franchise that was shortly to move to Los Angeles.

There was no furor over Baylor's move, but no move of Wilt Chamberlain fails to attract attention. Chamberlain is probably the only player widely believed to have been subsidized for playing in high school. As a record-breaking scorer and rebounder at Overbrook High School in Philadelphia, he was recruited by over two hundred schools. Of eleven major campuses he visited, six were in the Big Ten, and he also went to look at Oregon, Denver, Dayton, and Cincinnati (imagine how a Robertson-Chamberlain combination could have dominated the college game). But the one thing that was sure was that Chamberlain would make up his own mind and make a good deal for himself. He visited Kansas three times and was increasingly impressed by a basketball tradition that extended back before the turn of the century and had been enriched over the years by the presence of Dr. Naismith and Phog Allen.

He also learned that he was wanted so badly in Lawrence that he would want for nothing if he came. While other schools made concrete "unofficial" offers that went far beyond NCAA limits, Kansas stated no figures and led the Dipper to believe that the sky was the limit. The arrangement had long-range benefits: under oath Chamberlain could honestly say he didn't have an illegal salary or bonus setup and didn't know how much money he actually received. The Jayhawk alumni and friends had been very generous, but wise Wilt had deliberately never counted.

With Allen forced to retire, his assistant Dick Harp inherited the team for Chamberlain's sophomore year. Wilt earned whatever he got. Over 7 feet tall and well over 200 pounds, he was a prodigy of coordination, strength, and speed. He was also a marked man, facing special, exotic defenses in every game. He still managed to score 30 points a game, lead Kansas to a conference title, take them to the NCAA finals, earn them number two ranking, and bring about three rules changes. During the season Kansas lost only to Iowa State. In the tournament, they beat SMU when Jim Krebs fouled out trying to stop the Dipper, Oklahoma City by 20, and San Francisco by 24, before the championship showdown with top-ranked North Carolina.

The game went into three overtime periods before the Tarheels won by a point, 54–53, but Kansas really lost it in the first half when they shot 27 percent to North Carolina's 65 percent. Rosenbluth, playing Chamberlain as well as anyone had, fouled out at 46-all, but Frank McGuire's firm discipline controlled the pace and kept the game close enough to win on two last-minute free throws by Joe Quigg. The following season was even rougher for Wilt, though his scoring average improved slightly. The defenders were more aggressive and, it seemed, the officials were even less protective. Tex Winter's Kansas State, with Bob Boozer, barely beat Kansas for the Big Eight title and succeeded them as Midwest Regional champs. Kansas, at 18–5, had no postseason invitation.

Chamberlain quit, saying, "The game I was forced to play at KU wasn't basketball." Certainly it was not like what was being played anywhere else in 1958, not in the summer leagues in the playgrounds nor in most fieldhouses nor in pro arenas. But it was the Big Dipper himself who made the difference. With the offense built around him, Kansas forced opponents to radically archaic if not barbaric methods of defense, and with his growing defensive force he disrupted normal offensive patterns. Chamberlain toured a year with the Globetrotters, who are bound by few rules and fewer laws, until he could legitimately accept the NBA draft and become the superstar everyone who had seen him play knew he could be.

The case of Connie Hawkins is unique, as is his basketball brilliance, yet it is indicative of the manifold injustice of the collegiate athletic system. When Hawkins graduated from Boys High, he was already a legendary player in the Brooklyn and Harlem schoolyards. He had all the moves that anyone had ever seen and some they hadn't. The recruiters wooed him extravagantly, and he ended up at Iowa after a false start at Colorado. But he never played a varsity game. In a new outbreak of the old-type scandals, his name was mentioned in the investigations, his confused testimony in the Grand Jury was potentially incriminating, and he was dropped from school for academic reasons.

David Wolf's book *Foul!* tells the whole story, showing in detail that the case against the Hawk rested primarily on the fact that he knew Jack Molinas, one of the arch conspirators, and had innocently accepted a loan from him. But the plain irony is that Hawkins had no business being in college at all, not to mention a major university. He was passed through high school solely on his basketball credentials and couldn't pass any subject that actually required high school level reading. But this never fazed the recruiters, whose single-minded purpose was to remove him from the abject poverty of Bedford-Stuyvesant to their clean campus field-houses, where he would play winning basketball despite the alienating experiences of the campus and the disorienting encounters with higher education.

The hypocrisy that is the working principle in the symbiotic relationship between the colleges and professional leagues has produced a new phenomenon called "the hardship case." If a measurable financial need can be claimed, a collegiate player can declare himself eligible for a pro draft before his class graduates. The need need not have arisen since he matriculated, of course; in most hardship cases, the years in college have themselves been an improvement. But in a marketplace situation, commercial values obtain, so that a player must weigh the going price on his talent against a projection of that price after more college competition, opportunities for publicity, and prospective showcases for his skills.

Spencer Haywood is a perfect example. He was signed first by Ray Mears at Tennessee in the hope that a genuine black superstar could break racial barriers as well as scoring and rebounding records. But ten years of separate but equal education in Mississippi had left the reasonably intelligent Haywood without the reading skills to handle the SEC's minimum entrance requirements. Mears offered remedial reading programs and then, when Spencer balked, a cooperative junior college. Haywood then got a better junior college offer from another university's farm system, but after the season his outstanding play for the Olympic champions in Mexico City brought a new round of collegiate bidding. Detroit, including an implicit offer to his high school coach in the package, won the prize. But after one year, in which he led the nation in rebounding, Haywood jumped to the pros and the greater glory of gold.

Two years later a veritable plague of hardships descended upon the colleges. Julius Erving left Massachusetts after a sophomore year in which he seemed already in another league than anyone he played with or against. George McGinnis defected from Indiana, Tom Payne from Kentucky, Johnny Neumann from Ole Miss (the only white in this list, he led the nation in scoring as a sophomore), Phil Chenier from California, and—in mideason—Jim Chones from Marquette. The conditions were different in each case and the degree of need varied greatly, but there was one constant factor—the big money in the offer. There may have been a miscalculation on the part of Chones, since Marquette might well have gone far in postseason play and his value been increased; but financial pressures were immediate, and he jumped with Al McGuire's blessing.

Payne and Chenier are contrasts. One, the first black Wildcat at Kentucky, was troubled by his whole situation, by players and fans at home and away, and even by the law. But he might have earned a bigger reputation and price tag and learned some valuable lessons by playing two more years for the Baron. Chenier, on the other hand, was perfectly at home in Berkeley, socially and every other way but on the basektball court. The team was going nowhere, the coaching had nothing to offer him, and he rarely had challenging competition. By allowing him to

*Chenier, head and shoulders above college competition.*

*Haywood, in a class by himself.*

get an early start in NBA on-the-job training, the hardship clause gave Chenier a boost toward the status of all-star guard and its appropriate salary.

At Chapel Hill, another contrast may be found in two of Dean Smith's black stars, Bill Chamberlain and Bob McAdoo. Chamberlain, who seemed to be struggling against nature and himself to conform to Smith's concept of team play, completed his eligibility in a career that saw his talent dissipate and his market value diminish. McAdoo, whose individual style and skill often seemed at odds with the Tarheel patterns, played only one season, declared himself a hardship case, and was fast becoming a professional superstar before his class had graduated.

Sam Jones says that no coach, in good conscience, should discourage a player from accepting a possible hardship bonanza. If he chose the best deal in the first place, he should be able to take a better one now; and if he wants to complete his education, he can afford to do it in his own time. Charley Scott was able to improve his bargaining position by finishing his career (and taking his degree) at Chapel Hill. The social pressures, paralleled by Mike Maloy's at Davidson, and the collegiate as opposed to professional style on the court never hurt his game because Scott never let them. But though such independence is the exception rather than the rule, many others—David Thompson of North Carolina State, Fly Williams of Austin Peay, Marvin Barnes of Providence College, to name a few current examples—seem to resist the hardship road, while only a comparative few—like Mel Davis of St. John's—pick up their new-found option.

A final example is Maryland's Lenny Elmore. After a disappointing junior year, in which he played in Tom McMillen's shadow, failed to make the Olympic squad, was nagged by injuries, officials, and baiting opponents, Elmore took a long look at his situation at Maryland (who had failed to win their conference or survive the Eastern Regionals despite the schoolboy talent to stock two squads) and decided to be a hardship case. Instead of big offers, he got good advice: have a good year, help your team to high ranking and showcase performances, perfect your natural skills to prove your professional potential. Before the deadline Elmore withdrew his name from the hardship list and protected his eligibility. In helping to make a better deal for himself in the long run, he made a better season for his school.

Perhaps there is irony here, or at least poetic justice. The system tends to dehumanize the individual, treating him by standards based on his value as property. By accepting that value system, the individual player—if he is good enough and clever enough—can beat the system at its own game. The hardship clause, intended as a hedge against the whole hypocritical system being upset, has provided a means of subverting the system. It is like profit-sharing translated to the athlete as chattel, and if it has not helped "amateur" sport it has certainly helped individual players, particularly blacks, to the freedom provided by great marketplace value.

# Part 6

# The Playground Game

BY THE END of the Fifties and the beginning of the Sixties, all regional characteristics had virtually disappeared from the game of basketball. In any playground in any part of the country all of the five elements of the modern game could be seen on any afternoon—the gunner a la Luisetti and his descendants, the tricky dribbler and passer a la Cousy, the big man muscling in for his shots a la Mikan, the rejector and rebounder a la Russell, and the all-around offensive intimidator a la Robertson.

This was by no means the result of a leveling process but rather the development and integration of all the separate elements and styles into a national game universally understood, the American sport of universal participation. Urban playgrounds are crisscrossed with courts, and the driveway basket is a *sine qua non* of both rural and suburban architecture. The college game reflects this superdemocratization, this heritage of the playground: more free-lancing, more one-on-one play, more contact, more rugged defense, more accurate shooting, and more attention to individualistic moves. Some coaches have fought the changes by maintaining old ways and disciplines, and some have fought them by devising new strategies and postures; but most have adapted to them.

Several factors contributed to this advanced stage, many of them having to do with freer communication and exchange of ideas. Like the language itself, basketball lost regional peculiarities by widespread exposure in the mass media. There was also the mushrooming phenomenon of the basketball camp, an institution that was made possible when the job of basketball coach was finally seen to be a full-time year-round responsibility. This in turn led to larger staffs and expanded notions of developing and attracting material. Besides being an extra source of income for the coach and providing handy employment for assistants and players, the camps allowed coaches to make their pitch to future recruits and to develop a number of resources in the secondary schools. Prep coaches, treated properly, could make their schools client states in the sphere of a college's influence, and they would also make themselves candidates for future openings on the college staff. The pragmatic virtues of this system were apparent, but its educational contributions cannot be underestimated.

A parallel institution, perhaps even more important to the standardization of the complete basketball program, is the coaches' clinic. From fundamentals to sophisticated refinements, every approach to the game is part of the comprehensive curriculum of the clinics. Moreover, scores of books have been published since the Fifties, mostly written by successful coaches; and all those concrete moves that make up the plays and patterns of the game are rendered abstractly in diagrams and words. But the individual moves so basic to the playground game defy abstraction.

Contemporary basketball is the art of putting together concrete individual moves within coherent patterns of abstractable movement. No college coach can afford to keep a team ignorant of a wide variety of defenses—man-to-man and zone, pressure at full- and three-quarter- and half-court—and the offensive sets to use against them. Set plays are needed for specific game situations, and whatever the basic patterns a team uses, it must be able to change them when they aren't working. Careful preparation for particular games may include special devices for particular teams or individual players. But the fundamentals cannot be neglected for gimmicks, and the successful coaches always have their teams stress doing their own things well.

Many coaches are wedded to one particular style of offense and defense, and they recruit players to fit their system. But the best coaches get the best personnel they can and then mold their system to get the best possible results from their material. The point is to isolate favorable match-ups or favorable combinations to free a man for a shot he is likely to make. Whatever form of traditional movement or pattern is employed, whether fast-breaking or free-lancing or deliberate, the end result must be an individual move. This is where the playground skills come into play: in the three-man, two-man, or one-on-one maneuvers that are the quintessence of the game. And the bogarder, as they call the intimidator in the D.C. playgrounds, can do it on defense or on the boards as well as with the ball.

# 28

# *Free-for-All in the Cradle of Liberty*

THEY CALL themselves the Big Five, and they are Philadelphia's best advertisement this side of W. C. Fields's tombstone—La Salle, Penn, St. Joseph's, Temple, and Villanova. Though Penn plays in the Ivy League, and now La Salle, Temple, and St. Joseph's in the Middle Atlantic Conference, it is the intracity rivalry that provides the best competition and the natural attractions. Strangely enough, despite the long-standing tradition of basketball in Philadelphia, complete competition among the five did not start until the 1956 season.

Penn, of course, goes way back as an eastern basketball power, and they have always scheduled many games with their neighbors in Pennsylvania. By the early Twenties they had established series with Muhlenberg, Penn State, Lehigh, Allegheny, Susquehanna, Swarthmore, Franklin and Marshall, Pitt, Bucknell, Gettysburg, Carlisle, Lafayette, Haverford, Washington and Jefferson, Drexel, Dickinson, Penn Military, and Ursinus. Yet they only played Temple once, in 1921, before the 1956 season, and Villanova only twice, in 1910 and 1922. La Salle played them four times in the Thirties and beat them twice in the late Forties and once in the early Fifties before the Big Five inaugural. Only with St. Joseph's did Penn maintain long-term relations, playing them every year from 1923 to 1937 (losing three of the last six) and from 1944 to 1949 (losing four of the six). In 1945, when Penn under Howie Dallmar broke Dartmouth's stranglehold on the Ivy title, they beat St. Joe's by 17 points despite the presence of Al Guokas, the second of three future pros from that family to play for the Hawks.

St. Joe's has the best record of continuing play against the others of the Big Five. They played Temple as early as 1902, through most of the Twenties, and without an interruption since 1932. They played La Salle first in 1909 and without an interruption since 1934. And they played Villanova through the Twenties and occasionally in the Thirties. Starting in 1956, under Jack Ramsay, their overall record has improved remarkably, though they can look back to fine performances by Matt Guokas, Sr., in 1937 and by All-American George Senesky in 1943 when they were 18–4 under Bill Ferguson.

Temple began its basketball history against Haverford in 1895 (though not with five-man teams), and the Owls have often taken on the country's best even while shunning fellow-Philadelphians. But they've played La Salle with only one break since 1937 and St. Joe's without any break since 1932. With Don Shields, Meyer Bloom, and Ed Boyle, they won the inaugural NIT in 1938 for Jimmy Usilton. Under Josh Cody they went to the NCAA in 1944, losing to Ohio State. But they too prospered beginning in 1956 under the Big Five arrangement and Harry Litwack's coaching.

Still, it was the other two, Villanova and La Salle, that attracted the national basketball spotlight to the City of Brotherly Love in the Fifties. It was scoring that did it for the Wildcats of Villanova. Alex Severance's twenty-five years as head coach produced 416 wins, but this was a case of a player making a coach's reputation. Paul Arizin, with his spectacular low-trajectory jump shot, led Villanova to the nation's lead in scoring. In Arizin's junior and senior years, the Wildcats won forty-eight while losing only eight, scoring an average of 70 points a game. Their one tournament bid was in 1949 when they ran into tougher Wildcats, the NCAA winners from Kentucky.

With La Salle it was a combination of coach and player that made the Explorers celebrities. Charles McGlone turned it around for them after La Salle had had a dozen years of losing or mediocre records. McGlone arrived in 1947 and produced three straight twenty-game winners. In 1950 Ken Loeffler took over and went McGlone one better. The twenty-first win came in the NIT against Arizona, when Loeffler switched to a 3–2 zone to come from behind in the second half. Unfortunately they were edged by Dudey Moore's determined Dukes in the second round.

Loeffler, one of the most cerebral of coaches, was also one of the most colorful. A lawyer by education if not profession or temperament, he had coached Geneva College, Yale, Denver, and the St. Louis Bombers before coming to La Salle. In the 1951 season La Salle explored southward, going into Raleigh with a 13–2 record to play North Carolina State, which had lost only to Villanova in eighteen

222

*Loeffler (center), in his first year at La Salle, took the Explorers to the NIT, with Larry Foust (left) and Jim Phelan.*

games (they later got revenge in the NCAA Eastern Regionals). When Everett Case's Wolfpack won 76–74, Loeffler declaimed for all to hear: "This is the biggest steal since the Louisiana Purchase." After the season was over, and La Salle had once again gone out of the NIT in the first round to complete a 22–7 mark, Loeffler and Case were flying to a summer coaching clinic together. Case was dozing in his seat, when Loeffler shook him awake. "The plane's in trouble," he said, "and we may not make it. Quick, before we go down, admit those officials at Raleigh were terrible."

The La Salle coach had little to cry about in the next four years. Penn had Ernie Beck across town, but La Salle had the best player in the city, very likely the best in the country, and in the eyes of many the best college player in basketball history. Tom Gola, at 6 feet 7 inches, had the strength and timing to rebound with the biggest centers, the ballhandling and passing and outside shooting to play backcourt with the best, and the speed and inside moves to play All-American forward. Even as a freshman he displayed great poise and knowledge of the game, and he had the pure instinct to be wherever he was needed and do whatever he had to. Best of all, he had such marvelously quick hands that he defensed, shot, and passed without the elaborateness or spectacular quality that is usually needed to draw the attention of the press and All-American selectors. Gola was thus the prototype of the modern playground player, and since the Big Five organized in 1956, they have produced many outstanding players in that image.

For four years in Loeffler's and in Gola's hands La Salle was Philadelphia basketball. In 1952 as rank outsiders they won the NIT, with freshman Gola sharing MVP honors with teammate Norm Grekin. Their final record was 25–7, including losses in the Olympic trials to NCAA champ Kansas and the Phillips Oilers. In 1953 they were 25–3, the last loss a heart-breaker by 1 point to St. John's in the

*Mr. Everything for La Salle: Tom Gola.*

NIT quarterfinals. In 1954 they tried the NCAA and went all the way. The first game was actually the toughest. Eddie Conlin, Fordham's fine rebounder, kept the Rams ahead most of the way. Loeffler used two time-outs in 5 seconds to engineer a tie, and La Salle won in overtime.

They went on to beat North Carolina State (sweet revenge on Ev Case), Navy, Penn State, and Bradley. In the finals Gola picked up four fouls early, and La Salle switched to a 2–3 zone with Gola in the corner. On offense he concentrated on setting up Singley and Blatcher who scored 23 each, and he was able to play out the game, a 92–76 win. Gola was the MVP of the tournament and many thought the player of the year—over the likes of Pettit, Selvy, Hagan, Ramsey, Schlundt, Leonard, Ricketts, and Palazzi.

In 1955 they again went all the way to the NCAA finals, averaging over 80 points a game as Gola's four-year total went to 2,462. In the first game they swamped West Virginia by 34 as Gola was much hotter than Rod Hundley, in the second Princeton by 37, and in the regional finals Canisius by 35. Against Iowa, however, it was a struggle all the way. La Salle never trailed, but Bill Logan, Sugar Cain, and Bill Seaberg kept Iowa close, losing only by 76–73. In the championship game Gola was outplayed perhaps for the only time in his college career as San Francisco won 77–63. K. C. Jones up front and Bill Russell underneath kept Tom scoreless from the field for 21 minutes. He struggled to 23 points but could not dominate the floor against the Dons' defense. Nevertheless he was unanimous all-tourney choice, behind MVP Russell.

Ever the ironist, Loeffler claimed that his greatest triumph in 1955 was against Kentucky. Rupp's men had given La Salle one of their four regular season losses in twenty-six games and had lost only twice themselves before Marquette knocked them out of the Mideast Regionals. Both earlier losses were at the hands of Georgia Tech, and Loeffler said that Whack Hyder had followed Loeffler's own methods to pull off the upsets.

With Gola graduating and Loeffler moving on to Texas A & M, a new era began in 1956, the start of formal competition among all of the Big Five. Ned Irish had seen the potential back in the Thirties when he promoted double-headers at Convention Hall. And now, in the wake of outstanding players like Penn's Dall-

*Ernie Beck had more offensive moves than a MIRV stockpile.*

mar, Beck, Jack McCloskey, and Francis Crossin; Temple's Bloom, Bill Mlkvy, Nelson Bobb, Ike Borsavage, Angelo Musi, Jerry Rollo, and Jack Hewson; Villanova's Arizin, Tom Brennan, Tom Hoover, Larry Hennessey, Red Klotz, Jim Mooney, and Art Spector; La Salle's Gola, Jack George, Larry Foust, Jackie Moore, and Jim Phelan; and St. Joseph's Senesky and the brothers Guokas—now there began an unprecedented sequence of successes by a group of five schools in one city. Starting in 1956, they have never been without a postseason invitation, and only once has only one of them participated. Nine times, three of their number have received bids, and twice four out of five have been involved.

At the risk of repeating statistics, this record should be appreciated from a fuller accounting. In the period of seventeen years since their formalized membership in the Big Five, Penn has gone to the NCAA three times and reached the Eastern Regional finals twice. La Salle has gone to the NIT three times and the NCAA once, and in 1969, banned from postseason play because of academic and recruiting irregularities during Jim Harding's brief tenure, they were 23–1 and second-ranked nationally under Tom Gola; while St. Joseph's and Villanova went to the NCAA and Temple won the NIT, La Salle, having beaten them all, stayed home. Villanova has gone to the NIT seven times, finishing fourth, third, and second, and to the NCAA six times, reaching the Eastern Regional finals three times and the national finals once (second to UCLA in 1971). Temple has gone to the NIT seven times, finishing third once and winning it in 1969, and to the NCAA six times, winning the regionals twice and finishing third nationally in 1956 and again in 1958 after losing to champion Kentucky by 1 point. And St. Joseph's has gone to the NIT four times, finishing third once, and to the NCAA nine times, reaching the regional finals twice and winning it once, in 1961, when they finished third nationally after losing to runner-up Ohio State.

The coaches who have compiled the bulk of this remarkable record are Dudey Moore at La Salle, Dick Harter at Penn, Jack Ramsay and Jack McKinney at St. Joseph's, Harry Litwack at Temple, and Jack Kraft at Villanova. And among their star players who made it all happen are Hal Lear and Guy Rodgers, Temple's incomparable backcourt pair, along with other Owls like John Baum and Eddie Mast; from Villanova, Hubie White, Jimmy Washington, Bill Melchionni, Wally Jones, Howard Porter, Hank Siemiontkowski, Chris Ford, and Tom Ingelsby; from Penn,

*La Salle got Dudey Moore from Duquesne; he'd beaten them too often.*

Dave Wohl, Bob Morse, Phil Hankinson, and Corky Calhoun; from St. Joseph's, Matt Guokas, Jr., Cliff Anderson, Billy Oakes, Bob McNeill, Mike Bantom, and Steve Courtin; and from La Salle, Larry Cannon, Bernie Williams, and Ken Durrett.

As well as the Five has done against all outlanders, among themselves it has always been intense internecine warfare. And over the years the clear demarcations between, say, the Harry Litwack style and the Dudey Moore style, have been erased. Like basketball in the country at large, Philadelphia basketball has become standardized with the patterns, the rhythms, and the moves of the playground game.

*Coach Kraft with Chris Ford.*

*Wally Jones.*

*Jim Washington.*

Howard Porter (54) inside Bob Lanier (31).

# 29

# *Tobacco Road Madness*

OF THE MANY places in the country where basketball craziness has infected the population, perhaps none matches the area radiating out from North Carolina where the whole section rages at fever pitch at tournament time. The old Southern Conference, numbering as many as twenty-three schools in one season, was inevitably driven to a tournament following regular season play to determine a winner. More often than not, the surviving champion was not the team with the best record, but even when the SEC secession took place (1932) and then when the ACC–Southern Conference fission occurred (1953), the tournament tradition continued.

For a long time the teams in this confederation did not measure up in intersectional competition. Wake Forest (1939) and North Carolina (1941) went out of the NCAA regionals in the first round; and All-American players were few and far between—Morris Johnson of NC State (1930), Fred Tompkins of South Carolina (1934), Banks McFadden of Clemson (1939). But after the war things got better in a hurry. In 1946 Duke edged by Wake Forest to win the conference tournament, but North Carolina had a better overall record and received the NCAA bid. Coached by Ben Carnevale, a Howard Cann product from NYU, the Tarheels went all the way to the finals before Kurland and company proved too much for Jim Jordan, Jack Dillon, and Bones McKinney to handle.

*Banks McFadden.*

The arrival of Everett Case at North Carolina State in 1947 and his immediate success with the fast break made the greatest impact. For six straight years the Wolfpack finished first in the season's standings *and* the tournament, going on to the NIT twice and the NCAA thrice, with a third-place showing in each as their best performance. Dick Dickey and Sam Ranzino were Case's stars during this reign, but the league's best performer was Duke's Dick Groat.

Groat was a very gifted athlete who had come to Duke because of its baseball emphasis, but he was very fortunate for several basketball coincidences. In the first place he benefited from a brief stay of Red Auerbach (as an advisory coach between pro assignments) to learn the fine points of offensive moves. Second, Harold Bradley took over the coaching job at Duke for Groat's junior year (1951) to begin nine winning years of quality play. Third, early in his career, the Dixie Classic was initiated, bringing more tourney excitement to the area and providing a showcase for national recognition of local talent, as the four Tobacco Road teams (Duke, North Carolina, NC State, Wake Forest) competed in what was usually a very classy eight-team draw.

Groat led the nation in scoring in 1951, averaged more than 25 points a game for two years, led the nation in assists in 1952, and set free-throw records with 261 of 338 attempts in 1951. His greatest single performance was in the Dixie Classic in his junior year, against Tulane in the consolation game. It was a week of historic comebacks, the last week of 1950. Joe Culmone was driving hard at Tropical Park, shooting for Walter Miller's forty-four-year-old record of 388 wins in a year, while Willie Shoemaker was trying to come from behind at the Fair Grounds to catch Culmone for the national title. At halftime Tulane had an incredible 56–27 lead over Duke. On Saturday the 30th, after Culmone rode a triple for 385 wins, Shoemaker had four winners to tie him with one day to go. Groat took matters into his own hands in the second half, having decided that the Blue Devils were good enough to reverse the whole first half. On the 31st Culmone rode three winners at Oriental Park in Havana to tie Miller's mark, and then the Shoe matched him, winning his third of the day and 388th of the year in the eleventh and last race at Agua Caliente. Dick Groat, controlling the whole tempo and pattern of play, led Duke back to a 74–72 win. His 32 points gave him 71 for the tournament, but MVP honors went to Sam Ranzino of the champions from North Carolina State.

The Wolfpack's monopoly was broken in 1953, the last year before the formation of the ACC, when they finished first in the standings but lost by a point in the tourney finals to second-place Wake Forest, led by Dickie Hemric. Another important happening that year was the coming of Frank McGuire to Chapel Hill.

The first three years of the ACC witnessed a steady progression toward the first rank of college basketball leagues. While the abandoned Southern Conference produced scoring prodigies in Selvy, Floyd, and Hundley, the ACC produced formidable teams at Duke, Wake Forest, Maryland, North Carolina, and NC State. The most trouble they had was with each other, though each year the winner lost a cliff-hanging NCAA opener. It seemed as if the conference tournament took too large a toll before the Eastern Regionals.

*Ol' Ev Case (left) and MVP Sam Ranzino.*

First-place Duke in 1954 was upset in the tournament by NC State, with in-spired play by Ronnie Shavlik, Mel Thompson, and Skippy Winstead. Meanwhile Wake Forest beat second-place Maryland, Bud Millikan's best team in his fourth year at College Park, led by classy Gene Shue, in a deliberate game. The Demon Deacons then, with Hemric and Lowell Davis carrying the attack, played their third straight overtime affair before losing to NC State. The 7-point loss to even-tual champion La Salle seemed anticlimactic in Raleigh. In 1955 the first-place Wolfpack survived the tourney, but it was Duke that took the NCAA bid and the 1-point loss to Villanova. Virginia's Buzz Wilkinson and Clemson's Bill Yar-borough were helping to strengthen the league at the bottom. In 1956 NC State repeated, led by Shavlik, Vic Molodet, and John Maglio, but lost by a point to Canisius in four overtimes.

The ACC breakthrough came in 1957. McGuire's Tarheels went undefeated through all conference and nonconference games and through the ACC tourney as well. Len Rosenbluth was the All-American star and team leader, but he was ably assisted by Pete Brennan, Tom Kearns, Joe Quigg, and Bob Cunningham. In the NCAA North Carolina's high-scoring team rolled up big margins against Yale and Canisius, then beat Syracuse and Michigan State in more deliberate style, the latter in triple overtime, to set up a showdown with Kansas and their star Dipper.

*Len Rosenbluth.*

*Shue afoot.*

Top-ranked nationally, McGuire's team found themselves underdogs. While at St. John's, McGuire had successfully defensed another Kansas behemoth, Clyde Lovellette, though the Jayhawks had won the NCAA title game anyway. Now, five years later, he had similar plans for Chamberlain.

McGuire's defensive thinking began with his offense: control the ball. Harp had devised a diamond and one defense with Chamberlain under the basket and a shadow on Rosenbluth. North Carolina responded with outside shooting by Quigg and Brennan until Kansas had to go to man-to-man. Then Quigg drew Chamberlain outside, and Rosenbluth moved inside for his halftime total of 14 points. The New York area boys wearing the light blue of North Carolina—McGuire's "Yankee Rebels" they were called—shot 65 percent for the half, to Kansas's 27 percent, for a 29–22 lead. Chamberlain, who had looked silly at the opening tap when McGuire sent 5-foot 11-inch Tommy Kearns against him only to have North Carolina control the ball anyway, had been neutralized by 6-foot 9-inch Joe Quigg with help from Rosenbluth and Brennan whenever he got the ball.

In the second half Chamberlain and Kansas stormed back, with help from Maurice King and Gene Elstun, to get the lead and pull out to 5 points within 7 minutes. McGuire ordered a severe slowdown; deliberately playing for sure shots, North Carolina came back, tying the game at 46-all even though Rosenbluth had fouled out. North Carolina had won three overtime games during the season, but never without Rosenbluth. It was his replacement Bob Young that drove the lane for a Tarheel lead at 48–46, but Chamberlain tied it up with a jump shot. These were the only points scored in what was now a cautious, defensive chess game.

In the second overtime both teams probed for perfect shots that never came, and the most action occurred when both benches charged the floor after a loose-ball wrestling match. No one scored. Finally in the third overtime Kearns opened up. He shot and scored, shot again and was fouled, converting both free throws. Chamberlain came back with a 3-point play, and King made one of two from the line for a tie at 52. Two and a half minutes remained, and McGuire ordered North Carolina to play for one shot. They stalled away 2 minutes, but John Parker stole the ball from Quigg and Kearns deliberately fouled Elstun. He made one of two for a 53–52 lead. Kearns drove in for a shot, but Chamberlain rejected it; Quigg rebounded and was fouled. Six seconds remained as Quigg put North Carolina in front 54–53. Elstun's long pass to Chamberlain was knocked away by Quigg, who had played about 20 minutes with four personal fouls, and the horn sounded as Kearns threw the ball toward the Municipal Auditorium lights.

Since then the ACC has been recognized as a leading basketball conference, never failing to have at least one team in the top ten. In the early Seventies they have had as many as three teams ranked in the top five, an astounding figure when you consider that one place must always be conceded to UCLA. Many coaching changes have been interesting, if not productive. Clemson, laboring for many years in the second division under Banks McFadden, Press Maravich, and Bobby Roberts, seems to be on the rise under Tates Locke who took over in 1971, especially with the signing of 7-foot 2-inch Wayne "Tree" Rollins as a freshman for 1974. Duke was even more successful under Vic Bubas, a hardened Case alumnus from N.C. State, than they were under Bradley. And Maryland has had a resurgence under Lefty Driesell, who played for Bradley at Duke and led Davidson to high national ranking in his nine years there.

After Case's retirement and two years under Maravich, NC State lured alumnus Norman Sloan from Florida, and by 1973 he had produced an undefeated team. Over at Chapel Hill, Dean Smith, a Phog Allen product, moved up from assistant to replace Frank McGuire in 1962 when McGuire tried his hand in the NBA. Smith instituted a pattern offense, based primarily on the shuffle, and subsequently evolved a style of very quick continuity and dogged defense that demands total team dedication and frequent platooning. Within five years his Tarheels became a dominant factor in the conference again, and he has won accolades from his peers if not all his players.

Virginia, under Bus Male, Billy McCann, and Bill Gibson, has consistently been the league's poor relation, but finally emerged in 1972, with Barry Parkhill starring in Gibson's maddening four-corner offense, as a contender and NIT entrant. South Carolina drew Frank McGuire back from the pros in 1965 and within three years had become a national power. But they were unhappy with the ACC's restrictions and withdrew from the league in 1971, the year they upset North Carolina in their last appearance in the league's postseason tournament.

For eight years, Wake Forest was coached by the incomparable Bones McKinney. Coached as a pro by Red Auerbach, who called him "probably the

A rare view—Bones still on the bench.

*Dean Smith ( left), with Bill Chamberlain* (center) *and Dennis Wuycik.*

greatest competitor in the game," McKinney didn't live up to the retirement plans he announced to his teammates. He promised to set on his front porch in his ol' rockin' chair for about two years and then, just maybe, start rockin'. Instead, he treated fans down Winston-Salem way to the greatest show in town, a hymn-singing, referee-baiting basketball coach who even would tap the ball to his players when he could get away with it in the days when the benches were under the baskets on the endline. More recently, Jack McCloskey preached to the Demon Deacons before accepting a pioneer's challenge with the Portland Trail Blazers in the NBA.

The four Tobacco Road teams so dominated the conference that from 1958, when Maryland upset Duke in the tournament, until 1970, when South Carolina went undefeated through the regular season schedule, one of them finished first in the standings and one of them won the tourney—though four times they divided honors among themselves. Lee Shaffer, Doug Moe, Billy Cunningham, and Louis Pucillo starred for North Carolina, Len Chappell and Billy Packer for Wake Forest, John Richter for NC State, and across the border Grady Wallace for South Carolina.

During the mid-Sixties, Duke's dominating position in the league was maintained by a sequence of fine players beginning with Art Heyman, another New York product. In his sophomore year (1961), he led the scoring in nineteen games, with highs of 34 against Florida and 36 against Seton Hall in the Garden. For Georgia Tech he reserved his best rebounding performance, 21. Perhaps his best

236

game was against Marquette in the Dixie Classic when he exploded for 10 points in 2½ minutes as Duke outscored the Warriors 22–6 in a brief span to break the game open. After his sophomore year, Bubas said that the best thing about him was that he still had two seasons left, but Heyman went on to earn the title of Superflake in both pro leagues. In the wake of the flake, the following paraded to Durham: Jeff Mullins, Jack Marin, Steve Vacendak, Jay Buckley, Hack Tison, Bob Verga, Randy Denton, and Mike Lewis. The Blue Devils went to six postseason tournaments in eight years, making the NCAA semis three times and finishing second to UCLA in 1964.

When North Carolina resumed command in the late Sixties, it was with Larry Miller, Bob Lewis, and Charley Scott in starring roles. In 1968 they beat neighboring Davidson with Mike Maloy to win the Eastern Regionals and wound up second to UCLA. A year later they were beaten by Purdue with Rick Mount in the semis, and in 1972 they were third after losing the semis to Florida State. In between, they won the NIT as Bill Chamberlain won the MVP award. Dean Smith's newer generation stars also included George Karl, Steve Previs, Bob McAdoo, Dennis Wuycik, and Olympian Bob Jones. The 1970 champion Gamecocks were led by John Roche and Tom Riker, but it was Van Williford who led NC State to their upset in the ACC tournament. A year later the same South Carolina stars turned the tables on North Carolina during that typically mad week in Greensboro.

Perhaps the most exciting year in the ACC's history was 1973. North Carolina was the preseason favorite, but three challengers figured to be tough. Virginia, with young Wally Walker and Gus Gerard to go with All-American Barry Parkhill, proved disappointing. North Carolina State, on the other hand, might have been let down because NCAA probation prohibited postseason play. Olym-

*Quiet Norm Sloan in characteristic jacket and pose.*

*Lefty brought new excitement to Maryland from Davidson.*

*The Terps rose to power on the strengths of Elmore (left) and McMillen.*

pian center Tom Burleson and guard Monty Towe, 7 feet 4 inches and 5 feet 6 inches, respectively, were supposed to lead the Wolfpack, which was to have great depth as well. Instead, Norman Sloan came up with the player of the year, 6-foot 4-inch sophomore David Thompson, who looked like a young Oscar Robertson outside but leapt like a junior Elgin Baylor inside. With nothing to lose and nowhere to go, NC State simply played through the season and the ACC tourney without a loss.

The other power in the league was reigning NIT champion Maryland. Lefty Driesell had brought his formidable recruiting talents to College Park five years before and he now had an unprecedented collection of material: Olympian Tom McMillen, former Power Memorial schoolboy All-Americans Lenny Elmore and Jap Trimble, former high school All-American Tom Roy, former Illinois schoolboy player of the year Owen Brown, seniors Howard White, Jim O'Brien, Bob Bodell, and Darrell Brown, and two brilliant freshmen, Philadelphia schoolboy player of the year Mo Howard and Junior Davis Cupper from North Carolina John Lucas. Maryland seemed to suffer from an embarrassment of riches, overzealous press-agentry, and Coach Driesell's dogged adherence to the double-post offense he played in high school, played at Duke under Harold Bradley, and coached at two high schools and at Davidson. But the Terps' awesome firepower overcame these and a misfiring pressing defense to give Maryland a fine season, in which they earned second place in the conference schedule and the tournament, went to the finals of the Eastern Regionals, and played the game of the year against the Wolfpack.

The game was played in Cole Field House with a national TV audience preceding the Super Bowl, and it left fans gasping and sportswriters grasping for superlatives. McMillen got Maryland off in front, but Towe, Thompson, and Burleson opened up a 15-point lead for North Carolina State, Stoddard, Nuce, and Cafferky also hitting open shots. Then Maryland came back, as O'Brien, Lucas, and Elmore led the charge. Leading by 5, Maryland went into a stall—too soon. Some missed free throws gave NC State a chance, and the Pack came back. With seconds left and still 1 point up, Maryland's defense forced just the shot they wanted taken, Burleson from outside. It missed; but there was Thompson, soaring over the rim for the rebound, so high it looked like stop-action, and gently dropping it back through at the buzzer.

# 30

# *Traps for the Baron's Wildcats*

IT IS EASY to understand why the SEC has always been considered Kentucky's private reserve. Rupp's teams not only dominated the league but also proved their perennial excellence in ambitious intersectional scheduling. Rupp's players number almost half of all the SEC players who have won All-American honors and those who have gone on to professional careers. But the degree of dominance has not been so great within the conference as it has appeared from outside. All the other SEC schools peak for Kentucky, and the Wildcats have often had more trouble winning their own league than winning national recognition. Besides, for one reason or another, the SEC champion has sometimes not played in the postseason tournaments, yielding place usually to the Baron's charges.

Under Harry Rabenhorst, LSU had several outstanding teams and such star players as John Chaney, Frank Brian, and Joe Adcock even before Bob Pettit came along. Tennessee under Johnny Mauer and Emmett Lowery had Dick Mehen, Marshall Hawkins, Paul Walther, Art Burris, Carl Widseth, and Gene Tormohlen to test the Wildcats' mettle in Knoxville. In the Fifties, four coaches provided special challenges to Rupp in a conference where a single victory over Kentucky could make a season: Joel Eaves, Whack Hyder, Johnny Dee, and Babe McCarthy.

240

Eaves came to Auburn in 1950 and instituted a patterned continuity offense called the shuffle. Developed first by Bruce Drake at Oklahoma, who also originated the pass behind the endline to beat a full-court press, this attack weaved patiently in a basic 4–1 alignment designed to produce backdoor layups. Eaves's use of this pattern was so influential that it became known as the "Auburn Shuffle," and Eaves wrote the definitive textbook on it in 1960. It was designed, in Eaves's plan—like everything else in the SEC—to beat Kentucky.

Eaves reasoned that Kentucky normally gets twenty more shots than most opponents because of their traditional quick shooting and aggressive offensive rebounding. Therefore only a strict control game with high-percentage shooting could ever beat them. The Shuffle finally did the trick in 1958, Auburn's first-ever win over Kentucky. The Wildcats had their usual board strength with a front line of Ed Beck, Johnny Cox, and John Crigler, with Vern Hatton and Adrian Smith in backcourt. Rupp called this his "Fiddlin' Five," lamenting the absence of any real violinists. But he wasn't always such a music-lover: he once demanded that Artur Rubinstein rehearse somewhere else for a Memorial Coliseum concert so that his boys could concentrate on their practice.

When Auburn, playing strictly according to Eaves's discipline, beat Kentucky 64–63 in Birmingham, the Tigers had helped give the Wildcats their worst regular-season record in almost two decades. But Kentucky won the SEC anyway and then fiddled their way to the NCAA championship, whipping Miami of Ohio and Notre Dame with Tom Hawkins in the regionals. They beat Temple by a point on a last-minute basket by Hatton and faced Seattle in the finals. Castellani assigned Elgin Baylor to cover Crigler, and Rupp countered by having Crigler drive for the basket. Baylor drew three quick fouls and was rendered ineffective on defense and the boards. He scored 25 points, but Kentucky won 84–72.

A win over the national champions gave Auburn confidence. They had their best record ever in 1959, 20–2, led by Rex Frederick. But they were second best in the conference to Mississippi State, 24–1, to whom they gave their only beating. Yet they lost to Kentucky, who represented the league in the NCAA when

*Shuffle brought Eaves to top of SEC deck in 1960.*

Mississippi State declined to participate in the integrated event. In 1960 the shuffle again beat Kentucky, by a point, 61–60, and Auburn finally won the SEC title with an overall record of 19–3. But Auburn was on NCAA probation and couldn't go to the tournament. Georgia Tech replaced them, and the frustrated Eaves had to settle for the satisfaction of having beaten Rupp again and having kept out of the tournament a Kentucky team that had earlier beaten the eventual champion, Ohio State.

Hyder took over at Georgia Tech in 1952, and while the Engineers remained members in good standing of the SEC, had the remarkable anti-Rupp record of 9–15. No other coach ever beat the Baron nine times in ten years (1955–1964), including home-and-home sweeps in 1955, 1960, and 1963. These accomplishments are all the more remarkable in the light of the mediocre overall records of the Tech teams and the fact that only little Roger Kaiser in 1960 and 1961 was an outstanding player and All-American. Whack's strategy consisted primarily of getting five guys sky-high to go all the way against Kentucky and control the pace. Bobby Kimmel and Joe Helms did the damage in the first 1955 game that broke top-ranked Kentucky's home winning streak at 129. They scored 41 between them in the 59–58 win and then 44 in the 65–59 rematch victory in Atlanta. In 1958 Tech beat Kentucky's NCAA champs 71–52 as Terry Randall scored 26 points. In the 1960 sweep, Dave Denton led the way, as Hyder's defenders disrupted Kentucky's plays by pressuring the forwards. The 1963 sweep, including a double-overtime game in Lexington, helped Tech to a 21–5 record, far better than Kentucky's 16–9, but Mississippi State won the title.

Johnny Dee's four years at Alabama were climaxed by a 101–77 win over Kentucky in 1956. Dee had beaten Kentucky as a player (covering Beard for Notre Dame in 1946), and now in his third try he beat them as a coach. The win, paced by all-conference Jerry Harper's 37 points, was the first time anyone had scored a hundred against Kentucky, and it gave Alabama the SEC title (Harper was Alabama's first real star since Carl Schaeffer in the Forties). But Dee's starting five had been with him all four years in Tuscaloosa and were ineligible for the NCAA, so Kentucky went to the tournament anyway.

Babe McCarthy gave Rupp a lot of trouble, winning four of ten in his decade at Starkville (1956–1965), with another deliberate offense. For three years that offense was built around Bailey Howell, an overpowering one-on-one player, so that McCarthy designed his patterns to prevent any double-teaming. As a sophomore Howell got 37 against Kentucky, Johnny Ashmore added 25, and State beat the eventual SEC champs 89–81. As a senior, Howell had only 27, one under his seasonal average, but it paced a 66–58 win as State beat Kentucky for the SEC championship. Unfortunately, Howell was denied an NCAA tournament opportunity when his school declined to play against integrated teams. Kentucky as usual carried the SEC banner.

McCarthy won another title in 1961, though losing to Kentucky, but again

*Pettit looms above even the Wildcats in 1954.*

was kept from the NCAA. Kentucky won a playoff with Vanderbilt to get the bid, as Bill Lickert, Roger Newman, Larry Pursiful, Ned Jennings, and Dick Parsons all scored in double figures. Ohio State put them out in the regionals. A year later it was the same story: second-ranked Kentucky and ninth-ranked Mississippi State battling for the SEC title. The Bulldogs, led by W. D. Stroud, took an early lead and led 28–22 at halftime, infuriating the Lexington crowd with a spread-out shuffle style. McCarthy told his Maroons to dribble for 15 minutes and play defense for 5 in the second half, and they did, winning 49–44, hitting eighteen of twenty-six shots, mostly layups. Cotton Nash's 23 points weren't enough. At the end of the season these teams had tied for the league lead. The head-to-head win gave State the right to the tournament bid, but once again they declined, and once again Kentucky benefited.

The Mideast Regionals had a tough draw. Tony Hinkle's Butler team beat Bowling Green, despite big Nate Thurmond and high-scoring Howie Komives, but fell to Kentucky. Ohio State whipped Western Kentucky and then the top-ranked Buckeyes once again eliminated the Wildcats, despite Pursiful's 21 points, as Havlicek held Nash to 14 and Lucas scored 33. Nash was the first sophomore SEC scoring champ since Pettit, LSU's marvelous leader from 1952–1954.

Practically the only thing Pettit hadn't done in his career was beat Kentucky. He outscored Hagan 25–19 in the SEC tourney finals in 1952, but the Tigers lost 44–43. He led LSU to the SEC crown in 1953, but Kentucky did not play that season. LSU won the Eastern Regionals but fell to champion Indiana in the semis.

Then in 1954, in a playoff for the SEC, Hagan matched Pettit while Ramsey won it for Kentucky. This time it was Kentucky that declined the NCAA bid because of Hagan's, Ramsey's, and Tsioropoulos' ineligibilty; LSU lost to the regional champs from Penn State, but Pettit was everyone's All-American. The fact that he went on to be NBA rookie of the year next season and then MVP the season after that is a reasonable indication of the level of play in the SEC as everyone went gunning for the Baron.

In the Sixties another group of coaches arrived in the conference to try their hands at caging the Wildcats, including Roy Skinner, Ray Mears, Ken Rosemond, Press Maravich, and Tommy Bartlett. As an assistant to Bob Polk in 1959 and filling in for the ailing coach, Skinner had overseen a 75–66 upset of Kentucky. In his second year as head coach, 1963, he did it again, by 2 points in Lexington, helping to knock the Wildcats out of the SEC title. Ole Miss had classy Don Kessinger that year, but State won the championship. Finally they accepted the NCAA bid (and the law of the land) and fittingly were eliminated from the Mideast Regionals by the mostly black Ramblers from Loyola.

Skinner is a gentlemanly sportsman of a coach, and he likes to have his teams run the fast break and play tough man-to-man defense, even with big men in the middle. When he beats Kentucky, then, it is virtually at their own game, and he has had impressive success doing so. In an eight-year period, 1963–1970, Skinner and Rupp beat each other eight times. Led by Clyde Lee, Vandy swept Kentucky in 1965 en route to the SEC title, eventually losing to top-ranked Michigan in the regionals. Tommy Hagan, Bob Warren, and Roger Schurig led the 1967 sweep. In the 1969 and 1970 seasons, Kentucky lost only three conference games, and two of them to Vanderbilt, as Skinner got outstanding play from Hagan, Rudy Thacker, Perry Wallace, and Tom Arnholt.

*Hyder, Skinner, Rosemond, and Mears—a quartet of answers to the question of how to beat Kentucky.*

Ray Mears, Tennessee's coach since 1963 though he sat out that first year because of illness, has an entirely different conception of the game from Skinner's. An intense competitor who deploys any available showmanship for psychological value, Mears developed a 1–3–1 trap zone defense and a disciplined 1–3–1 patterned offense at Wittenberg College, and he has made only minor adjustments at Tennessee. Mears takes on prominent opposing personalities as a personal challenge, whether it's a team, a coach, or a player. Sometimes it has seemed as though the pride in winning a game has been secondary to that of winning a test of wills, like forcing Rupp into a zone defense, breaking the back of Skinner's fast break, or defensing Pete Maravich. And when Ken Rosemond came to Georgia in 1966, there was simply a battle of personalities that was waged on the court and in the press. But Mears has been a winner, largely because of his defensive genius and his ability to develop the skills of promising players.

His first stars were point-man Danny Schultz and high-post A. W. Davis. Rupp sprang a 1–3–1 trap of his own and beat the Vols twice. The Baron said, "We never have played a zone. That was a stratified, transitional, hyperbolic paraboloid defense." When Mears got a measure of revenge the following season, he credited Tennessee's win over Kentucky to an "iconoclastic defense with disharmonious tendencies." In 1966 Tennessee was the only team to beat Kentucky, Rupp's Runts, until the NCAA finals. Mears had some good big men on this team, Howard Bayne, Red Robbins, and Bobby Hoggsett, but it was Tennessee's greatest all-around athlete, Ron Widby, who won it from the high post.

The best proof of Mears's ability to develop the big man is Tom Boerwinkle, who progressed from massive immobility to competent pro prospect under Mears and their shared dedication. Along with Canadian Bob Croft, Knoxville's Billy Justus, Spook Hendrix, Billy Hann, and the ubiquitous Widby, Boerwinkle helped the Vols to the SEC title in 1967 when they swept Kentucky and second place in 1968 when they split with Kentucky. The 1967 Vols were edged by Dayton 53–52 in the regionals, as Don May outduelled Widby, and the 1968 Vols—after whipping Kentucky 87–59 in Knoxville—lost their league lead and a chance to repeat on a last-minute play by Jaracz and Issel at Lexington.

Only once more did Mears beat Rupp, in the 1971 game in Knoxville, when the Tennessee defense rendered Tom Payne inffective and the offense kept isolating Jimmy England for one-on-one jump shots. The Vols have challenged for the SEC title each year but have not quite made it since 1967. They have had their share of good players, little men like Mike Edwards and John Snow, bigger men like Larry Robinson, Don Johnson, and Len Kosmalski, and there have been others who got away, like Rudy Kinard, Larry Mansfield, and Rupert Breedlove; but their best performance was third place in the 1969 NIT, led by Billy Hann. Hann, a schoolboy All-American from Ohio, was perhaps the slickest all-around player ever to come to Tennessee. But Mears's system demanded an unselfish point man, and Hann spent three years as a playmaker, setting records for assists but

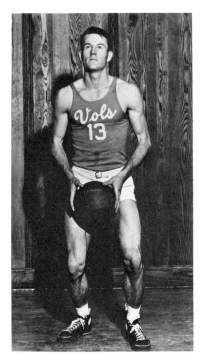

Harry Anderson.

Dick Mehen.

Paul Walther.

*Three decades of stars
in Tennessee's galaxy . . .*

A. W. Davis.

Ron Widby.

Carl Widseth.

Gene Tormohlen.

Danny Schultz.

Red Robbins.

Tom Boerwinkle.

Billy Hann, Jimmy England, Bill Justus.

losing his shooting touch, playing a disciplined college-type game to perfection but losing the natural playground skills that might have brought him a professional career.

Croft had been recruited for Tennessee by dynamic little Stu Aberdeen who replaced Tommy Bartlett as Mears's top assistant. Bartlett, who also coached Tennessee tennis but strengthened his elbow elsewhere, succeeded Norman Sloan at Florida, which seems to specialize in Vol coaches (for example, Johnny Mauer and Doug Dickey). Bartlett did even better against Rupp than Mears, splitting twelve decisions in six years (though the ailing Baron did not accompany the team to Gainesville for the 1971 loss). Mears's patterns were worked well by tall Gators like Gary Keller, Jeff Ramsey, Andy Owens, and All-American Neal Walk. Even more deliberate than Tennessee and Florida was Georgia under Rosemond since 1966, but everything was permissible against Kentucky. Only once did the stall work, in 1967, when the Bulldogs kept the score down to 8–6 at the half, winning 49–40 with Jim Youngblood and Bob Lienhard in control. Rosemond's only other win over Rupp was more satisfying: the Bulldogs ran with the Wildcats in Athens and beat the SEC champs 85–73 with Ronnie Hogue leading the way.

"Beat Kentucky" has always been the cry in the SEC, and coaches and players alike are made or broken by their performances against them. C. M. Newton (a Rupp alumnus) won at Alabama with Wendell Hudson as his star, and such prodigious scorers as Johnny Neumann of Ole Miss and John Mengelt of Auburn are among those who have risen to occasional splendor against the Wildcats. But only in one instance has national attention to SEC basketball been totally preempted from Kentucky, and that was during the reign of the Maraviches at LSU.

It was Jim Corbett, the LSU Athletic Director, who engineered the deal to bring Press and Pete to Baton Rouge and then died before seeing the results. It was a package deal—a five-year contract for the much-traveled coach, provided the Pistol would sign up. The arrangement was a mixed blessing. The coach father abandoned most of his disciplined-pattern ideas in order to showcase the player son. The result was much more scoring and publicity than winning. Pete had been given an extra year at Edwards Military Academy after his graduation from high school to develop his physical capacities and perfect his amazing talents. Then, in 1967, he came to LSU when his father made the move from North Carolina State.

While Press's first varsity squad won only three of twenty-six, Pete's freshman team won seventeen of eighteen. The one loss was 75–74 to Tennessee, with Kerry Myers guarding the Pistol in a zone-and-one defense and holding him way under his 43–point average. Perhaps everyone in Louisiana expected miracles, but they came only for the star and not for the team.

The Bayou Bengals got off to a good start in 1968, were 10–3 when they got into the heart of their SEC schedule. Then Kentucky beat them 121–95, Vanderbilt 99–91, Kentucky again 106–96, and Tennessee 87–67. The pattern was thus established for Pete's career: LSU would not beat the top teams in the conference; Maravich would roll up big individual totals, but the opponents would run up big margins; for Tennessee, Mears would devise a defense to stop the Pistol, and incidentally the Vols would win the game. In that first meeting, Billy Hann held Maravich to 21 (9 of 34 from the floor) before Pete fouled out while Press berated the officials. When the coach worked at it, he could find a winning strategy, as when he devised a combination defense to stop the Auburn shuffle, in a 76–72 LSU win. But that rarely seemed to the point; more satisfying was the Pistol's 59 against Alabama. He finished the season with a country-leading percentage of 43.8, but the team was a disappointing 14–12. And then Pete along with other hotshots Calvin Murphy and Rick Mount failed to make the Olympic squad.

The next year was better, and it was worse. Pete was MVP in the All-College Tournament in Oklahoma City, and he averaged 44.2 for the year. But LSU, starting 7–1, then lost five straight conference games and finished 13–13. Finally in 1970 they had a good year together. They upset Southern Cal 101–98 as Pete had 50, beat St. John's in the Rainbow Classic 80–70 as Pete outscored all the Redmen in the second half, and they finished 20–8 for an NIT bid. Never mind the 133–84 loss to UCLA, never mind the 97–94 loss to Yale, and never mind that LSU barely made the first division of the SEC—the NIT wanted the Pistol in the Garden. But he misfired: only 20 as they beat Georgetown 83–82 with Danny Hester scoring 30, the only time in his college career that Pete was outscored by a teammate; 37 in the 97–94 win over Oklahoma; and 20 again as Marquette eliminated them 101–79.

His senior average was 44.5, his three-year total 3,667—records for a father to be proud of, but little solace to a coach who wanted to win games. The problems were many. Pete had a whole arsenal of offensive moves, not just shooting but passing, dribbling, and even rebounding. But he played over the heads of his teammates instead of with them, and he played a gambling, free-lancing defense. There was good college material there, with Hester, Jeff Tribbett, Bill Newton, and Apple Sanders, but they were never integrated with their star. The coach had never put the potent ingredients together in a coherent whole, but the father had provided a showcase for his son's solo talents that produced a seven-figure pro contract.

But the Maraviches, like the Pettits and the Howells, come and go, while the big story in the SEC remained Adolph Rupp. With the level of play improved throughout the league and everyone gunning for the Baron, he still managed to lead Kentucky to conference championships in his last five years as coach. After the disappointing 1967 season, when injuries to Pat Riley left the Wildcats with little help for Dampier and Thad Jaracz, help came in the tripartite form of Mike Casey, Mike Pratt, and Dan Issel. Issel became Rupp's best-shooting big man ever and led Kentucky into three Mideast Regionals, where they lost in successive years to Ohio State, Marquette, and Jacksonville.

Finally there were Larry Steele, Tom Parker, Tom Payne, Kent Hollenbeck, and Jim Andrews to carry the Baron through to compulsory retirement after the 1972 season. His 874 wins are not likely to be surpassed, and his winning percentage of .821 will take some beating too. That Joe Hall, in his first year in the Baron's seat, was able to take the Wildcats to another title as further tribute to Rupp's judgment. The Kentucky tradition seems self-perpetuating, and the present plans for a palatial new coliseum are not likely to hurt, especially with the pervasive spirit of the Baron as a constant inspiration.

*With Tom Parker after last home game, the Baron with heart full.*

# 31

# *Big Ten: Contact*

THE MYSTIQUE of Big Ten basketball has several elements to it. First, there is the tradition: dating back to the formation of the Western Conference in 1905, these schools contributed mightily to the early development of the game. Raycroft's teams at Chicago, with Schommer and Page, Meanwell's at Wisconsin, Olsen's at Ohio State, and Lambert's at Purdue set standards of style and excellence that influenced large areas of the country. Star players and coaches carried the tradition with them, extending the dominance of the Big Ten's reputation: John Wooden, Osborne Cowles, Bennie Oosterbaan, Dutch Lonborg, Everett Dean, Branch McCracken, Sam Barry, Harry Combes, Tippy Dye, John Kundla, Lou Boudreau, Tom Harmon, and Otto Graham are some of the prominent names up to World War II.

No doubt the football prominence of the conference helped, not only by attracting outstanding athletes, but also concretely by building ample fieldhouses from huge stadium successes. Moreover, the comparatively early emphasis on recruiting black football players by some Big Ten schools has made the pitch go down easier with black basketball prospects. Two final elements in the mystique may have borrowed coloration from football as well: that Big Ten basketball is the roughest in the country, with more contact allowed and expected, and that (perhaps because of this) it provides the best training ground for professional basketball.

The record hardly supports the total image here projected. The influence of coaches with Big Ten backgrounds is unquestionably extensive, but it is far from monolithic. Meanwell's and Lambert's patterns themselves could constitute a workable set of polarities. Dean and Barry brought quite different styles to the Pacific Coast, Wooden's made a third, and Cowles went east with his own brand from the Big Ten irons. It is the size, the duration, and the comparative success of the basketball programs at Big Ten schools that matters, not a consistent way of playing the game.

Since the initiation of the NCAA tournament, the Big Ten champion has survived the regionals fifteen times in thirty-five tries. When there were only two regionals, East and West, only three Big Ten teams (the first three) went to the finals out of thirteen, runner-up Ohio State and champions Indiana in 1940 and Wisconsin in 1941, though in all fairness the Illinois Whiz Kids in 1943 would have been the class of the tournament. That was the only year the Big Ten was not represented, and it was their own choice, a bow to wartime austerity.

Since 1952 the Big Ten champion has had an automatic placing in the Mideast Regional semifinals and has failed to survive almost half the time. More often than not, the tournament performance has placed them lower than the polls had them. Of the twelve Mideast champions, seven have gone on to the finals and two have won. In 1953 Indiana lived up to its top ranking, and in 1960 Ohio State won in a mild upset. The greatest disappointments were the failures of top-ranked Ohio State in 1961 and 1962 and Michigan in 1965.

The intent here is merely to put the Big Ten in perspective, not to minimize its considerable contributions. It is well to remember that Ohio State and Northwestern played to a record crowd of 22,822 in Chicago Stadium in 1946, but that they were the preliminary game to the feature between Notre Dame and DePaul. A year later the conference contributed to another record of sorts: Purdue led Wisconsin 35–34 at half-time when the whole bleachers collapsed; two weeks later the game was completed and Wisconsin won 72–60 for the longest comeback win in the books.

Certainly worthy of note are some of the star individual players and outstanding coaches in the last two decades of Big Ten basketball. And more extensive mention should be made of the great teams from Ohio State in the early Sixties and Michigan in the mid-Sixties. At Michigan State a distinguished sequence of coaches has presided. Pete Newell spent four seasons in East Lansing before returning to the West Coast. He was followed by Forddy Anderson, who had coached at Drake and Bradley, but brought a Big Ten tradition with him from his own college training under Indiana's Everett Dean at Stanford. Anderson is known as the leading proponent of the change of direction on offense. According to Bernie Bickerstaff, himself a product of the Pete Newell–Scotty McDonald–Phil Woolpert tradition on the West Coast, that's what team offense is all about: get the defense moving one way, then change direction and go to the hoop. Anderson led the Spartans to their first league title in 1957 and again in 1959, with Jack Quiggle and jumping Johnny Green their first All-Americans since Al Ferrari.

In 1966 John Benington took over. He had played for Newell on the San Francisco NIT champions, but after almost a decade in the Missouri Valley at Drake and St. Louis, his system was less deliberate than his mentor's and thus not so drastic a change from Anderson's. At Benington's untimely death just before the 1970 season, his assistant Gus Ganakas inherited the team and all-star Ralph Simpson. With his son Gary at guard, Gus became another in a long line of coaches to have his son play for him. And with Ganakas teamed with high-scoring Mike Robinson, the Spartan backcourt was outscored only by Notre Dame's Brokaw and Clay in two years. Early in his senior year Robinson became Michigan State's all-time leading scorer, surpassing Julius McCoy and Stan Washington.

At Minnesota, where Cowles had produced jump shooters like Skoog, Garmaker, Mencel, and Kalafat, John Kundla returned to his alma mater and had considerable success with Archie Clark and Lou Hudson as stars playing in the penumbra of Michigan's conquering heroes. Later, Jim Brewer and Ron Behagen were towers of strength for the Gophers. At Purdue, Mel Taube and Ray Eddy carried on the fast-breaking tradition of their mentor, Piggy Lambert, but without outstanding success. George King moved over from West Virginia with his own Kentuckiana style in 1966 and finally produced a title in 1969. Boilermaker stars were Bill Keller, Terry Dischinger, Dave Schellhase, Rick Mount, and Herm Gil-

*Two Michigan State Coaches: Anderson (left) and Benington.*

*Hottest of the Boilermakers were Terry Dischinger, Dave Schellhase, Rick Mount, and Herm Gilliam.*

liam, all cut in the mold of running, shooting, high-scoring Hoosier basketball.

Down the road in Bloomington, the Hoosiers themselves were running under Branch McCracken's direction right through the 1965 season. Indiana couldn't repeat the national championships of 1940 and 1953, though they had powerful teams in 1954, 1960, and 1965. Bill Tosheff, Archie Dees, George McGinnis, and Walter Bellamy were some of their stars, though more typical of their hustling style were Bob Leonard, Jon McGlocklin, and the Van Arsdale twins. After some lean years, in 1972 they hired Bobby Knight, whose emphasis on defense and control had made Army a consistent winner, and he led them to the NIT under their altered style (and relaxed conference rules) and to the NCAA final four in 1973.

At Illinois, Harry Combes held sway for twenty years. His predecessor Doug Mills had coached him his senior year, and they both had been coached by Craig Ruby, who in turn had been coached by Doc Meanwell at Missouri. This line of descent may account for the somewhat more disciplined patterning of the Illini teams. Andy Phillip of the Whiz Kids was probably their best advertisement, though several subsequent products have been outstanding, including Skip Thoren, Don Freeman, Jerry Colangelo, Wally Osterkorn, Dave Downey, Don Ohl, Dave Scholz, and especially Big Red, John Kerr. Most recently the Spoon, Nick Weatherspoon, has eclipsed all the Illini scoring records under Coach Harv Schmidt.

Over at Iowa City, Bucky O'Connor's teams in the Fifties finished fourth and second to San Francisco, with Deacon Davis, Bill Logan, and Sugar Cain.

254

Sharm Scheuerman, who succeeded O'Connor in 1959, also played on those teams, and Iowa went on to produce such fine players as Don Nelson, Don Smith, George Peeples, and Fred Brown. Illinois and Iowa are also famous for the ones that got away: Jerry Sloan, who could not focus his fierce powers of concentration on the huge Champaign campus and transferred to little Evansville, where he felt more at home, though he credits Coach Combes with teaching him a great deal about defense; and Connie Hawkins, the booty of one of the most outrageous recruiting wars, who was booted back to Bedford-Stuyvesant without due process, never having played a varsity game for the Hawkeyes.

But the Big Ten's still considerable reputation for basketball excellence rests on the great teams at Ohio State and Michigan, while its reputation for permissible contact has been enhanced by the infamous Ohio State–Minnesota confrontation. Fred Taylor is the coach who took Ohio State to its NCAA championship, but it was Floyd Stahl who began to assemble the team that won it. Tippy Dye had had Dick Schnittker and Bob Donham in Columbus, then Neil Johnston, and Stahl had Paul Ebert, Robin Freeman, and Frank Howard. Taylor, however, put it all together with senior Joe Roberts, junior All-American Larry Siegfried, and three sophomores, Jerrry Lucas, John Havlicek, and Mel Nowell.

These three, along with Gary Gearheart, had played together as Ohio's high school all-stars in their annual series with Kentucky and Indiana. The object of vigorous recruiting campaigns, they all decided to stay together at the home school.

McCracken with Van Arsdales, Dick at left, Tom at
right—or is that Tom left, Dick right?

Harv Schmidt (33), now Illinois coach, looks
for a call while Jumpin' Johnny Green performs.

Taylor had played for Dye, and there was some Meanwell thinking in his lineage,
but he preferred the running game and had the gunning crew to handle it. Taylor, however, was a thorough and driving leader, so that his Ohio State teams
could run precise patterns to beat any kind of press or zone in case their fast break
and free-lancing offenses were stymied. On defense they simply outmanned their
opponents, especially the Nowell-Siegfried combination at guard. Like many great
teams, this one was a blend of complementary talents with unselfish players, bench
strength, and confidence in each other carefully instilled by Taylor's thoroughness.

In the 1960 season they won twenty-five while losing only three en route to
the Big Ten and national titles. They peaked at tournament time, beat Western
Kentucky by 19, Georgia Tech by 17, and NYU by 22. In the finals, with Lucas
stifling Darrall Imhoff, they beat Newell's Cal team at their own disciplined
game by 20 points, 75–55. The only regret was that they never faced Oscar Robertson and Cincinnati, who felt snubbed by Ohio State's refusal to play them—Cal
had dominated the Bearcats in the semis. If there ever had been a doubt about
the greatness of this Ohio State team, however, it was dispelled in the championship game when they shot 84 percent from the floor during the first half and
almost 70 percent for the whole game as thirteen Buckeyes played.

256

The next year Ohio State seemed even better. Richie Hoyt replaced Roberts in the front line, and they still had Gearheart and future coach Bobby Knight on the bench. Their twenty-seven straight wins took them to the number one ranking and the NCAA finals, including a narrow win over Peck Hickman's Louisville team that surprised them with a slowdown and easy, running wins over Kentucky and St. Joseph's. The finals matched them at long last against second-ranked Cincinnati. Lucas outplayed Hogue and Siegfried's shooting kept them in the game, but Jucker's patterns worked to perfection and Ohio State lost in overtime.

If there was any falling off the following year, the record barely revealed it. Only one loss during the season marred their drive toward a rematch with Cincinnati and sweet revenge. Dick Reasebeck took Siegfried's place at guard and Doug McDonald joined Lucas and Havlicek in the front line. Gearheart was still available and a strengthened bench also had Jim Doughty, Don Elatt, and big Gary Bradds. In the NCAA, Western Kentucky tried triple-teaming Lucas, as Ed Diddle hoped Hickman's strategy would work for him. It worked on Lucas, but the open men more than made up the difference this time; they won 93–73. Third-ranked Kentucky went down 74–64 as Havlicek picked Cotton Nash apart, and then Wake Forest 84–68 with Lucas dominating Len Chappell.

The end of the Lucas-Havlicek-Nowell era was not as programmed in Columbus, however. Lucas got hurt in the semis and was less than half-speed for the finals. Bradds picked up the slack, but again second-ranked Cincinnati executed their game to perfection and won a clear-cut victory 71–59. Ohio State has never regained that level, though they finished a surprising third in the 1968 NCAA and won the Big Ten in 1971, eliminating second-ranked Marquette before losing the Mideast Regionals to Western Kentucky. Bill Hosket, Dave Sorenson, Luke Witte, Allan Hornyak, and Jim Cleamons have been outstanding players who have kept them close to the Big Ten top, though their greatest notoriety came in a violent three-ring ruckus in 1972.

Michigan meanwhile had taken over as the dominant school in the conference. Ron Kramer and George Lee had been stars in Ann Arbor, but it wasn't until Dave Strack's fourth year as coach, 1963, that they challenged Ohio State and Illinois for the title. Strack had been an assistant at Michigan for eleven years under Cowles, Ernie McCoy, and Bill Perigo, and he had played for Oosterbaan, so that he was a died-in-the-wool Wolverine. When he returned from one year at Idaho to take over at Ann Arbor, he began recruiting in earnest in the spring of 1961 and brought Larry Tregoning, George Pomey, and Bill Buntin into the fold. A year later he signed Oliver Darden, Jim Myers, John Clawson, John Thompson, and Cazzie Russell to complete the black-dominated bonanza. This is the squad that brought three straight Big Ten titles to Ann Arbor.

The first came in 1964 when their 23–5 record took them to the second ranking in both polls. They won the Mideast Regionals but missed a showdown with top-ranked UCLA when third-ranked Duke upset them in the semis 91–80. With

*Cazzie the wonderful Wolverine (33) and Buntin (22).*

virtually the entire squad back, they held number one ranking throughout the 1965 season. After an early 1-point loss to Nebraska, Cazzie really got them going against Dave Stallworth and a tough Wichita State team. Trailing for most of the game, Michigan came back to win 87–85 when Cazzie scored 23 points in the last 9 minutes, including a long jump shot at the buzzer.

During the Christmas break Michigan came to New York for the Holiday Festival Tournament. There, in the semifinals, the long-awaited confrontation between Russell and Bill Bradley occurred; only they never played head-on because Bradley had to match up against one of the bigger Wolverines. For 36 minutes, Bradley was superb, rebounding, assisting, holding Darden down, and scoring 41 points. When he fouled out, Princeton led by 13. Strack switched to a 3–1–1 zone press, forcing Princeton into constant errors when they could not pass or even see over the pressure of Michigan's big front line. And Cazzie took over the game. In a 66-second span he made two steals, one assist, and 6 points to cut the margin to 4, with 2½ minutes left. Van Breda Kolff tried to steady his Tigers, but Cazzie had all the answers. His 3-point play tied the game in the last minute and then, with 3 seconds left, his jump shot won it.

In the finals against St. John's, Michigan had the tables turned by Lapchick's Redmen. With 9 minutes to play and trailing by 16, St. John's applied the identical defense, the "3–1–1 half-court combination press" as Lapchick called it. They caught Michigan and beat them 75–74, and Lapchick went on to finish his final season with yet another upset win in the NIT over Villanova. Michigan meanwhile went about their business of winning the Big Ten and retaining their ranking in the polls. They lost only once more during the season and went into the NCAA as the favorites. In the regionals, Dayton was easy, but Vanderbilt extended them to an 87–85 win. Cazzie needed 11 points in the last 7 minutes to save the game.

Despite Bradley's heroics the rematch with Princeton in the semis wasn't close. In the other bracket UCLA breezed by Wichita State, which had done remarkably well after Stallworth's graduation, with Kelly Pete and Jamie Thompson taking up the slack. In the finals Michigan fell before UCLA 91–80 as Goodrich's 42 points (including eighteen free throws) dwarfed Russell's 28. Michigan led early in the game, but when Kenny Washington replaced injured Keith Erickson, he turned it around with steals and long-range shooting as UCLA pulled away to 47–34 at the half. That was as close as Michigan would come to the title, though Russell led them to the regionals again in 1966. There top-ranked Kentucky shot them down in the finals, and they have not been back since—though Rudy Tomjanovich and Henry Wilmore, under new coach Johnny Orr, have brought them winning seasons.

Big Ten basketball has at least as much variety as any other conference. Traditions of Kentuckiana style at Purdue, Illinois, Ohio State, and Indiana are as likely to be flouted by disciplined game plans as followed by running up high scores. The reputation for muscle and contact can be matched in actual play in the Missouri Valley, in the Big Eight, or among neighboring independents like Toledo, Dayton, Marquette, and Notre Dame. This myth along with that of basketball as a noncontact sport can be dispelled anywhere in the country, as the legacy of the playground comes to Connecticut with Toby Kimball, to Miami of Ohio with Wayne Embry, to Louisville with Wes Unseld, to SMU with Jim Krebs, to Houston with Elvin Hayes, to Western Kentucky with Jim McDaniels, to Tennessee with Tom Boerwinkle, and to South Carolina with a series of imported bogarders.

But the Big Ten maintains its tradition and has ways of breathing new life into it. It carries over from the gridiron where Ohio State's Woody Hayes is known as the coach who put the foot into football coaching and where his apt pupil Bo Schembeckler at Michigan treats national TV audiences to violent sideline tantrums. Worst of all, it comes from the sorry spectacle of the spitting, kicking, punching, and wrestling brawl between Ohio State and Minnesota during their nationally televised game in 1972. The game was crucial as they fought for conference honors, and Bill Musselman had his team so high that they were at an emotional breaking point for the Buckeyes. Fred Taylor's big men easily prodded or pushed them over, and when the violence came it had the ugly overtones of a racial rumble on top of the schoolyard fracas.

The very physical and emotional nature of the game as it is now played (bearing some resemblance still to the indoor-rugby aspect of its original conception) makes such outbursts likely, particularly under the pressures of rival polarities and the all-too-frequent inconsistencies of officiating. But even in the playground itself, the sporting nature of basketball usually maintains its own order, and in organized play other factors keep the lid on potentially explosive stuff. The coaches concentrate mainly on execution, and the players have more to lose than the games by outbursts. Even in the Big Ten a player soon learns how much contact the heavy traffic under the boards and in the lane will bear.

# 32

# *The Elegant Ivies*

DESPITE a practice of athletic deemphasis in recent decades, the Ivy League has retained more than its fair share of publicity. Whether it is the aura of ancient and honorable tradition or a matter of snob appeal getting to sportswriters, especially in the East, no outstanding performer among the Ivies fails to get noticed and good notices at that. There is a mystique here, too: that the Ivy League is the last refuge of pure amateur sport on the college level, that its teams perform in a classy and classic style, and that basketball being a game for the quick-witted players the intellectual centers should produce the sharpest teams. A number of talented players have given some substance to these ethereal notions, though the matter of distinctiveness may be called in question.

As far as coaching is concerned, the Ivy League seems to have had as its most outstanding mentors men who have earned their fame elsewhere—Ken Loeffler, Howard Hobson, Butch van Breda Kolff, Jack McCloskey, Howie Dallmar, Doggie Julian, Dave Gavitt, Lou Rossini—or in other fields—Red Rolfe, Elmer Lampe, Rip Engle, and Weeb Ewbank. The exceptions are Osborne Cowles, who successfully perpetuated a dynasty at Dartmouth; Gordon Ridings, who guided Columbia to the top of the league in his first two years as coach (1947–1948); and more recently Dick Harter, who has led Penn to legitimately high national ranking, perhaps more for competing successfully among Philadelphia's Big Five than for leading the Ivies. But for the most part it has been the players, rather than teams or coaches, who have captured the attention of press and public and kept the traditions alive.

Back in the late Forties there were many Ivy League players competing for All-American honors and even getting professional contracts: Dartmouth's Audley Brindley, George Munroe, and Ed Leede; Cornell's Ed Peterson and Nat Militzok; Harvard's Wyndol Gray and Saul Mariaschin; Penn's Howie Dallmar and Frank Crossin; Brown's George Grimshaw and Coulby Gunther; and Columbia's Walt Budko, Norm Skinner, and John Azary. At Princeton, contrasting teammates were van Breda Kolff, with his dogged, hustling play, and Bud Palmer, with his casual flamboyance and pioneer jump-shooting. And it may not be stretching the vine too far to include Colgate's Carl Braun and Ernie Vandeweghe.

The most elegant of this vintage was Yale's Tony Lavelli who for four years received some All-American notice and was considered the best player in New England, though Kaftan and Cousy were playing for Holy Cross at the time. Lavelli, who played the accordion as well as basketball, had a graceful, balletic move that made his sweeping hook shot beautiful to behold and difficult to stop. Since he had great range with the shot and a delicate touch with a one-hand foul shot, his scoring was prodigious. Yet it is a mistake to suppose that such grace was typical of the play in the league. Even at Yale, for one of Lavelli's years he was teamed in the front line with Paul Walker, an All-American end whose rugged play in the Payne Whitney Gym bore resemblances to what might be seen in the Bowl, in the playgrounds, or in the Big Ten.

Lavelli's failure in the pros gave some credence to the notion that Ivy League basketball was a thing apart, a noncontact activity for effete intellectuals. But he was a slim 6 feet 3 inches, lacking the strength to play forward and the speed and skill to play guard. He was unique, by no means typical of his league except for the disproportionate publicity he received. In his senior year he finally led Yale to a league championship, though they failed to survive the first round of the NCAA. Indeed, from Dartmouth's 1944 win in the Eastern Regionals it was twelve years until an Ivy League team won another NCAA tournament game (Dartmouth won one in 1956, two in 1958, Princeton one in 1961, one in 1964) and twenty-one years until one survived the Eastern Regionals (Princeton, in Bradley's senior year).

The next generation had fewer players who drew serious attention, though there were some good ones who perhaps should have, like Penn's Jack McCloskey, Brown's Mo Mahoney, and Princeton's Mike Kearns. Dave Sisler was noticed at Princeton, but not because of his basketball playing, and his fellow pitcher and future teammate, Pete Burnside, who was probably the best basketball player in his time at Dartmouth, wasn't eligible because of his baseball contract. Most of the attention went to Ernie Beck. He had the statistics, leading the league in scoring and rebounding for three years and ranking high nationally as well. His baseline turn-around jump shots were very accurate, and by his senior year (1953) he had brought Penn a conference championship and himself a first-team All-American berth. But though he was stronger and closer to the model of pro players than Lavelli, he was never better than mediocre in five seasons for the Warriors. Beck dominated the Ivies in weak years, his statistics won him the honors, and in fact he was never the dominant player on the court that he was on paper.

An exact contemporary of Beck was better, Jack Molinas of Columbia. Molinas was as good as he wanted to be whenever he wanted to be. He would beat Beck head to head and not bother elsewhere because he wasn't challenged. His inconsistency was testimony to the lowered quality of play in the league. Molinas, when motivated, was the complete player, and he was equally at home in a thinking game in Cambridge or a playground game in Brooklyn. If deception, as Leonard Koppett would have it, is the essence of the game, Molinas was the essential player, deceptively strong, fast, quick, accurate, canny, and perceptive. But his moves were choreographed to a beat that defied all systems, and we'll never know how good he was or could have been.

It was during this period that Doggie Julian pulled off one of the biggest upsets in New England basketball history. The game attracted little attention at the time, a dismal winter on the Hanover plain, when Holy Cross, coached by Buster Sheary, lost to Dartmouth, coached by Sheary's predecessor. Holy Cross was between the peaks of the Kaftan-Cousy teams and the Heinsohn teams, but with Togo Palazzi, Ronnie Perry, and Earle Markey they were still on their way to a 20–6 season that would carry them to the Eastern Regional final against LSU with Bob Pettit. They had beaten Dartmouth seven straight times, twelve of the last thirteen, and Julian had never beaten his old school. Dartmouth, on the other hand, was going through its longest slump, its fifth straight year of losing records and second division among the Ivies. Memorial Gym was virtually deserted for home basketball games, and even the Crusaders didn't attract many fans.

But this time Julian had the Green ready, and led by captain Fred Gieg they shot with unwonted accuracy and defended with desperate diligence. By halftime they held a 4-point lead, and with the news spreading across the campus and students pouring into the gym they grimly held on through the second half. Holy Cross was frustrated mostly because Dartmouth never let up and never hit the cold streak that was habitual to Hanover. The final score was 67–61, and it is a good measure of the dimensions of the miracle to note that in their return match in Worcester Holy Cross beat Dartmouth the way they should have, 99–50.

When Dartmouth regained their accustomed eminence, it was on the rugged shoulders of Rudy LaRusso, who personified the return of the Ivies to the mainstream of big-time basketball. In the mid-Fifties the biggest story in the league was the prodigious scoring of little Chet Forte for Columbia, and there were

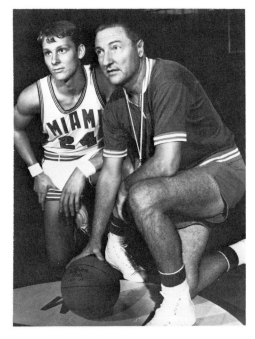

When Doggie Julian coached son Toby at Dartmouth, they joined a throng of father-son combinations, including the Maraviches of LSU, the McGuires of Marquette, and father-in-law Bruce Hale and son-in-law Rick Barry of Miami, and the Allens of Kansas, the Keaneys of Rhode Island, the Enkes of Arizona, the Ganakases of Michigan State.

*One of a long tradition of Dartmouth
All-Americans, Gus Broberg in 1941.*

*TV producer Chet Forte was a mighty
productive scorer for Columbia.*

other creditable showings by Bart Leach at Penn, Johnny Lee at Yale, and Gerry
Alaimo at Brown. But LaRusso restored credibility to the whole league. The only
thing elegant about his style was the way he could take complete command of a
game when it counted, as in the final minutes of the 1959 playoff with Princeton
to determine the championship and the NCAA bid. At 6 feet 8 inches and 220
pounds, with the intimidating moves at both ends of the court bred of his Brooklyn playground background, LaRusso was the picture of a contemporary professional player and stepped directly into the NBA without any loss of stature.

In the Sixties and into the Seventies the Ivies have on occasion ranked high
in the polls and even been favored to win a game or two in the Eastern Regionals. In 1972 their runner-up accepted an NIT bid. Among the outstanding players
were Columbia's Dave Newmark and Jim McMillian; Penn's Dave Wohl, Corky
Calhoun, and Bob Morse; and Princeton's Brian Taylor, Geoff Petrie, and John
Hummer. But the biggest story of all was 1965's college player of the year, probably the college player of the decade, perhaps the Ivy League player of all time,
and the apotheosis of basketball elegance—Bill Bradley.

It is difficult to avoid superlatives in talking about Bradley. Too many experienced observers have singled out his performances as the greatest they ever saw.
Bradley had the basketball disadvantage of growing up rich in Crystal City, Missouri. But his long hours of practice at his own backyard basket and in school
gyms made up for any loss of schoolyard competition. And all the thinking he did

Mens sana in corpore sano, *in spades:*
*Mr. Bradley (42) of Princeton.*

*LaRusso* (left) *toys with Dave Gavitt, now
coach at Providence.*

about the game made up for his being essentially a loner. One of the most cerebral of athletes, he became an accomplished team player by the way he perceives patterns abstractly. Among the primary elements of his game are these: a natural shooting touch, perfected by diligent practice and deliberate concentration; the size and reach to rebound, enhanced by a fine sense of timing and concentrated attention on position; the hands and eyes to make passes and plays that are like the computerized comprehension of immediate situations and variables; and the will to keep moving at both ends of the court that enables him to run faster players into the ground or out of the gym. No wonder Walt Hazzard, his Olympic teammate, paid him the supreme compliment of calling him "the white O."

After leading Princeton to the league title in van Breda Kolff's first year as coach, Bradley almost got them by St. Joseph's in the NCAA first round. He scored 40 points and held Tom Wynne to 9 before fouling out with less than 4 minutes to play. In his junior year he averaged over 30 points a game and again led Princeton to the Ivy championship and the NCAA. This time they beat VMI in the opener before losing by 2 points to Connecticut as rookie coach Fred Schabel's deliberate game plan provided the upset.

As a senior Bradley was even better. Against top-ranked Michigan he did everything but operate the clock for 36 minutes. He rebounded, set up plays for Princeton scores, held big Oliver Darden to 1 point, scored 41 himself, and left Princeton with a 13-point lead when he fouled out. The Garden crowd gave him

a 2-minute standing ovation. That Michigan had the explosive power to pull that game out is only further testimony to the greatness of Bradley's performance. Joe Lapchick said, "I have never seen one player so humiliate a whole team, and a top-ranked team at that." Princeton won the Ivy League again and this time the Eastern Regionals as well.

In the first round they beat Penn State, John Egli's best team in all his fourteen seasons at University Park, 60–58. Then Press Maravich had North Carolina State try a zone press, but Bradley handled it with aplomb and Princeton won 68–40. Maravich thought that the Wolfpack was hypnotized from the way everyone was watching Bradley. The regional final matched them with fourth-ranked Providence, who had just knocked off third-ranked St. Joseph's. But Bradley not only scored 41 points but also inspired great play from teammates Robbie Brown, Ed Hummer, Gary Walters, Bob Haarlow, and Don Rodenbach; Princeton won 109–69.

Even Bradley could not make the rematch with Michigan close. He scored 29, to Cazzie Russell's 28, but Buntin, Darden, and Tregoning all had more than the next high scorer from Princeton. Bradley fouled out with 6 minutes left, and Michigan coasted to a 93–76 win. His final game was the consolation match with Wichita State. With 9 minutes left, Bradley had 32 points and Princeton an 84–58 lead. In the next 4 minutes he added 8 points but picked up his fourth personal and expected to come out when Princeton called time. But van Breda Kolff, with his other players' eager assent, said, "Bill, this is your last chance; for once, be a gunner." He was, and he couldn't miss. He shot eight times—jump shots, hook shots, and driving layups—and made them all, plus two free throws. His 58 points and twenty-two field goals broke Oscar's 1958 NCAA records, his 177 points in five games beat West's 1959 record, Princeton's 118 beat West Virginia's record, their forty-eight field goals beat a UCLA record, and their 173 field goals in the tournament beat Loyola's 1963 record by twenty-one.

In this case the statistics bear out the greatness of Bradley's performance, but they fail to indicate his excellence as a team player. After two years at Oxford on a Rhodes Scholarship, Bradley's playing on the Knickerbockers would demonstrate the completeness of his game. While his accurate shooting in key situations would contribute to his new nickname "Dollar Bill," his main contribution to the team was playmaking, passing, moving without the ball. Bradley had finally found a home on a team that could act out the finer patterns of his distant cerebration.

# 33

# *The Big Little Men of PC*

SPORTS, like all other forms of surrogate religions, are both rich in rituals and profligate in the production of traditions. It is difficult to say exactly when a practice, drill, or routine becomes a ritual, that is, when it passes from a purely practical action over into a ceremonious repetition or celebratory reenacting of the original usefulness. Often it is simply a superstitious belief in an efficacy that was likely to have been coincidental with the particular action. But in sports, the transition from a perceived pattern to a tradition is obvious, because it is instantaneous with the repetition of the pattern.

Providence College (PC), a small Dominican school, started basketball in its fourth year of existence, 1921, and began winning some games six years later, including an upset of St. John's. Ed Crotty, a Notre Dame man, began coaching in 1928 and within a year had established a winning tradition while scheduling some of the major powers in the area. During his eleven-year tenure he won almost 70 percent of his games, including big wins over Dartmouth, Holy Cross, Yale, Harvard, Princeton, Manhattan, St. John's, Seton Hall, Rhode Island, Brown, and Villanova. Indeed, CCNY was the only big one that got away from the Friars without a defeat. Their first prominent star was high-scoring Eddie Wineapple in 1929, and the next was John Krieger who led the win over the St. John's Wonder Five that was their only loss in 1930. Allen Brachen followed in 1933 as the Friars continued to attract national attention.

PC resumed its winning tradition in 1956 when Joe Mullaney, who had learned his winning ways during championship play at Holy Cross under Doggie Julian, took over. By this time the NIT draw was largely made up of Catholic schools, but it took four impressive years for the Friars to beg a bid. In 1958 they had beaten Boston College, who went to the NCAA, and St. John's, who went to the NIT, and lost by a total of 4 points to Fordham and St. Francis of Pennsylvania, two other NIT teams. The breakthrough came in 1959, when they could no longer be denied, having beaten three tourney-bound teams in an 18–5 season, and they went on to postseason play for nine consecutive years.

The difference came in the form of an instant tradition, that of the dominant little man, the Providence guard who would control an entire game. The first was Lenny Wilkens, who went about his domination in such a quietly competent and consistent way that you didn't notice he was leading in points, in assists, and in steals in virtually every game. In short, he was already perfecting the skills that would make him many times an NBA all-star. It was Wilkens who led PC to fourth place in the NIT, losing to champion St. John's in the semis.

The next year they were even bettter, beating St. Joseph's, the best of the Big Five, and going into the NIT with a streak of eighteen out of nineteen. This time Wilkens, a senior, played costar to junior John Egan, as spectacular as Lenny was efficient. Egan was a fiery 6-footer who could suddenly break a game open with a flurry of brilliant plays—shots, drives, passes, steals—all performed at a kind of fever pitch that would inspire his team, excite the crowd even in the Garden, and demoralize his opponents. Three times Egan and Wilkens brought the Friars from behind, to beat Memphis State, St. Louis (who had beaten them early in the season), and seventh-ranked Utah State. But in the finals fourth-ranked Bradley was too much for them. They stopped Chet Walker with 9 points, but Mack Herndon, Mike Owens, Dan Smith, and Alpha Saunders all scored in double figures, as the Braves came from 12 down to win. Egan had 20 points but only five field goals and was never permitted to perform any of his charismatic prestidigitation. Wilkens, however, in his final collegiate game, scored 25 in an almost flawless performance that won him the MVP award.

The Egan mystique carried Providence all the way in the 1961 NIT, but there was an even smaller guard who was even bigger in the hearts of the fans. Tow-headed sophomore Vinnie Ernst, 5 feet 8 inches, won the MVP award for his cool playmaking, while Jack "the Shot" Foley was high scorer in the tournament for third-place Holy Cross. Ernst, the lowest-scoring Friar in the finals against St. Louis, simply controlled the tight 62–59 game with his sure ballhandling and clever quarterbacking.

Surprised a year later by Temple in the first round, Providence returned to win the title in 1963. Ernst was still in control, but his three-year running mate Ray Flynn was the tournament high scorer and MVP. After all this, Providence had still failed to win top-ten ranking, in part because NIT regulars were considered second-class citizens in the basketball hierarchy. For the next three years they tackled the big boys in the NCAA, losing in 1964 to seventh-ranked Villanova in the first round.

In 1965 they were back with a star in the backcourt, Jimmy Walker, discovered in the Boston playgrounds by Sam Jones and farmed out to Laurinberg Institute for academic as well as athletic seasoning. Walker's manifold skills earned him the traditional accolade of "the new Robertson" and finally earned PC its high national ranking. Incidentally he led them to twenty-two wins out of twenty-three games during the season, then an easy win over West Virginia in the Eastern Regionals. The next game was supposed to decide the regional winner, with nationally third-ranked St. Joseph's against the fourth-ranked Friars. PC won it 81–73 but were humiliated 109–69 by Princeton as Bradley and for once every other Tiger performed to perfection.

Barely tenth-ranked in 1966, though 22–4 and with Walker a bona fide All-American, they lost in the first round to St. Joseph's; and a year later they were back home in the Garden, losing in the second round of the NIT to runner-up Marquette. There followed two mediocre years, ending with Mullaney's defection to the pros and the simultaneous arrival of Dave Gavitt, the young coach from Dartmouth, and Ernie DiGregorio, the new big little man. Ernie Di, who grew up in Providence knowing he would go to PC, was a 6-footer with all the Cousy and Maravich moves he could study. Lacking speed, he perfected quickness, and he never lacked the flash or the cockiness needed for center-stage presence. As a sophomore he led the Friars to twenty wins and back to the NIT, where they lost to champion North Carolina in the second round. In his junior year there were twenty-one wins and a first-round NCAA loss to third-ranked Pennsylvania. In his senior year, with Gavitt coolly integrating the DiGregorio flash into a cohesive team performance, PC went through to the Eastern Regional title, beating mighty Maryland in the finals, only to lose to Memphis State in the national semis when imposing center Marvin Barnes was injured.

DiGregorio pulled out some close games against the team of touring Russians, then accepted an astronomical pro contract, following Wilkens, Egan, and Walker into the NBA. So strong is the tradition of PC's guard play that hardly noticeable is the fact that they have had outstanding players in all positions right along. Big Jim Hadnot was a mighty force in the Wilkens-Egan-Ernst era, with help from Moynahan, Zalucki, and Flynn. Then came John Thompson, who went on to the pros and now the head coaching position at Georgetown, with Stone and Kovalski as important teammates.

Contemporary with Walker were Dexter Westbrook and Mike Riordan, who because he played reserve guard for the Knicks is thought of as another Friar lit-

*Big Barnes* (right) *and Little Di share a victory toast.*

tle man. But Riordan, called "Iron Mike" because of his tireless hustle, played all positions in his years at Providence and always got things done. Though he has been described as "doggerel in motion," Riordan has both a dedication to the game and an ability to concentrate his quick Irish wit on court situations that have made him one of the most successful PC graduates in the pro ranks.

Finally, on the DiGregorio teams were Barnes, Frank Costello, Kevin Stacom, and Nehru King. These were the backbone and heart of the team, even if Ernie was the head that bore the halo. But so deeply is the sports fan imbued with the tradition that in 1974, with Barnes and Stacom returning, everyone wondered who would be the big little man. Thus do sports traditions strive to perpetuate themselves, as many college baskeball stories are ongoing scenarios. Like the biggest one of all, to which the final section of this history is devoted.

# Part 7

# Plastic Man, Wooden Soldiers

TALKING TO some Washington sportswriters who were trying to get him to badmouth Lefty Driesell, his rival around the Beltway, John Thompson of Georgetown said, "How can you knock him when he's done so well? By your standards there's only one good coach—and he wins them all."

John Wooden is as much a product of our times and its systems as George Allen, John Wayne, Mrs. Robinson, Walt Disney, Ronald Reagan, Bob Haldeman, and Richard Nixon. It is probably neither coincidental nor incidental that they have all shared at one time a southern California provenience as well as a made-to-order reactionary political persuasion. The plastic man is a public personage, all shiny surface, a facade that projects to the masses through the media the image that is supposed to be admired. The magical properties of plasticity being what they are, the facade and image can shapeshift without altering the integrity of the product. The projection is itself a mask composed of features that are abstract, insubstantial, formless virtues and pieties.

For the most part the plastic man is after results and effects no matter what. But for Wooden (like Disney) the means and processes and causes are important too. There is neither hypocrisy nor cynicism here: Wooden (as Disney did) believes in the absolute rightness of his beliefs, that his beliefs motivate his actions, and that their rightness has produced his success.

Wooden has gone so far as to define success as "peace of mind which is a direct result of self-satisfaction in knowing you did your best to become the best that you are capable of becoming." And his "pyramid of success" has no doubt inspired thousands who wished to emulate his own. But the pyramid itself does not stand long under careful examination. Its blocks—its qualities—are all more or less admirable in the way the Boy Scout creed is, but their interrelationships are often questionable or overlapping if not actually contradictory. And near the apex is "faith through prayer" which is the strongest argument that Wooden's analogy of life with sports is not as soundly constructed as a pyramid should be. I have always thought that if colleges—particularly liberal arts colleges with strong interests in the humanities—have to have invocations before athletic contests, it should be the Muses who are invoked.

The irony of the Wooden pyramid of success is that it is an after-the-fact construction, a rationalization of what should have been in terms of what should be. "Patience" at the apex opposite "faith" is a case in point; Wooden now is patient with success, but he was always impatient to achieve it and remains impatient with failures. "Self-control" on the second level is interesting too: Wooden's remarkable aplomb and his public pronouncements of judicious diffidence are the product of his success: he achieved it in a history of emotional outbursts. He has become, in short, the model of what he thinks one ought to be. But that is hardly what got him there.

Wooden began to achieve his phenomenal success by a diligent devotion to a program he believed in. By commanding the respect and response of his troops, he led them to the top. And he did it pretty much on his own. It was only after his initial championships that the enormous resources of support for athletic domination in southern California were marshaled in his behalf. And then the perpetuation of the dynasty was made more secure by a variety of methods which the coach was in a position to blink.

Wooden went quietly, even piously, about his business of molding the blue-chip material he was now getting into successive champions. To his credit, and perhaps this is the key to his unparalleled success (the hidden, fluid key to the plastic pyramid), is his ability to adapt and integrate the talents of his material into a flexible but controlled system. Each UCLA team has had its own personality, true to itself despite the unmistakable Wooden imprint. This too is plasticity, like his ability to bend his ways where necessary to accommodate small corners of changing, awakening social consciousness.

274

# 34

# *Building the Pyramid*

WOODEN brought to Westwood Village in 1948 much more than an abstract formula, hackneyed definitions of qualities, and a taste for homiletic versifying. He brought a concrete program for successful athletic performance and a solid background of winning basketball from the competitive tradition of Kentuckiana. Three years he had been an All-Indiana high school player, three years he had been an All-American at Purdue, eleven years he had coached high schools in Kentucky and Indiana, and two years he had coached at Indiana State in Terre Haute. The major influence on his thinking all those years was Piggy Lambert and his fast-break style, and the style fit in perfectly with his ideas about the importance of conditioning. Only in his first year as a high school coach had Wooden had a losing season.

The key word is tradition. Wooden's steadfast devotion to the moralistic traditions of his background may make him (again like Disney) a sociological anomaly in contemporary southern California, but Lambert-Kentuckiana basketball traditions gave him the methodology for immediate success at UCLA. In the first place, he was bred in a milieu where basketball was paramount; even at the high school level, it was big-time sports. This in turn produced a drive to win

*John Wooden—they call him coach; they better.*

honed on the whetstone of keen competition. Then under Lambert he learned the virtues of controlled fast-breaking that extended beyond immediate game strategy; while at the same time, playing in the Big Ten, he learned the limitations of the disciplined pattern game as taught by Meanwell and his disciples. The Lambert-Meanwell polarity was then carried to the West Coast and recapitulated in the Wooden-Newell opposition.

Another important tradition Wooden brought to the West from Indiana was color-blindness in sport. However insensitive he may be to the subtleties of racial awareness, the fact is that he has been remarkably consistent, even rigid, in his concept that "team" obliterates "color" or any other factor of distinction. Perhaps his admiration for the Rens, against whom he played when he was moonlighting with the Kautsky Grocers, contributed to his acceptance of blacks. In any case, when his first Indiana State team was invited to the NAIA tournament in 1947, he promptly, quietly, firmly declined because he was informed that a black reserve on his team would not be welcome. A year later this barrier was dropped and Wooden's team went to the finals before losing to Louisville, led by Jack Coleman.

These traditions formed the cornerstone of the UCLA pyramid, when Wooden arrived for the 1949 season, having lost a chance to fulfill his ambition of coaching in the Big Ten. Minnesota had offered him a job but balked at hiring his assistant, Eddie Powell. They promised to call back if they could arrange for Powell to come, too, while Wooden asked UCLA to wait until the appointed time for his answer. The time came with no call from Minnesota; Wooden accepted UCLA; the Minnesota offer came an hour later, delayed by a Minneapolis snowstorm, but Wooden had given his word and stuck by it. His first choice was Minnesota, so that the decision hurt, but to him it was ennobling pain brought on by honorable action. Two years later Wooden wanted to accept an offer to return to Purdue. Again his sense of honor prevailed when he was reminded that there remained one year on a three-year contract that he had insisted on.

The UCLA program he inherited was a loser. Red Sanders, the football coach, controlled the athletic budget. There were no facilities, winning traditions, or recruiting. That Ralph Bunche had once played for the Bruins was of interest in some spheres, and Jackie Robinson's prodigious accomplishments counted for something. But the whole history of UCLA basketball had produced only three genuine stars, Dick Linthicum in 1930, Bill Putnam in 1945, and Don Barksdale, who had just graduated from a team that finished last in the conference. All Wooden did was win the conference Southern Division championship his first year.

He did it with a system of practice that he has varied only slightly during his career: long, vigorous workouts for conditioning; constant repetition of drills on fundamentals so that they become second nature; tight organization so that every minute is used for a specific purpose; and scrimmaging at the end, so that the team is used to playing tired. He did it in the old Men's Gym, capacity 2,450, popularly known as B.O. Barn. And he did it with a team consisting of Eddie Sheldrake, Alan Sawyer, Carl Kraushaar, Chuck Clustka, Ron Pearson, and George Stanich, an Olympic high jumper and All-American rebounder. UCLA lost the conference playoff to Slats Gill's Oregon State, but Wooden's pyramid was well under construction.

The next year, with Ralph Joeckel and Jerry Norman joining four returning starters, they beat Washington State in the playoff to earn a berth in the NCAA regionals. They led Bradley by 7 with less than 6 minutes remaining but fell victim to costly turnovers and a 10-point blitz from which they couldn't recover. Bradley lost the finals of both the NCAA and NIT to CCNY, the Cinderella team that UCLA had beaten by 7 points earlier in the season. The next two years continued the pattern: Southern Division champions in 1951, losing the playoff to Washington and big Bob Houbregs; conference champions in 1952, beating Washington, but losing to Santa Clara in the regionals.

Wooden thought the 1952 team might go all the way. Jerry Norman and All-American Don Johnson were cocaptains, Ron Livingston and Mike Hibler were experienced players, and two freshmen earned starting places on their way to All-American careers, Don Bragg and John Moore. In these years, virtually all of UCLA's players were from California, and most of them junior college transfers. But Moore was a significant exception, a black star from Gary, Indiana. The ability to attract blacks from other sections of the country would become a major building block in the Wooden dynasty.

Despite four straight Southern Division titles, Wooden had not sold the California press or public on the Bruins' style. The carefully controlled fast break still seemed messy. Piggy's old dictum that the team that makes the most mistakes will win the game seemed contradictory in California, but then so did Wooden himself. Even later, in the late Fifties, when Wooden's teams widened the breaking lanes and the runners held up to gun the open jump shots from around 16 feet, UCLA's style still seemed formless and unstylish. It wasn't the Luisetti-Bunn tradition that dominated in California but the influential style of James Needles of Loyola in Los Angeles and his colorful successor Scotty McDonald. Pete Newell at San Francisco and then Berkeley, Phil Woolpert at San Francisco, and Forrest

*Before Wooden came to UCLA, Jackie Robinson, a star athlete, incidentally played basketball.*

Twogood and Bob Boyd at Southern Cal all won with Needles-McDonald principles of controlling the opponent, disciplining the offense, and dictating the tempo. Wooden resented the McDonald presence (and the man himself) and its success. The others seemed to resent Wooden's presence, a mixture of smug piety and fiery competitiveness—a coach who built unemotional confidence in his players before a game by having them believe in their team and that they would win by playing their own game, but who would scream at, cajole, wheedle, and needle the players on both teams, the officials, and opposing coaches during a game.

Through the Fifties several factors worked against the completion of the pyramid. Beginning in the 1956 season, with the gym ruled unsafe for more than a thousand people, UCLA played their home games at Venice High School or Pan-Pacific Auditorium or Long Beach City College or the Los Angeles Sports Arena or Santa Monica City College or the Long Beach Arena—anywhere but home, until Pauley Pavilion opened in 1966. The arrival of great players like Willie Naulls and Maury Taft in 1954 and Walt Torrence in 1957 kept up their winning seasons, but they also coincided with other, better teams on the West Coast: Southern Cal in 1952, 1954, and 1961, Oregon State with Swede Halbrook in 1955, California in 1957–1960, and San Francisco in 1955–1956.

Worst of all, scandals involving payoffs to football players led to NCAA sanctions against Washington, Cal, UCLA, and USC and the conference temporarily dissolved. Recruiting, never a strong point in Wooden's program, was virtually impossible. Then, when a recruiting coup was accomplished, it backfired. Ron Lawson, a bright black graduate of Nashville's Pearl High School, broke UCLA's freshman scoring records in 1960, clashed with Wooden, and left school after his sophomore year in the wake of the new round of point-shaving investigations. Lawson had been guilty of associating in a basketball camp with some players who were involved and of not reporting a couple of tentative bribe offers. He left UCLA without any imputation of guilt, highly critical of Wooden's methods. Wooden, in turn, lashed out at Lawson's character in a statement that exonerated the player from actual wrongdoing but unfortunately left room for suspicion.

These were the low points—the 14–12 record in 1960 and the internal strife in 1961. Yet the missing ingredients for the success pattern were fitting into place. One of the most important was the hiring of Jerry Norman as assistant. Norman had challenged Wooden in many ways during their player-coach relationship, but they had come to respect each other's complementary talents very much. Norman became three things for Wooden that the coach would never be himself: an able, avid recruiter; a catalyst for change and innovation in the preparation of strategy; and a decisive, quick reactor in game situations.

A subtle change in practice routine for the 1961 season was the result of Wooden's detailed analysis of every part of his program, a program that had produced winning seasons, even conference crowns, but no national championship

*Hazzard in action against Washington.*

and little recognition. The conditioning that frequently carried them through a season seemed to break down in postseason play, especially when key substitutions led to loss of team coordination. Wooden's solution was to have a seven- or eight-man team work as a first unit in practice scrimmages, moving men in and out quickly to establish cohesive patterns of teamwork among all combinations of the regulars.

Another building block was J. D. Morgan, who took over as UCLA Athletic Director in 1963. Morgan relieved Wooden of the responsibilities of making budgets and schedules, dedicated himself to national titles at whatever cost, and helped in every way except providing the Bruins with first-rate nonconference opponents. And then came the building—just the breaking of ground was a great incentive to the basketball program, long before the Pavilion was finished.

Of course the major ingredient was the players. The postwar population boom in California provided a much greater pool of material, and Norman's recruiting efforts began to pay off. The 1962 team started slowly, losing seven of their first eleven games. But then they jelled and rolled. There were two slim blond forwards, Gary Cunningham and Pete Blackman, a blocky black 6-foot 5-inch center, Fred Slaughter, a skinny guard with a cue-ball haircut, Johnny Green, and the man now known as Mahdi Abdul-Rahman, Walt Hazzard.

It was Hazzard who made the team sputter at first and then it was he who made it go. He was simply too good for his mates at first. Recruited out of Overbrook High School in Philadelphia by Willie Naulls, Hazzard spent a year at Santa Monica City College and then moved right into UCLA's starting lineup to run the offense. His passes so often bounced off unready teammates' heads, shoulders, and chests that he was ready to quit and go back east. Naulls convinced him to stay, Wooden rode him to settle down and play team ball—model himself on Oscar Robertson, and the others finally caught on.

They won the conference, taking two out of three from a fine Southern Cal team led by John Rudometkin and Ken Stanley, and then broke their regionals jinx by beating Utah State and Oregon State, with Hazzard MVP. In the semis they faced Cincinnati and fought the Bearcats down to the wire. The game turned on two questionable calls in the last 2 minutes. With the score 70–70, Paul Hogue was called for an offensive foul to give the ball to UCLA. Just 25 seconds later it was Hazzard ditto to give it back. The men in the striped shirts had simply exchanged possessions. Tom Thacker hit his only basket of the game to win it for Cincinnati at the buzzer.

Hazzard and Slaughter were joined for 1963 by Keith Erickson, Gail Goodrich, Jack Hirsch, and Freddie Goss. For inexplicable reasons they played erratically and had to come from three games behind to tie Stanford for the conference. They won the playoff 51–45 with a full-court man-to-man press, but in the regionals they ran into a hot Arizona State team led by Joe Caldwell and Art Becker and were outrun and outgunned 62–31 in the first half, losing 93–79.

Two final blocks were needed to complete the pyramid as all five starters returned for 1964: the zone press and the great sixth man. Convinced that he had the right material for the press and strongly urged by Norman, Wooden had installed it midway through the last season. Now he planned to use it full time. The primary object was to dictate the tempo of the game. The teams using the McDonald-Newell style had consistently been able to cut off UCLA's fast break and determine the tempo by controlling the ball. But the pressing defense could hurry opposing offenses as well as allowing itself to convert instantly to offensive blitzes.

There was nothing new in the press. Wooden says that Lambert used a form of it in the Twenties to force Meanwell's patterns back toward midcourt. He had experimented with it at Indiana State himself and used it sporadically since. Nat Holman recalls Cincinnati, coached by John Wiethe, pressing all over the court to beat LIU in the Garden in 1950. San Francisco under Woolpert and Cal under Newell had used varieties of pressing defenses, and elsewhere West Virginia, Kansas, and Bradley had pressed with good results. Perhaps most influential, as Johnny Bunn says, was the zone press used by Penn State under Elmer Gross in 1954, when they upset Notre Dame in the Mideast Regional finals.

It was clearly a technique whose time had come. UCLA's full-court zone press took them to their first two NCAA championships, and in 1965 the College Division champions from Evansville, the NAIA champions from Central State in Ohio, and the AAU champions from the Armed Forces all used pressing tactics. That same year Bob Cousy brought Boston College into the NIT with a press against Joe Lapchick's Redmen. St. John's planned to run a disciplined offense, but BC speeded up the tempo by pressing. The plan worked but without the desired result. St. John's, forced to run to break the press, broke up the game and ran up a 114–92 score.

Perhaps more than any other strategy the zone press requires the proper personnel. Wooden had it in 1964. The 2–2–1 zone press had the quick Goodrich and Hirsch attacking the ball as soon as it was inbounded; Slaughter and Hazzard were on the second line, the big man to force the turnover on the long pass and the great ballhandler for the instant conversion to attack; and Erickson was the safety man and signal-caller. Doug McIntosh was the relief man for Slaughter, but the vital substitute was Kenny Washington, who had come to UCLA from Beaufort, South Carolina, by way of a summer in Philadelphia's playgrounds and Walt Hazzard's coattails. Washington could and did fill in anywhere on the court, often sparking the blitz that would decide a game and become the trademark of UCLA's pressing teams.

By the second game of the Los Angeles Classic in December, the dynasty was enthroned. The press blitzed second-ranked Michigan, with Hirsch doing a job on Cazzie Russell. The Bruins then ran through the entire season without a loss. There were some close calls: Illinois almost caught them with their own zone press; Cal, under Rene Herrerias, broke the press and controlled the tempo, but Hazzard's foul-shooting down the stretch preserved a 2-point win; and SC extended them to 91–81 in the last regular-season game. In the regionals Seattle (John Tresvant, L. J. Wheeler, Charlie Williams) tried to run with them and lost 95–90. Then San Francisco (Ollie Johnson, Erwin Mueller, Joe Ellis) tried to control the ball, but the Bruins came from behind to win 76–72, with McIntosh and Washington coming off the bench to make key contributions.

Both games in Kansas City were difficult. First Tex Winter's Kansas State team had a thirteen-game streak working, including upsets over ranked Texas Western and Wichita State in the regionals, and they had lost earlier in the season to UCLA by just 3 points. Willie Murrell scored 29 points, and the Wildcats' 1–3–1 zone gave the Bruins trouble. Hirsch and Slaughter had poor games, but Erickson took up the slack with 28 points. With 6 minutes left, UCLA had tied Kansas State at 75 with 5 straight points and Winter called for time. At this point help arrived for UCLA in the miniskirted persons of Kathleen Johnson, Pat Shepherd, Margie Bryant, and Sheri McElhany, their cheerleaders who had been delayed by a snowstorm. From there they pulled steadily away to a 90–84 win.

Meanwhile, Duke avenged an earlier loss by beating Michigan. Bubas had a formidable double-post offense with Jay Buckley and Hack Tison at 6 feet 10 inches plus Jeff Mullins, Jack Marin, and Steve Vacendak. The favored Blue Devils got an early lead, and Wooden, who compulsively resists calling the first time-out, overcame his scruple. With McIntosh and Washington in the game and switching to a 1–2–2 zone, UCLA scored 16 consecutive points in 2½ minutes for a 43–30 lead. This blitz, in effect, settled the game, which ended at 98–83. Goodrich had 27, but it was Washington, with 26 points and twelve rebounds, who provided the spark.

For the defense of the championship several changes had to be made. Goodrich had to take over for Hazzard as the playmaker, with Freddie Goss as the other guard, and Edgar Lacey and Mike Lynn were the sophomore forwards, while McIntosh and Washington were back where they finished the last season—center and sixth man. Wooden changed the zone alignment to 1–2–1–1, and in the opener against Illinois, they got blitzed 110–83. The loss was a mixed blessing, taking off the pressure of an undefeated season and streak, and the only other loss of the season was to Iowa with George Peeples two months later. In between they had beaten Minnesota with Hudson and Clark, Utah with Jerry Chambers and Granny Lash, and several conference teams. Then they swept through the rest of the schedule and buried Brigham Young in the regional opener. Pete Polleta had his strong San Francisco team back, and they extended UCLA to a 101–93 game in the regional finals.

In the semifinals, Wichita State was easy, but the finals promised to be tough against top-ranked Michigan. It wasn't. UCLA blitzed them in the first half, going out to a 47–34 lead, then took only good shots in the second half to win 91–80. As usual it was Washington coming off the bench to lead the blitz. Goodrich had eighteen free throws and 42 points. Cazzie Russell joined Washington, Goodrich, and Lacey on the All-Tournament team, but it was Bill Bradley as the MVP.

Half of the AP All-Americans for 1965 were on that tournament team, Bradley, Russell, and Goodrich. The others were Fred Hetzel of Davidson, Rick Barry of Miami, and Wayne Estes of Utah State. Barry had wound up a spectacular career in which he had become an outstanding scorer, averaging 19 his sophomore year while leading Miami to a 23–5 record and the second round of the NIT, 32 his junior year with a 20–7 record and the NIT again, and 37 his senior year with a 22–4 record. At sixteen years of age Barry had chosen Miami from about forty scholarship offers because of his respect for Coach Bruce Hale, and before he left Coral Gables he had developed into a strong rebounder (eighteen a game as a senior) and married the coach's daughter. He had failed, like Goodrich, to make the Olympics in 1964, but a year later, like Goodrich, he was drafted high on his way to a successful professional career.

Estes's honors came posthumously: during the season he was second only to Barry in scoring average, with a high of 48 against Denver, when he was electrocuted, brushing his head against a high-tension wire after a traffic accident. Earlier in the season, Utah State had played in a tournament in Hawaii, and Coach LaDell Anderson had overzealously berated an official, Creighton Richards. Richards's father-in-law James Aiona, also a basketball official, ended the rhubarb by knocking Anderson cold.

Wooden's quest for a record-breaking third straight NCAA was knocked cold even before the season started. He had hopes for a good team, and he still believes they might have continued their string of championships. Lacey, Lynn, Goss, Washington, and McIntosh were back, and to replace Goodrich they had an imported black star from South Bend Central, Mike Warren. Wooden blames the illness of Goss and the injury to Lacey for their failure, and there were minor illnesses affecting McIntosh and Lynn for their crucial trip to Corvallis and Eugene. But the fact is that the spirit of this team, which went 18–8, was killed in the preseason exhibition game that opened Pauley Pavilion on Salute to John Wooden Night, with a large local TV audience as a bonus.

The UCLA varsity was humiliated in that game by the UCLA freshman team, coached by Gary Cunningham. The starters were Kent Taylor, a walk-on from Houston, and Jerry Norman's best recruiting crop: two star California schoolboys, Lynn Shackelford and Kenny Heitz; the player of the year from Kansas, Lucius Allen; and one Lewis Alcindor, now Kareem Abdul-Jabbar, from Power Memorial in New York. Wooden did not try to defense Alcindor in any special way, not because he didn't think it necessary to win, but because it seemed more important in his pragmatic coach's mind not to make the big man unhappy. The contented giant scored 31 points, took twenty-one rebounds, blocked several shots, broke the press by handling the inbounds pass, and forced the varsity shooters outside where they hit only 35 percent. The freshmen won 75–60 and were ahead 62–44 when Cunningham cleared his bench. Despite Wooden's disclaimers, the varsity players were not great enough to recover from the psychological blow. It was almost as if the whole season had been sacrificed to insure the next three, the triumphant Alcindor Era.

# 35

# *Peaking with the Big A*

WOODEN HAD changed in some perceptible ways. He hadn't been ruined by success, he had been improved by it. The championships and the recognition they brought made it possible for him to project a new image. The fierceness of his competitive drive had earlier burst out in displays of temperament during games and in petulant explosions with reporters. The man who made the pressing defense work, one wag noted, was notably offensive to the working press. But back-to-back NCAA championships had put Wooden in very exclusive company, and he was now able for the most part to practice in public the gentlemanly piety he had always preached. The problem was that if success is conceptualized as a pyramid, there is no room for company at the apex. Wooden correctly perceived in Alcindor the potential for unparalleled success, and he subordinated everything to the realization of that potential.

Alcindor of course was the object of more recruiting attention than anyone since Chamberlain. He was well over 7 feet tall, he was agile and quick and coachable, and he was a very bright and mature though introverted young man. His coach at Power Memorial, Jack Donahue, was moving up to Holy Cross, but there were no strings attached, and among the Catholic schools St. John's and Boston College seemed to have impressed Lewis more. Michigan and NYU were also in the running. The UCLA campaign was waged, in a dignified fashion, by big guns like Jackie Robinson, Willie Naulls, Arthur Ashe, and even Dr. Ralph Bunche. Wooden's own posture in recruiting has always been what he thought it should be: stay low key, stress academic virtues, display strength of character, and imply that a student should be honored if offered a scholarship to UCLA. He did make a rare trip east to meet Alcindor's parents—at J. D. Morgan's and Jerry Norman's urging—but without bending that posture. And Lewis was sold. Incidentally, he stopped en route in Kansas City to reinforce Lucius Allen's determination to get out of Kansas and away from the Big Eight, still dominated by the Iba tradition of ball control.

While the 1966 team was finishing second in the conference, the freshmen were breezing through an undefeated season. Alcindor averaged over 33 points a game, Allen over 22, and Shackelford almost 21. As a team they shot 56.8 percent from the floor (Lew was 68 percent) while their opponents shot 31 percent. UCLA had a special assistant, Jay Carty, a strong 6-foot 8-inch Oregon State graduate, who went one-on-one with Alcindor for many practice hours, developing his shots, his rebounding, and his ability to sustain physical pressure. And Wooden was working as many extra hours, studying the patterns of a low-post offense which he had never used.

For all his moralistic traditionalism, Wooden is an adaptable and pragmatic man. With the end being the maximum accomplishment by a team, the means must include using the individual players' talents best for the team. Thus he employs all sorts of psychological gimmicks to motivate different players—and only rarely are they counterproductive. And he acknowledges sliding standards for behavior depending on individual temperaments—and abilities. In Alcindor he recognized one of the most remarkable basketball talents ever to come along, and he designed his team plans to make use of that talent. Incidentally, he contributed to the development of that talent, so that Kareem could step into the NBA and become rookie of the year, MVP, and hub of a championship team.

With Alcindor at low post, Wooden would have a formidable offensive weapon. With Lew rebounding defensively, he could also trigger a potent fast break. At guard the combination of Warren and Allen already appeared to rank with the great Hazzard-Goodrich tandem, and they learned to slow down—if there was no immediate advantage in the break—to wait for the big guy to set up. At forward, however, there were problems. Lacey's knee had not recovered after surgery and he would have to sit out the season. Then, shortly before the season started, Mike Lynn was lost for the year too, suspended because of arrest (and subsequent conviction) for illegal use of a stolen credit card. Jim Nielsen and Neville Saner both had chances at starting but did not earn it. Wooden wound up with the other two scholarship players from Alcindor's and Allen's freshman team, Shackelford and Heitz.

Wooden turned this weakness at the corner to an advantage. Shackelford had

*This is called dominating the scene: Alcindor (33) the Big A.*

problems. The no-dunk rule had come into the game, aimed directly at Alcindor, but it only made him a better player offensively while making him a far more devastating defender. The dunk was virtually the only offensive weapon he couldn't handle under the defensive basket. Wooden's main problem was personnel. He had too much, and he made a change in his offense to accommodate the troops that probably weakened the team (though the record indicates no weakness at all). He switched from single low post to a high-post/low-post setup, with Shackelford alone in the corner. Heitz was shifted to guard behind Warren and Allen, and Lynn and Lacey shared the high post.

Wooden knew that both Lynn and Lacey were better all-around players than Shackelford, but he believed that Shack complemented Alcindor so well that the team was better off with him in the corner. The high post made another, greater difference: it cut down the penetrating area for the two All-American guards. The opener against Purdue was a scare. Rick Mount's 28 points, Herm Gilliam's fine floorplay, and an effective diamond-and-one defense against Alcindor almost engineered an upset for George King's Boilermakers. But at 71-all, Mount missed a jump shot, Alcindor rebounded, he threw the outlet to Shackelford at midcourt, Shack hit Sweek at the circle, and Sweek hit the jump shot at the buzzer.

The middle remained clogged, but the team was so overpowering it made no difference. In the sixteenth game of the season, at Berkeley, Alcindor got 44 points and a finger in the eye. He missed the next game at Stanford, as Wooden resurrected the high-post offense with Lynn in the middle, but UCLA won easily anyway, stretching their record to 17–0 and their winning streak to forty-seven. But the abrasion was serious and Lew was doubtful for the Houston game that was to have 55,000 in the Astrodome and a TV audience of many millions. In the event, Wooden allowed Alcindor to decide for himself that he would play despite vertical double vision.

Guy Lewis's team was even better than the previous year. Hayes was at forward along with Theodis Lee, 6-foot 9-inch Ken Spain was the center, and Chaney was back at guard along with George Reynolds. The game proved to be an exciting but undisciplined affair. Alcindor was definitely under par and only Lucius Allen played well for the Bruins. Lacey was benched for not following instructions on how to play Hayes, and Chaney kept stifling the UCLA offensive patterns from the point of the 1–3–1 while Hayes controlled the baseline.

It was the Big E's night, and he made the most of it, scoring 29 in the first half as Houston led 46–43. The second half was less artistic than the first, but the Cougars went to Hayes when they needed 2 points and he kept them in front. His 38th and 39th points came on free throws with 28 seconds left to make it 71–69. Chaney and Reynolds then double-teamed Allen with the ball at midcourt. Lucius spotted Shackelford open and tried to hit him with a crosscourt pass, but Mike Warren thought it was meant for him and lunged at the ball, knocking it out of bounds to end the Bruins' hopes.

*Guy Lewis sometimes cried in his towel but never threw it in.*

*In their rubber match Alcindor and UCLA overwhelmed Hayes and Houston.*

UCLA lost more than their number one ranking and their winning streak in that game. They lost Edgar Lacey, their best forward, who withdrew from the team. Lacey had turned down a Boston Celtics' contract to play out his eligibility, but he could no longer accept Wooden's demands that he sacrifice his individual skills for the sake of the team. Wooden's judgment might be called in question, but the fact is that for the rest of the season UCLA was a better team, considered by many the greatest college team ever.

They went back to a single low-post offense and alternated their 2–2–1 and 1–2–1–1 zone presses. And they ran every opponent out of the gym. The NCAA semifinals brought Houston to Los Angeles for a rubber match, and it was no contest. Jerry Norman suggested a box-and-one on Hayes; Wooden changed it to diamond-and-one, with Lew underneath and Shack shadowing Elvin. It worked so well that UCLA led by 95–51 when Wooden pulled his starters. The final score was 101–69. In the finals Dean Smith had North Carolina, with Larry Miller and Charley Scott, play a disciplined four-corner offense. UCLA countered with a man-to-man press and won 78–55, a performance as convincing as the one before, considering the style of play.

Now Wooden was the nonpareil, and he could tell his players as the clock ran out not to jump around or dance on the floor or act like fools. And from the serenity of unparalleled records he could write, "Just give me a group of gentlemen, who play the game hard but clean, and always on an upward path. Then the championships will take care of themselves if the overall ability of the team warrants them."

For Alcindor's last year Wooden faced again the question of how to avoid losing. Mike Warren was graduated and Lucius Allen was lost for academic reasons, though a second arrest for possession of marijuana was thought to have something to do with the decision. Lucius, without rancor, simply says that Wooden never betrayed knowledge of either the legal charges or the academic problems. Indeed the coach's communication with his players dealt with basketball and nothing but basketball. Whereas parents of potential recruits have responded positively to the image of Wooden *in loco parentis* for their sons, the fact is that this is another role that others have assumed for him. Sam Gilbert, whose official standing is merely that of alumnus and fan, is the man who most often performs this function; he is a sounding board for players' pressures and problems, and he is an active agent in helping them to provide for the future and advising them for the present to help themselves by staying to help the team. Wooden, paradoxically, seems both relieved to relinquish this responsibility and resentful that his players look elsewhere for counsel.

Heitz and Sweek did not seem the answer in the backcourt, and there was competition from Donnie Saffer, Terry Schofield, and Kenny Booker. The man who took over, however, was a junior college transfer, John Vallely, who came to UCLA despite the recruiting campaign of Jerry Tarkanian at Long Beach State.

Shackelford's position was in danger because Curtis Rowe, Sidney Wicks, and Steve Patterson all looked strong. These were among the last of Norman's blue-chip recruits. Norman had retired from basketball to stockbrokerage, and Wooden replaced him with Denny Crum, who had also fought with him as a player and had that combination of fierce competitiveness and intelligent decisiveness that Wooden believes is good for any team.

Too much talent was again a problem. Saffer quit. Sweek walked out but returned after a shouting match with the coach. (Somehow Wooden always seems to appreciate the man who gives him trouble but comes back for more.) Wicks and Rowe were unhappy playing part time, and Shackelford played poorly under the pressure of being the fair-haired boy in the corner. But Vallely had taken charge and Alcindor rolled on with his overpowering play at both ends.

They went through twenty-three games without a serious challenge, though Rick Mount and Austin Carr had good individual efforts against them in the Purdue and Notre Dame visits to Pauley. Then, with the conference title and NCAA berth clinched, they went cold. Against Cal, Rowe's two free throws saved a tie at 74, and they won in overtime in what Wooden called their toughest game in three years. Then there came two games with Southern Cal. The first went two overtimes, saved by Shack's 30-foot shot, and the Bruins won 61–55. But Boyd got the Trojans ready to play their control game again the next night, and this time they held on to win 46–44.

UCLA recovered quickly for their NCAA defense. New Mexico State held the ball but was an easy 53–38 victim. Santa Clara tried to run but UCLA blitzed them 90–52, using the 2–2–1 press for the first time all year. Drake, coached by Maury John, defensed Alcindor well, but Vallely scored 29 before fouling out. This game marked the loosing of pent-up hostilities. The pressures of coaching the Alcindor teams, that were supposed to win every game, took their toll on Wooden. Sweek seemed to respond reluctantly to the coach's call for a substitute; Wooden sent him back to his seat, but Sweek went straight to the dressing room. Schofield came in cold, played poorly, and almost blew the game, which ended 85–82. Wooden blasted Schofield and then went one-on-one with Sweek in the shower room.

They made peace the next day in a team meeting, and the Bruins went on about their unprecedented business, beating Purdue 92–72 with Kenny Heitz doing a dogged defensive job on Rick Mount. Alcindor had taken them to the summit and kept them there three years running, three straight NCAA championships, eighty-eight wins in ninety games, a career average of 26 points on a .639 shooting percentage. Many called him the greatest collegiate player ever; Wooden called him the greatest big man at both ends of the court and—the highest compliment of all—a great team player for all his individual ability. Now the coach could go back to trying to win games instead of trying to avoid losing.

# 36

# *Plateau and New Peak*

WITH ALCINDOR and Walton towering above memories of the great UCLA teams, it is difficult to assert that Wooden has always been a guard-oriented coach. Yet down through the years he has depended on the backcourt men to control both the ball and the tempo of the game, no matter how much scoring and rebounding are done up front, and he has had more All-American guards than forwards and centers together. He could thus look forward to the 1970 season with great comfort.

There was a powerful front line: Steve Patterson, an ideally unselfish high-post center; Curtis Rowe, a consistently excellent returning regular; and Sidney Wicks, most talented of all, who had been erratic as a sophomore but who would now have his driving game unleashed without the big man in the low post. John Vallely would be the experienced hand in control, with Terry Schofield and Kenny Booker both ready to fill in. And up from the freshmen was a long-range gunner from Franklinton, North Carolina, Henry Bibby, another black import to complement the home-grown troops.

This team could run, press, and shoot with the best of Wooden's teams, and they had the best balance of all of them. Perhaps this was why the coach relied so heavily on the starting five. Yet many of their performances were flat, uninspired. They won several close games, but they seemed overly cocky rather than confident,

*Rebound to Wicks; Rowe in matching knee brace, at left.*

and Wooden's statesmanlike notions of gentlemanly efficiency seemed to have gone too far—they were unemotional to the point of nonchalance.

They beat an average Minnesota team 72–71 on a Bibby jump shot, Princeton 76–75 on a Wicks jump shot after Geoff Petrie and John Hummer had almost sprung the upset, and Oregon State 72–71 on a John Ecker hook after Wicks had fouled out. It all caught up with them five games later against Oregon. Stan Love inside and Rusty Blair outside gave the Bruins their first loss of the season, 78–65, and the team acknowledged their problems. Wicks and Rowe were playing two-man basketball and so were Patterson and Vallely, a matter of habit rather than a consciously racial thing. It was the sophomore, Bibby, who spoke out, and from everyone's desire to win they began to play together as a team again. To the UCLA players a single loss had become a traumatic experience.

When they lost again, it was after they had clinched the conference title, and again it was Boyd's Trojans that beat them at Pauley. Joe Mackey and Paul Westphal led the 87–86 upset as SC shot 53 percent to UCLA's 43 percent. The next night at the Sports Arena, SC jumped on top again. Midway through the first half Wooden yanked Wicks, chewed him out for not trying, sent him to the end of the bench, and told him to come back when he was ready to play. In this case the school-marm tactic seemed to work, because when Sidney returned to action 5 minutes later, he sparked the comeback that took them to a 91–78 win with 31 points on eleven for eighteen from the floor and sixteen rebounds. And now they were up for the NCAA.

First Jerry Tarkanian's Long Beach State team, with George Trapp, went down 88–65 as Bibby bombed over the zone. Utah State went down 101–79 as Wicks and Rowe scored 52. New Mexico State, with Jimmy Collins and Sam Lacey, went down 93–77 as Vallely had 23. And then came Jacksonville, unimpressive winners over St. Bonaventure who had played without injured Bob Lanier. Joe Williams, however, a Guy Lewis laissez-faire type with his players but sartorially a Johnny Carson type, had the kind of material to give UCLA trouble. In the backcourt were Roy Wedeking, the little quarterback, and Rex Morgan, at 6 feet 5 inches dangerous all over the court. On the front line were 6-foot 10-inch Rod McIntyre, 7-foot Pembrook Burrows, and 7-foot 2-inch Artis Gilmore, who was being hailed as the new Alcindor.

The day before the game, as Wooden wondered how to defense the Dolphins, Andy Hill and Steve Patterson asked him if they could wear Yale jerseys on the victory stand. The coach was aghast. It took him a little time to understand that the point was to protest the NCAA sanctions against Yale for allowing a basketball player, Jack Langer, to play in the Maccabean Games without NCAA approval. Wooden disapproved, not just because he opposed antiestablishment gestures, but because he could not understand why his players were not, like him, concentrating on Jacksonville. Later on, UCLA caught a glimpse of the Dolphins frolicking through a Globetrotter-style warm-up drill, and this seemed to inspire them with the kind of angry attention to business that Wooden admired.

For 10 minutes Jacksonville looked like number one. Wooden had Wicks fronting Gilmore, with Patterson dropping off to help out, but Morgan was getting the ball over Wicks to Gilmore and Burrows hit open shots when Patterson left him. Wicks was so frustrated by Gilmore at first that he dunked the ball for a costly turnover. Wooden called time and made an adjustment: Wicks to play behind Gilmore, Patterson to help out against the left-hand hook, Rowe to help out on Burrows, and Vallely to tighten up against Morgan. For a while it didn't help. Jacksonville went up by 24–15, but then Wicks stopped the big man cold and the Bruins' fast break began to click. From down 36–33 they blitzed for the last 8 points of the half and simply drew out to coast home 80–69: four straight titles, six in seven years.

At the senior banquet the dissension became public. The starting five had jelled to win another championship, but the bench had continued to seethe with resentment. Bill Seibert's farewell speech criticized the whole program: basketball at UCLA was an unhappy experience; there was a double standard for starters and subs; there was no communication between coaches and players. Many in the crowd hooted and catcalled, but the rest of the squad gave him a standing ovation. Wooden reacted badly. He and Crum and Cunningham singled out Ecker, Schofield, and Hill and interrogated them, accusing them of being the worst thing imaginable—left-wing political activists.

The team did act, sending a letter of protest to President Nixon about Southeast Asia and Kent State, with copies to Bob Haldeman (who helped raise the funds for Pauley Pavilion) and the *Los Angeles Times* (which promised but failed to print it). At a subsequent team meeting, Wooden tried to have each man speak in turn to lodge specific complaints, lamenting that the whole incident was sure to damage the UCLA basketball program and ruin their chances for another championship. Wicks's response was a classic. He reminded the coach that the team was living up to his fondest wish—they were acting as a unified team.

Wooden did not laugh, but neither did he kick over the benches. He did make some effort to change, to have his consciousness raised, and he showed it in subtle ways.

The next season began with only one starter gone, Vallely. Bibby was shifted over to handle the ball, while Booker and Schofield battled for the fifth slot. Booker started most of the games but Schofield played just about as much. In his annual preseason letter to the team Wooden spoke to the communication-gap point, saying he would work to close it and urging the players to be open. On the matter of double standards, there were occasions early in the year when even Wicks and Rowe were disciplined. But there remained a sullenness on the squad that resulted in a kind of methodical performance on court. The method and the talent produced wins, but there was no exuberance in play or in victory. Bibby did all that was asked by his coach, but his added responsibilities threw off his shooting. Wicks and Rowe, their eyes on big pro contracts, had things their own way most of the time on court.

There were some close calls—Bibby pulled one out in Eugene, Wicks in Corvallis, and Booker against Paul Westphal and Boyd's top-ranked SC team—and they lost one against Johnny Dee's Notre Dame team in South Bend, when Austin Carr scored 46 points in the 89–82 game. Carr couldn't be stopped in that one, and Wooden even tried Larry Hollyfield, a big, mobile left-hander, against him. But in the NCAA it was business as usual. Brigham Young with Kresimir Cosic was no competition, but Long Beach State made it a contest. Tarkanian had an effective zone and the brilliant Ed Ratleff to run the attack. But getting good performances from reserves Ecker and Farmer, UCLA came from behind to win 57–55.

Back in the Astrodome, UCLA disposed of Kansas easily, Bibby having his best scoring game of the year, despite angry words between Wooden and Crum at the start. Crum was on his way to Louisville as head coach and Wooden was annoyed that he hadn't been consulted first—the Victorian father asked by a suitor if he could call. The result was that he bridled at Crum's strategic game-time suggestions, though he had come to rely on assistants for just that function.

In the finals with Villanova they faced another tough zoning team, coached by Harry Kraft, with Hank Siemiontkowski, who had scored 31 against Western Kentucky's Jim McDaniels, and All-American Howard Porter. UCLA led 45–37 at the half on Patterson's outside shooting for 20 points, then opened the second half with a stall, Rick Betchley replacing Booker. Villanova fought back in a man-to-man, but Bibby was the steady man down the stretch in a 68–62 win.

Five straight NCAA titles, seven out of eight. In those seven championship seasons they had lost a total of seven games, five to total team efforts by Illinois, Iowa, Oregon, and Southern Cal twice, and twice to supreme individual efforts by Elvin Hayes and Austin Carr. And twice they had had a run at San Francisco's record of winning sixty straight games. This seemed the only significant record that UCLA under Wooden had not broken.

Enter Bill Walton: the new peak, the dominant force at both ends of the floor, the big man with all the moves, all the skills of an accomplished basketball player. Wooden installed him at the low post, but this time he had the ideal high-post man to go along with him, Keith Wilkes. Now instead of another forward in the corner, UCLA set up in a 1–3–1 with Larry Farmer and Captain Bibby at the wings and Greg Lee at the point, spelled by Tommy Curtis. Larry Hollyfield was the first reserve at forward, and at center Swen Nater provided Walton with occasional relief. And the 2–2–1 zone press was back, with Walton as anchor man. There wasn't a serious challenge through the entire season, which saw another championship, a third undefeated year. A new record was their average margin of victory, 33 points.

With Walton catching everyone's eye and a lot of elbows, too, the Bruins were an indomitable team. Perhaps Marquette with Jim Chones might have given them a good game, but Chones finished the season as a pro. In the NCAA semis, Wooden faced his former assistant Crum, but Louisville, even with Jim Price's 30 points and tight man-to-man defense, was no match for Walton and Wilkes

*Upsets over UCLA were accomplished by Notre Dame's Austin Carr (left), then John Shumate.*

and the rest. In the finals Hugh Durham's Florida State Seminoles made it close for a while, with Ron King hitting outside and center Lawrence McCray giving Walton all he could handle. But McCray got in foul trouble before Walton did, and UCLA pulled out to 67–51 and then held off the Florida State comeback to win 81–76.

Between seasons, Walton's political activism and even his arrest were matters of concern to the coach. But Wooden had mellowed with success to the point where he wouldn't react to anything that didn't interfere with the playing of the game. Wooden answers now, with perfect cool, needling questions that would have rubbed naked nerves before. Nor can some heart trouble and some hearing loss account for this change. It is success, the proof of the everlasting rightness of his way: One Way, the slogan has it, with the finger pointed up to the top of the pyramid.

In the 1973 season the old San Francisco record fell and many new standards were achieved. Walton and Wilkes at the posts, Farmer and Hollyfield on the wings, Curtis or Lee at the point, with Nater, David Meyers, and Pete Trgovich coming on. UCLA worked themselves up with a pregame dunk drill. And they went right on winning, without even showing any pressure as they approached sixty straight wins and then the sixty-first. In the NCAA semifinals Indiana, with freshman Quinn Buckner quarterbacking the Hoosiers, was surprisingly close at the end, but a bigger surprise was Memphis State, upset winners over Providence, with DiGregorio, Barnes, and Stacom. In the finals Walton removed all doubts about his quality with an individual performance that ranked with the greatest of all time, including twenty-one of twenty-two shots from the floor.

The streaks went on, seven straight championships, nine out of ten, and a new standard every time they won a game. In 1974, for once, UCLA played a difficult nonconference schedule, including highly touted Maryland, San Francisco, the same NC State team that had gone undefeated in 1973 but had been banned from postseason play, and Notre Dame home-and-home. After a tune-up with Iowa, they entertained Maryland at Pauley. Driesell had the Terps sky-high with confidence, and with Elmore battling Walton evenly on the boards, the Maryland comeback fell just a point short as Lucas could not get a shot off in the closing seconds.

Against Norman Sloan's Wolfpack on a neutral court in St. Louis, the two undefeateds played for what should have been the championship of the previous season. Walton sat out half the game in foul trouble, but State could not take advantage. Ralph Drollinger played well in relief, and Keith Wilkes proved the outstanding player on the floor, not just offensively with his scoring and passing, but especially on defense where he held David Thompson down to mortal dimensions and consistently boxed him out from the offensive boards. UCLA won comfortably by 16 points.

The streak stood at eighty-seven when UCLA traveled East again, but Walton was injured and a questionable starter. Wooden said if he couldn't go against Iowa he would be left home and miss Notre Dame as well. He skipped the Iowa game, number eighty-eight, but he was there for the Irish. For 37 minutes the Bruins had things their way. They led 70–59; Walton had hit twelve of thirteen shots, and no one for Notre Dame had reminded the crowd of the Austin Carr spectacular three years earlier, the last time UCLA had lost anywhere. Shumate was playing well, and so were Dantley, Brokaw, and Ray Martin; no Bruin was brilliant either, but they seemed home free—for 37 minutes. In the last 3 minutes it all turned around. UCLA kept turning the ball over and Notre Dame made each exchange count. Shumate scored over Walton, Dantley scored on a steal, Brokaw scored on a jumper, and suddenly it was 70–69. One last time UCLA turned it over, on a Wilkes baseline drive that was called for charging, as Wooden shouted "you crook" at the ref for all lip-readers in the national TV audience.

The coach had gone to sleep on the bench as the team had on the floor, and Dwight Clay hit the baseline jump shot that dug the streak's grave for Digger Phelps's biggest win. Walton got one more shot and Meyers tried to tip it in, but Shumate rebounded for number one Notre Dame. He had taken the ball right to Walton for 24 points, as no one had ever done before (as no one has ever done to Abdul-Jabbar). In the return match at Pauley he did it again, but not quite so effectively and with not quite such good support. UCLA never let down in this one and regained their accustomed top spot with an 18-point win.

But a funny thing happened on the way to the NCAA. UCLA went on a lost weekend to Corvallis and Eugene, losing two disciplined games to lowly Oregon State and hungry Oregon on successive nights. Suddenly they were number three, Walton had lost one more game than Alcindor, and Wooden was in a dogfight for the conference title.

That fight did not end until the first round of the NCAA had been played. On that same day the ACC championship was decided in Greensboro, top-ranked NC State beating Maryland 103–100 in overtime in the finest game of the year. Meanwhile the Big Ten remained undecided as Michigan and Indiana tied. Purdue, eliminated on the last day, promptly accepted an NIT bid. Under Fred Schaus the Boilermakers won the tournament, beating Bill Foster's young Utah team in the finals despite the all-around play of MVP Mike Sojourner.

UCLA played a half of flawless defense for an incredible 47–13 lead against SC. With Walton playing one of his authoritative games, shooting better than 80 percent, and Andre McCarter and Marques Johnson providing traditional Bruin sparkle in substitute roles, it looked like Wooden's real troops had emerged for the title defense. They stumbled some in an overtime win over Dayton but demolished San Francisco to win their regionals. NC State won their regionals with greater ease over Dave Gavitt's Friars and Buzz Ridl's Pitt Panthers. Kansas came through the close Midwest draw, and the Mideast was even closer.

In a playoff for the title, Johnny Orr's Michigan team upset Indiana. Bobby Knight's team went on to an easy win in the inaugural Collegiate Commissioners Association tournament (runners-up from eight conferences), whipping SC in the finals. Other postseason winners were West Georgia, coached by former Tech star Roger Kaiser and led by Foots Walker, in the NAIA and top-ranked Morgan State in the NCAA College Division. Meanwhile Michigan, led by Campy Russell, shocked Notre Dame out of their hopes for a rubber match with UCLA. Marquette edged by Vanderbilt and then Michigan, giving Al McGuire's Warriors their first regional title after eight attempts. When Marquette came back to beat Kansas in the semis at Greensboro, McGuire said he felt as if he had won the B championship as he prepared to watch UCLA, second-ranked but favored, against the top-ranked underdog Wolfpack.

The climactic game measured up in excitement if not in excellence. The UCLA dynasty ended in a double-overtime loss, but it was not a good death. Walton played well and so did Thompson as Wilkes got in early foul trouble. But both teams did a lot of standing around, playing tentatively at both ends of the court. Not only the players but the coaches went out of their customary patterns in the second half; in the last 30 minutes of play Sloan used only six men, Wooden unaccountably only five. UCLA blew an 11-point lead by poor shot selection and turnovers in regulation; even worse, they led by 7 in the second overtime and gave it all away—the game, the title, and the unprecedented streaks of seven championships and thirty-eight straight wins in NCAA tournaments. Gracious in defeat, Wooden said he would enjoy watching the championship game. Anticlimactic though it was for them, NC State survived McGuire's antics, Marquette's deliberation, and their own premature slowdown to win the title 76–64. The king had been dethroned, and the heir apparent was for real.

*Walton's wonders paled somewhat in comparison with David Thompson's (44) miraculous play.*

# Overtime

A FEW LAST shots before the buzzer. There are implied and even explicit judgments expressed in these pages which will be viewed with hostility by the sports establishment. Criticism of sacred institutions is always likely to evoke a love-it-or-leave-it reaction. But I have always believed in caring enough to make things better. And I do care about basketball and about college sports, so this book has been a labor of love.

Basketball is a beautiful game, and I believe it is the great American sport. College basketball is worthy of the devotion it inspires, yet it stands clearly in the need of repair. It is thus with affection, nourished by many years of attention, that I offer the following suggestions.

The recruiting is absurd. It has no place in institutions of higher education. The spectacle of a university president, who takes no part in faculty recruitment even at the senior level, greeting a high school prospect on a rolled-out carpet is a striking example of an inversion of values and priorities. Virtually every off-court ill that besets basketball comes from the corruption of standards that accompanies recruiting practices. It should not be supported and it certainly should not be subsidized, however indirectly, by academic institutions. Since it is nearly impossible to draw a clear demarcation between the permissible offers and promises and the impermissible, why not just outlaw the whole procedure? Eliminate the whole atmosphere of slave market, high bidding, and closet pandering. In practice, it would be much easier to police contact with high school players by representatives of colleges than contact by "known associates of gamblers."

Next, take some of the money saved from these mushrooming recruiting budgets and support an NCAA training program for officials. In no other sport is the whole play so totally at the mercy of officiating as in basketball, and in no other sport are the officials so haphazardly prepared and disharmonious among themselves. The nature of the game demands that referees control the tenuous balance between legitimate contact and aggression, between legitimate movement and violation, between legitimate duration and too much time, and between the rights and privileges of offense and defense. But in practice the whistling is so erratic, inconsistent, antagonistic, and provocative, that the blowers should be arrested for incitement to riot. The preponderance of "judgment calls" in basketball is overwhelming. Judgment calls for the steady wisdom born of education and mutual understanding. Only an ambitious nationwide school for referees could produce the climate, if not the temperament, for such judgment with wisdom; it need not be so elusive as peace with honor.

Two major rules changes are needed to improve the play of the game. College basketball games are too often destroyed by stalling tactics, and I believe a time-clock is the solution. But the strategic options open to coaches should not be limited, so that various defenses would put the burden of variety of attack on the offense. In other words, the team with the ball should be able to identify a defense, run a pattern against it with all its options given a chance to develop. This rarely takes more than 18 seconds according to my figures. If one pattern is thwarted, a team should have the opportunity to set up once more and run another pattern. That's a maximum of 36 seconds, which might be extended to 40 to include a little extra time for transitions. The virtues of such a rule are manifold, but above all it would put equal burdens on offense and defense to control the pace of a game and equal responsibility on the leading team and the trailing team to continue the action, the actual playing of the game.

Equal responsibilities should suggest, as well, equal opportunities. Bring back the dunk. This shot—and never mind the excitement it generates for crowd and player alike—reduces the intimidating domination of the overwhelming big man and allows smaller men with equivalent skills to use all their moves and do their stuff inside.

# *Bibliographical Note*

Invaluable in researching this book were Zander Hollander, *The Modern Encyclopedia of Basketball*; William Mokray, *Ronald Encyclopedia of Basketball*; Alexander Weyand, *The Cavalcade of Basketball*; and Spalding's *Official Collegiate Basketball Guide*. Also of considerable help were Forrest Allen, *Better Basketball*; Clair Bee, ed., *Winning Basketball Plays*; Nat Holman, *Holman on Basketball*; Ed Jucker, *Cincinnati Power Basketball*; James Naismith, *Basketball: Its Origin and Development*; Pete Newell and John Benington, *Basketball Methods*; and Adolph Rupp, *Rupp's Championship Basketball*.

From the twenty-two shelves of basketball books in the Library of Congress, I recommend the following miscellany: Arnold Red Auerbach and Paul Sann, *Red Auerbach: Winning the Hard Way*; Pete Axthelm, *The City Game*; *Clair Bee's Basketball Quiz Book*; John Bunn, *Basketball Techniques and Team Play*; Doc Carlson, *Basketball: The American Game*; Dwight Chapin and Jeff Prugh, *The Wizard of Westwood*; Bob Cousy with Ed Linn, *The Last Loud Roar*; Jack Gardner, *Championship Basketball with Jack Gardner*; Leonard Koppett, *24 Seconds to Shoot* and *The Essence of the Game Is Deception*; Tev Laudeman, *The Rupp Years*; Joe Lapchick, *50 Years of Basketball*; Ken Loeffler with Ralph Bernstein, *Ken Loeffler on Basketball*; John McLendon, *Fast Break Basketball*; John McPhee, *A Sense of Where You Are*; George Mikan as told to Bill Carlson, *Mr. Basketball*; Sandy Padwe, *Basketball's Hall of Fame*; Buzz Ridl, *How to Develop a Deliberate Basketball Offense*; Bernice Larson Webb, *The Basketball Man: James Naismith*; Jerry West with Bill Libby, *Mr. Clutch: The Jerry West Story*; David Wolf, *Foul!*; and John Wooden, *They Call Me Coach*.

# *Index of Names*

The index is arranged in two cross-referenced sections: (A) Coaches and (B) Players. Coaches and players have their respective schools indicated parenthetically. References to illustrations are underscored.

## B. PLAYERS